SYNGRESS®

JOURNEY
TO THE CENTER OF THE
INTERNET

Pamela Rice Hahn

Jesse Flores Animator

KEY	SERIAL NUMBER
001	Q3ERT945T5
002	9PLDT4MLE4
003	SXT6L3N54N
004	H5J74B39UN
005	NY3KMU6N7H
006	NFG4RN2VC7
007	BWBVHTU83W
008	QPB9R5MF5A
009	83N5M446H7
010	GT6YH2J7SS

PUBLISHED BY
Syngress Publishing, Inc.
800 Hingham Street
Rockland, MA 02370

Journey to the Center of the Internet

Printed in the United States of America

1 2 3 4 5 6 7 8 9 0

ISBN: 1-928994-75-x

Animator: Jesse Flores   Cover Illustration by: Lee Macleod
Copy Editor: Laura Roberts   Cover Designer: Michael Kavish
Indexer: Jennifer Coker   Page Layout and Art by: Shannon Tozier
Developmental Editor: Jonathan Babcock   CD Production: Michael Donovan

Distributed by Publishers Group West in the United States and Jaguar Book Group in Canada.

From the Publisher

This book is the result of my not being able to answer my fourteen-year-old daughter Sasha's most basic questions about how the Internet actually works. Most Syngress Internetworking books are written by and for experienced network engineers, and I had trouble not referring to DNS lookups and IP configuration commands while answering her question "how does e-mail work." *Journey to the Center of the Internet* attempts to answer this question and others in a way that is both entertaining and educational. It was created in the spirit of the classic Jules Verne book *Journey to the Center of the Earth*, and hopefully it conveys some of the same sense of adventure and wonder. Sasha, I wish I could have as much fun answering all your *other* questions.

—*Chris Williams*
President, Syngress Publishing

Sasha and Chris

Syngress Acknowledgments

We would like to acknowledge the following people for their kindness and support in making this book possible.

Karen Cross, Lance Tilford, Meaghan Cunningham, Kim Wylie, Harry Kirchner, Kevin Votel, Kent Anderson, and Frida Yara of Publishers Group West for sharing their incredible marketing experience and expertise.

Jacquie Shanahan and AnnHelen Lindeholm of Elsevier Science for making certain that our vision remains worldwide in scope.

Annabel Dent of Harcourt Australia for all her help.

David Buckland, Wendi Wong, Marie Chieng, Lucy Chong, Leslie Lim, Audrey Gan, and Joseph Chan of Transquest Publishers for the enthusiasm with which they receive our books.

Kwon Sung June at Acorn Publishing for his support.

Ethan Atkin at Cranbury International for his help in expanding the Syngress program.

Jackie Gross, Gayle Voycey, Alexia Penny, Anik Robitaille, Craig Siddall, Darlene Morrow, Iolanda Miller, Jane Mackay, and Marie Skelly at Jackie Gross & Associates for all their help and enthusiasm representing our product in Canada.

Lois Fraser, Connie McMenemy, Shannon Russell and the rest of the great folks at Jaguar Book Group for their help with distribution of Syngress books in Canada.

Finally, a special thanks to Sasha Williams, inspiration for this title. Sasha is a 14-year old young lady who takes on the world with the maturity of a person double her age. Thanks for all your help at Syngress Sasha!

Author Dedication

To Taylor, Charlie, and Courtney—for teaching gramma that learning can always be fun!

Author Acknowledgements

Thank you...

For their help and support, I would like to thank everyone at Syngress Publishing: specifically Jon Babcock and Andrew Williams. For his animations: Jesse Flores. For all of their hard work and perseverance, I would like to thank my agent Sheree Bykofsky and her associate Janet Rosen. For help and assistance in making this book a reality: Eric J. Ehlers. For finding answers to research questions in a pinch: Jodi Cornelius.

I also want to thank my daughter and joy of my life, Lara Sutton.

Additional thanks go to...

For help when needed: my newest "adminstrative assistant" Katie Bonvillian, my niece Nicole Teeters, my former "administrative assistant" and artist friend Michele Nagel, and my nephew Andrew Rice. For being there: my sister-in-law and "personal shopper" Ann Rice, mom, dad, and the siblings. For your encouragement and sharing the laughter: my photographer friend who makes house calls Bill Grunden; computer guru buddy Don Lachey; my online friends: David Hebert, the elusive Bishop Ra Fiki, Stevie Harris, Ed Williams, Troy More, Dolf J. Veenvliet, Erin Klitzke, and all the other #Authors on the Undernet regulars.

Animator Dedication

The animations are dedicated to Jennifer, Molly, and Sophie. Thank you for your constant companionship and positive enthusiasm. We've created this project together.

Author

Pamela Rice Hahn is a full-time freelance writer who's worked with and written about computers since 1969, starting with a college-era job that involved using alcohol and cotton swabs to clean the tape heads on humongous IBM 364 computers. In addition to serving as a contributing editor to a national computer magazine and frequent columnist and reviews contributor to others, Pam works as a writer and technical editor for technology publishers, among them Macmillan Computer Publishing, Sybex, Osborne, Quessing, DDC, and Syngress Publishing. She was lead author on *How to Use Microsoft Access 2000* (ISBN: 0672314916).

Pam's experience goes beyond just writing about computers. In fact, only one of her last two books is computer- and Internet-related: *The Unofficial Guide to Online Genealogy* (ISBN: 0028638670). She's also the author of *Macmillan Teach Yourself Grammar and Style in 24 Hours* (ISBN: 0028638999), published almost 100 general interest articles in the past year, and is writing two cookbooks. She designs and maintains several Web sites, among them her personal site (www.ricehahn.com), CookingWithPam (www.cookingwithpam.com), the Webosaurus online companion guide for this book (www.webosaurus.net), The Blue Rose Bouquet online magazine (www.blueroses.com), and GenealogyTips (www.genealogytips.com).

If you are like Pam, you use your computers to streamline and enhance your working, educational, and recreational life. Pam has spent her entire adult life working with computers in some form or another. Join Pam on this fun and informative *Journey to the Center of the Internet* and soon you'll be an expert.

Animator

Jesse Flores is an independent digital animator and illustrator located in Boston, Massachusetts. His work includes 3D characters, company and new product promotions, medical and technical simulations, and architectural environments. Recent projects feature an ambitious clean room technician, machines that squeeze plastics, sculpture towers of Asia, pumping human hearts and a variety of flying, spinning, twirling logos! These projects were used in CD-ROM, video, print, tradeshow, and Internet presentations. A sampling of his best image and animation efforts can be viewed at www.bestofjesse.com.

Jesse's home-based studio consists of an assortment of Macs and his software tools include the Adobe product line and Electric Image's Universe. His animation upbringing included use of an old super 8 camera prior to his digital evolution. He has extensive fabrication experience with many real world tools and materials that have proven to be helpful with digital 3D modeling and scene construction. Jesse is originally from Flint, Michigan and is a Fine Arts Sculpture graduate of San Jose State University in California.

About the CD

The CD that is included with this book contains an e-book copy of the book itself, as well as a series of animation clips illustrating various aspects of Bert's journey to the center of the Internet. The animation clips elaborate on the material presented in the book, and are a fun way for readers to join Bert on his journey. You will notice as you read that at certain points in each chapter there are CD icons (like this one) in the text; these are to alert you to the fact that there are animation clips on the CD that correspond to that particular chapter material. As you read through the chapters, watch the accompanying clips on your computer to get the full *Journey to the Center of the Internet* experience.

There are two programs that you will need in order to view the animations and the e-book. These are Adobe Acrobat Reader and QuickTime, both of which we have conveniently included on the CD for you. To install Adobe Acrobat Reader, put the CD in the drive tray, close the door, and browse to the CD-ROM drive (it is usually the **D:** drive on most computers). Open the file named **Install Adobe Acrobat Reader** and follow the easy installation steps. Once you have Adobe Acrobat Reader installed, browse to the CD-ROM drive again and open the file named **setup.exe**, which will bring you to the Main Screen of the *Journey to the Center of the Internet* CD. To install QuickTime, simply click on the button labeled **Install QuickTime** and follow the simple installation steps.

Subsequently, any time you want to access the CD, simply put it in your CD-ROM drive and close the door. It will autorun automatically, and you will be presented with the Main Screen. If your computer does not have autorun enabled, the CD will not start up automatically. If this is the case, browse to the CD-ROM drive and open the file named **setup.exe**, which will bring you to the Main Screen. For optimal viewing of the animation clips, you will need at least a 4X CD-ROM drive.

The Main Screen is where you can access either the animation clips or the e-book. When you first get to the Main Screen, you will see that it is divided in half. On the right hand side is the Animation Clips Table of Contents, which lists all of the clips according to the chapter they correspond to. Simply click on any clip to view it. You will be presented with a warning screen which tells you that you are opening a file that could potentially contain viruses; be assured that none of them do. Click **Open**, and the QuickTime Player will pop up. Press **Play**, just like on a VCR (it's the large button on the bottom, right in the middle, that looks like an arrow pointing to the right side of your screen), and the animation clip will begin. When it is over, click on the **X** in the upper right hand side of the QuickTime Player to exit the player.

On the left hand side of the Main Screen you will see a menu. The top menu item says **Main Screen**; click on this at any point to bring you back to the Main Screen. Below this is a link to the e-book. Clicking on the **E-Book** link will bring up an onscreen version of the book on the right hand side of the screen. You can scroll up and down to move through the text of the e-book, or you can jump back and forth to any chapter by clicking on the chapter numbers from the menu on the left. If you click on any of the CD icons while reading through the e-book, they will automatically start the corresponding animation clip.

Contents

Introduction

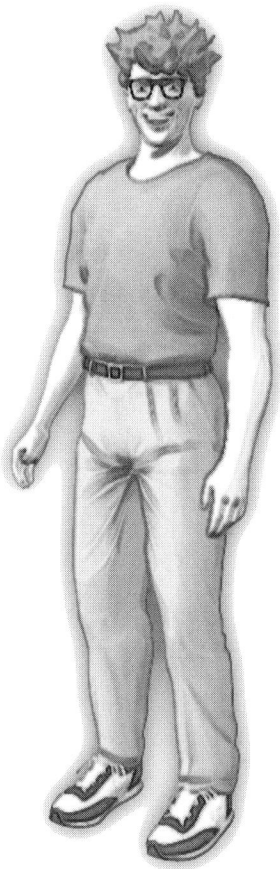

I imagine this is the first book you've read that's written by somebody who's inside of a computer, instead of just seated at one typing in his story. In fact, now might be a good time for you to boot up that CD that came with this book. You'll need it later in the journey anyhow, and for now it'll give you a chance to see what I look like and allow me to officially introduce myself.

I know. That still doesn't answer how I got inside of here in the first place. Be patient. We'll get to that. First, in order to understand how that happened, you need to know about Dr. F.

His full name is Dr. Mortimer Franklin.

While we're on the subject of names: you'll recall from that CD intro that mine is Albert. My friends call me Bert; however, Dr. F. usually just calls me "BT." That's short for Beta Test. Sometimes he calls me Beta, or just "B." When I first met him and he'd get really impatient, he'd mutter "baloneyforbrains" under his breath, like it was all one word, while his eyes rolled so far back in his head you'd think he could see behind him. Of course, with all that Dr. F. *can* do, maybe he can do that, too. But I digress....

Dr. F. is well known throughout our town as being a bit eccentric. His tinkering with his latest invention often subjects the local townspeople to what he called "beta tests." People still talk about the time he outfitted his dog, Data, with The Ultra Animal Translator. Equipped with the UAT, Data could fetch your morning newspaper and read you the front page!

As with many of his inventions, Dr. Franklin was soon asked to dismantle the device when Data began telling humans how dogs really felt about them. The final straw was when Data got really upset when one of the neighbors tried to feed him steak that was well done.

"You obviously don't know the first thing about gratitude," Mr. Gordan, the well-meaning neighbor, said to Data when he complained about the steak.

"And you know even less about canine cuisine," Data reportedly retorted.

Things went downhill after that and got downright ugly, with Mr. Gordan doing lots of growling, and not in the least amused when Data tried switching to witty repartee in an attempt to diffuse the situation.

Being his neighbor, my family and I constantly heard strange noises from Dr. Franklin's lab.

Before I actually met him, I would often sneak towards his workshop, careful to avoid the various out-dated circuit boards, motors, antennae, and scrap metal

that littered his lawn. I'd get up on the tips of my feet and peek through a hole in the wall at Dr. F's latest creation.

They were almost always too abstract to identify. So, I would usually only be treated to a glimpse of patchwork metal humming away in the corner and would have to guess at its intended purpose.

One day I noticed that Dr. F's car wasn't around, so I figured he wasn't home and that I could finally be assured some privacy while I checked things out. I mean, who would have guessed that there was a mechanic in town who could work on his car? It's a cross between a Model T and a spaceship, and it's a wonder that it works at all. It has running boards and one of those old flip-up seats in back with headlights that resemble infrared heat-seeking missiles. One minute the car's a convertible and the next minute, before you've even had a chance to see anything happen, the car has a top. So, I'm almost afraid to speculate what it has under the hood. Choreographed lemurs, for all I know. Anyway, when I didn't see the lemurmobile burrowed in its rightful place among what I've come to think of as Dr. F's lawn ornaments, I got a bit more bold about looking around. In fact, I was leaning against a pink flamingo that I figured Dr. F. had put next to some artistically arranged copper tubing to add a bit of contrasting color and was about to venture in closer for my latest look inside of his lab, when I felt something that I can only describe as "squishy."

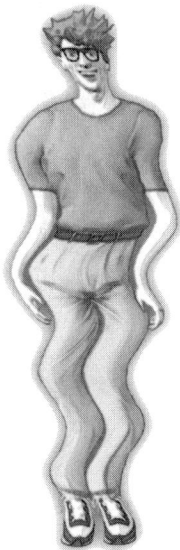

I never have found out for sure what it was. You can bet I didn't stick around at that moment to find out. I just knew that there was no physical reason why my left shoulder and then other parts of my body, from my right elbow to my earlobes, should be getting that strange, prickly sensation. It was kind of like how your foot feels when it falls asleep. After the first squish, I knew my body was on full alert and totally awake. After I'd felt a few of those squishes, anybody watching me run from Dr. F's lab window would have thought I was a member of the Olympic track team instead of a World Class Marathon Sit-On-My-Behind Computer Whiz.

Can you believe that there are actually people out there who make fun of others just because they're smart? I, for one, find learning new stuff to be one of the greatest adventures there is. But, I guess I digress again....

In my opinion, curiosity didn't kill the cat; it's how she gained the knowledge to become aloof and confident enough not to care about what other people think. Curiosity is one of the things that leads to learning. I become curious about how something works and I want to take it apart to find out.

Maybe that's why Dr. F's lab beckoned to me like a Christmas gift box hidden in the closet. I just couldn't wait to get a chance to look inside. My compulsion was enough to drag me away from my computer for hours at a time. I gained a renewed affinity for my tree house. It became my lookout post from which I waited to see what exactly Dr. F. was up to in his lab.

One day I climbed the ladder, took a look around, and found my reward! The lemurmobile was back in its rightful place among the lawn art. Now all I had to do was watch and wait. I knew it was just a matter of time. Someday I'd catch a glimpse of Dr. F. driving away in that strange car of his. I could be patient, knowing that I'd soon get my chance to do some first-class, uninterrupted exploring again. I didn't figure the guy could stay at home all of the time! Nobody lives on delivery pizza and Chinese food forever. At the very least, I figured he'd have to go out and buy toothpaste or something.

Within a few days I got my wish. From my perch inside the tree house, I saw Dr. F. exit the lab. His lab coat trailed behind him, caught up just as much from the momentum of his step as from the wind that had just started to whip the limbs of the trees. With Data yapping at his heels, he pulled what I imagined was a beeper from his pocket, and from where I stood, crouched in the tree house, it looked like he pressed a button. The next thing you know, Dr. F. and Data have disappeared from next to the car, which is suddenly speeding down the driveway, Data sitting almost cross-legged in the rumble seat, his head hanging out the back window.

I waited for what I thought was a respectable (and safe) length of time and then climbed down from the tree house. Once I hit the ground, there was a sense of urgency in my step. The wind was picking up and the sky seemed to be darkening as well. Had I known at the time that I'd eventually be telling you about what happened, I wouldn't have picked a time as clichéd as "a dark and stormy night" to do my exploring.

That night, I feared we must be in for a monster of a storm because not only was the sky growing dark at an amazing pace, but the blue roses that surround Dr. F's house were already hunkered down for the night ...literally. The stems holding the buds seemed to shrink almost to the ground and, while I watched, the leaves began forming umbrella-like canopies above the tender blue blooms.

As fascinating as it was looking at Dr. F's strange flowers, I didn't have time to spend that night watching them. I began to weave my way among and between the flotsam and jetsam that littered—or decorated, depending on your perspective—the yard, working my way toward the lowest lab window, all the while glad it was apparent that Dr. F. had left the lights on inside. Otherwise, on a night like this, I knew I wouldn't have been able to see a thing.

Like an old school teacher who refuses to forego the chalkboard and embrace the overhead projector or other new gadgets, I saw that Dr. Franklin had found a way to reach a compromise in his lab. Before that night, I'd seen blackboards. I'd also seen the kind of boards that are green. But, I'd never seen a blueboard. *Must be his favorite color*, I thought, the rain-sensitive roses still fresh in my mind. Lining all the bare walls in the lab, and suspended from chains like some sort of psychedelic, descending

movie screen in front of the dozens of filled bookcases, I
saw boards of every shade of blue one can imagine. Gone
were the misshapen chunks of metal whirring away that
had once filled every available space in the lab. In their
place was board after board after board. Light blue ones
with navy lettering and vice versa. Others had an almost
eerie metallic glow reminiscent of those holograms I'd
once thought I'd find in the lab. And covering every surface on every one of the boards were formulae I couldn't
begin to decipher. The only similarities I was able to discern in the short time I had to look around was that
somewhere on each board were the letters "J-T-C-I" with
arrows and icons and numbers leading to and away from
the letters. "JTCI," I heard myself mutter aloud, as a gust
of wind blew the hairs on the back of my
head so they tickled my neck and
another cloud rolled in to further mask
the sun. Then I felt something else. And
this time, it was definitely squishy!

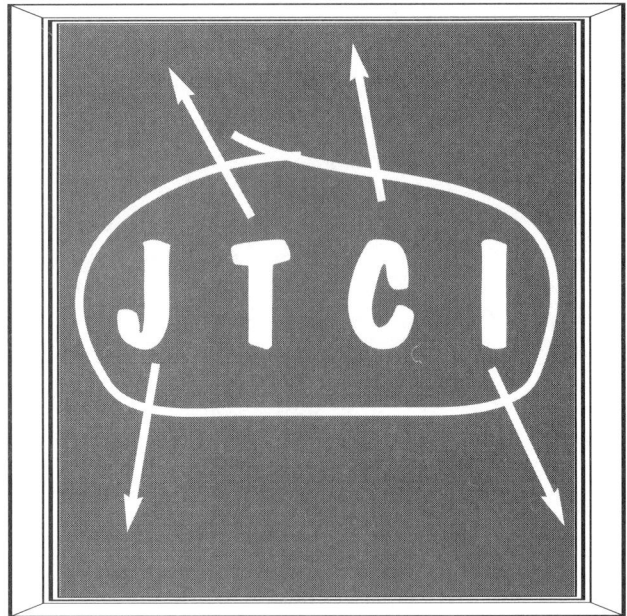

"A bit jumpy tonight, aren't you?"
The reality of a voice behind me
made me jump again.

"Whoa there, boy. Calm down."
Who can be calm at a time like this? I
thought as I tried to coordinate my
jumping with my efforts to discern what
had caused the squish.

"Get a grip, Bert," I said out loud.
The sound of my voice brought me
back to reality, if not to earth. Other than the jumping,
I'd only seemed to be running in place anyhow. In a
voice that sounded like chalk scraping across one of
those boards in the lab, I heard myself ask, "Who's
there?"

"Shouldn't I be the one asking the questions, young
man? After all, *you're* the one trespassing on *my* property." That said, I felt a hand on my shoulder as he
turned me around to face him.

"Dr. Franklin?" I asked.

"Up close and in person," he answered. Before he could say anything else, I had a flashback remembrance of something decidedly squishy and started looking back and forth over my shoulders, trying to find what had caused that eerie sensation.

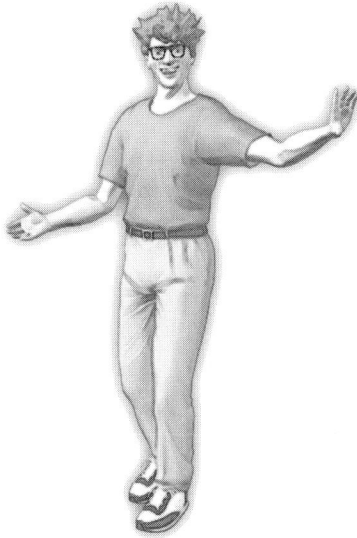

Dr. F. harrumphed as only an impatient adult can harrumph, and grabbed hold of my nose this time, turning me toward him. "I'm over here, son. Stay focused."

"But..."

"Perhaps you're looking for this?" he asked, as he opened his palm to reveal what I'd likened to a beeper earlier. As I watched, he pressed a button and I felt that weird squishy sensation move through my fingers and then simultaneously tickle my thumbs. This time he chuckled. "Gets your attention, doesn't it?"

"What...?" I managed to stammer.

"We don't have time for trivia tonight," he said, with another one of his distinctive harrumphs. "You need to get home before the storm hits, and I have work to do."

Dr. F. punched another button on the tiny control panel he held in his hand and I watched as his strange car pulled up alongside him. With another press of a button, the engine shut down, the lights went out, and Data jumped out of the backseat just as the roof appeared over the car. The only thing that surprised me was that a garage didn't suddenly appear around the car. I guess even Dr. F. can only take technology so far.

A few days later, I was up in my tree house again when I heard voices in the yard. Some people may think I'm getting a little old to be spending so much time up there, but it's a peaceful place. I like spending time alone. It's easier to think without having others around to distract me. So even though I'd decided there probably wasn't a foolproof way to spy on Dr. F's lab, I still spent time there. Who knows? Maybe deep down I thought that in a moment of solitary contemplation the perfect plan would occur to me. As it turned out, I didn't need a plan. I was about to gain carte blanche access to the lab. Yes! To the *inside* of the lab.

Anyhow, that night I happened to be gazing up at the stars through this set of binoculars my granddad had given me. Dad told me later that Dr. F. wandered into our yard and asked if it was okay if he joined me in the tree house. Dad said he'd wondered how the "old guy" was going to handle the rickety steps, but he told him if he was up to the climbing, he was welcome to join me.

I didn't hear him approach, so I almost jumped out of my shoes when he tapped me on the shoulder. I guess I can be thankful he didn't do that squish thing to announce his arrival. Dr. F. shrugged when I realized who he was, and without saying a word, reached into his pocket protector and pulled out what I thought was a laser pointer like the one I carry with me (I mostly use it to give my dog Broccoli Spears something to chase when I'm busy trying to read or do other stuff). Anyhow, I heard some clicks and, before I knew what was happening, he'd unfolded the device into something that looked like a miniature telescope. I got a closer look at the planets that night than I ever did at the local university planetarium. I got my first up close look at a lone neutron star. I saw the black hole in the spiral galaxy M87 in greater detail than I'd ever seen on the NASA Web site. Literally seeing for myself that Dr. F. has something that powerful in his tech arsenal was enough to make me believe the rumors

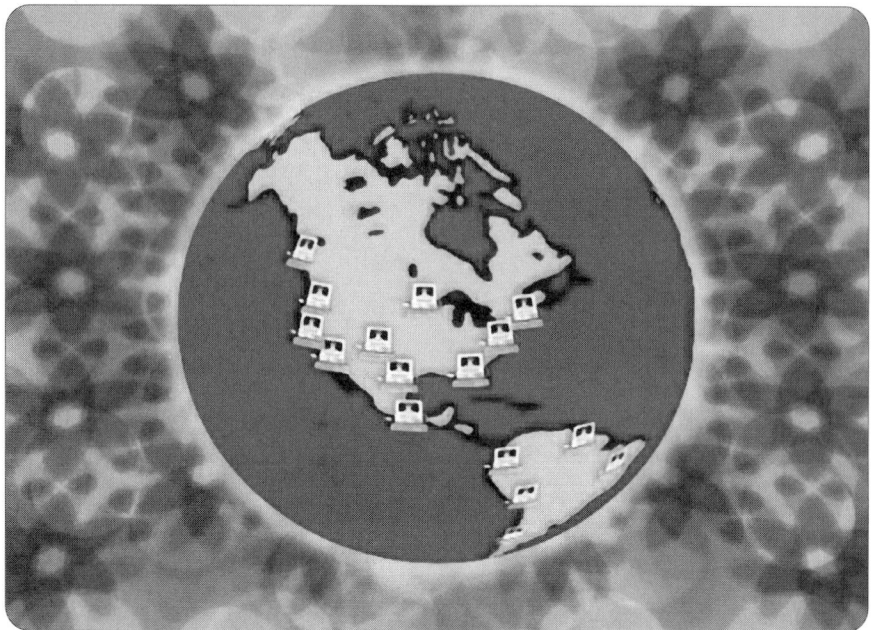

that he communicates with aliens, even though I've still never seen him do that.

I lost track of how much time we spent stargazing. Dr. F. would give me what he obviously thought was time enough to stare in appreciation at something before he'd take the telescope away from me, make a few adjustments, hand it back to me, and point me in another direction. I could have spent the entire night gaping at the skies, but without any indication that I was handing the telescope back to him for the final time, I sadly watched as Dr. F. folded it up and put it back in his pocket protector.

"You still curious about what I've got in my lab?" he asked me.

"I guess so." I wasn't sure where this conversation was going. I didn't want to risk sounding too eager or anything.

"Your dad says it's okay if you come over to help me out occasionally. Think you'd like that?"

Think? "That wouldn't be too bad, I guess."

We shook hands and the deal was struck. We climbed down out of the tree house, and after I'd hung around long enough to eat some of the pizza mom had brought out to the patio, I went upstairs to my room and settled back down in front of my computer.

After that night, I frequently visited Dr. F's workshop. One night, however, I noticed something familiar to me, but new to the lab. Dr. Franklin had set up a computer in his workshop. There was a hard drive, a monitor, a keyboard, and a mouse. All the usual stuff. Which was actually unusual for something normally found in his lab. Just as I made this discovery, Data came bounding up from behind where I was examining the computer and unleashed a flurry of barks. Dr. F. burst through the front door and found me cowering beneath Data's mercifully untranslatable outbursts.

In hindsight, Dr. Franklin did seem a little too glad to show me his latest creation. He fixed me a cup of herbal tea in a glass beaker held over a Bunsen burner. He was always telling me that "kids these days drink too much of that sugary soda pop," so I soon learned it was easier to just drink the tea, rather than hope to find something else in one of those coolers or refrigerators he kept here and there throughout the lab. (Now I'm actually starting to like the stuff, but I don't let on.) Anyhow, he began to introduce the computer that sat upon his desk like it was an actual person or something.

"This, my young man, is a computer..." he began , as if I didn't already know that. "I affectionately call her *Preemptive Portal Packet*," he continued. I decided right then and there that this guy really needed to get out more. Find somebody to date. Something. "Through 3P and the use of the Internet, I will be able to bring the people of the world a wealth of knowledge that they have only dreamed about."

Of course, I knew all about the computer and the Internet. "Doctor," I said gently, so as not to hurt his feelings, "the computer and the Internet have been around for awhile."

Sometimes, as I think I've already mentioned, Dr. F. isn't known for his patience. "I know that, Beta," he retorted, rather forcefully. "But, do they know how it works?"

It suddenly dawned on me why lately Dr. F. had seemed emphatic that I understand some stuff that he referred to as Time Division Multiplexing and Modified Real/Time Theory of Relativity.

However, like he so often does with my nickname, once he tells you a term, he resorts to the acronym, so it's been TDM this and MRTTR that in a lot of his recent conversations with me, although perhaps conversation is the wrong word, as I barely get to say anything.

Although I sometimes find my self doing it in class, I don't dare zone out while Dr. F. is talking. He really hates to repeat stuff. Little did I know how risky it would be to have missed one of his earlier explanations. It wasn't until later that I knew understanding what he was talking about was easier when I could associate the words with the acronyms. I'd spent the past few weeks pondering just what exactly he meant every time he talked about "JTCI." I didn't plan to repeat that mistake! Or maybe I just assumed I'd missed it. Knowing Dr. F., he might have kept that one on a need-to-know basis. After all, it *was* the acronym I'd seen written repeatedly on all of those mysterious blueboards, so I'd think that no matter where my mind was at the moment, hearing the doctor mention those letters should have gotten my attention. Doesn't matter now, I guess. Besides, I'm digressing again.

Getting back on topic: TDM and MRTTR are the terms that Dr. Franklin uses to explain the ability to observe nanosecond operations using one's real time senses.

Dr. F. is also a firm believer in immersing oneself in study in order to comprehend a subject. I never dreamt he meant that literally when he was telling me about how, much like when an adrenaline rush brought on by a crisis can make things seem to happen in slow motion, TDM and MRTTR technology takes the brain's subconscious ability to comprehend data quickly and translates it to real-time, conscious observation.

Aside from that, I couldn't help wondering what TDM and MRTTR were going to have to do with the

Internet. Everybody knows things are transmitted quickly over the Internet. I couldn't understand why Dr. F. felt they needed something as esoteric sounding as TDM and MRTTR technology to comprehend that.

"Most people don't really care how the Internet works, do they?" I asked. "Beyond learning how to turn on the computer and click the mouse, that is. Once they learn how to log on, what else do they need to know?"

"Do you want to settle for being like *most people*? Don't answer that, B. It was a rhetorical question." Even though he'd called me "B" again, I could tell he was over his impatience. He was now into one of his preoccupied modes. Or so I thought.

"Now sit here, my young Beta Testee," he continued.

His modification of the name he used to address me did concern me a bit, but I did as I was told. I sat down.

"Allow me to demonstrate my latest invention."

As he spoke these words, I was suddenly aware of what the eccentric doctor had in mind. He muttered something about "Inverse Particle Projection—IPP, if you will" while he adjusted the Web cam that until that moment had been walking back and forth across the top of the monitor on tiny little legs. I began to think about whether or not I should panic.

Before I could react further, he pointed the Web cam directly at me and pushed a large blue button.

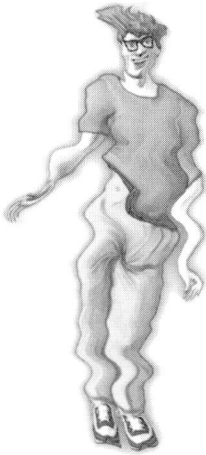

"JTCI, BT," I heard him say, almost as if he were speaking through a megaphone held backwards. "Now you begin *your* Journey to the Center of the Internet!"

I was suddenly drawn into what should have seemed like a series of tiny cables but actually became these huge circular walls on all sides. Lights flashed about me as I beheld the digital scenery rushing past me. Or was I rushing past it? While I tried to push my stomach back down to its proper place and get a grip about what was going on, Dr. F's workshop became a chaotic stew of swirling images from my past and my mind became a firing range for random synapses. I was soon overcome and fell into an almost semi-conscious state. Actually, it felt more like what I imagined somebody undergoing hypnosis might feel like as everything around me seemed to slow down and the lights about me seemed to pulse less frequently than my racing heart beat.

I closed my eyes for a bit in order to steady my breathing. When I opened them again, I found myself in what almost looked like a large, well-ordered city. *Networkopolis or something*, I thought to myself.

Okay, I told myself. *Things are now under control.*

"How are you doing in there, Beta?"

Okay. Maybe not so good. Either I'm hallucinating or that hub just talked to me!

Chapter 1

Home Computer Terms

So now you know how I got inside the computer network.

At that point, I still didn't know how that hub connection was talking to me. Or why it sounded so much like Dr. F. I already knew the guy was a genius when it comes to technology. I'd never suspected he was a ventriloquist, too.

In the meantime, I bounced back and forth between things I couldn't name, while I had this eerie feeling that I was somehow being broken apart and reassembled... repeatedly. Other times I felt like my thoughts were coming to me in quadraphonic. All around me I heard these digitized sounds and saw what I could only assume was data speeding by in bits of bytes or bytes of bits or something. It was like I was in some sort of thought-driven vehicle. The scariest thing of all was that I couldn't be entirely sure it was my thoughts that were doing the driving.

"Do I have access to any brakes here?" I asked nobody in particular, since I wasn't certain who was even around to ask. At the same time, I was trying—and failing miserably—to mask the shakiness in my voice.

"Son, you're on a journey; you're not the driver." The voice that came from somewhere behind a router to my left still sounded like it belonged to Dr. Franklin. I just couldn't get myself to slow down enough to get a good look at who—or what—was doing the talking. "Think of

Hubs, Routers, and Packets

A **hub** connects all necessary computers and communications devices together as the hub of your bicycle connects all the spokes of the wheel.

A **Router** sends data (or packets of data) from one network or area to another. **Routers** decide what is the most efficient way of sending information much as when a delivery person must decide which streets to drive on to save the most amount of time.

In order to send information efficiently, computers package information into **packets** much as we put our letters in an envelope to send through the mail.

yourself as an interactive passenger and things will go a lot easier for you."

There was a brief moment of silence as I felt myself bounced off of one satellite link and into another.

"You ever ride on a tandem bicycle?"

"Yes," I told him. (The voice was distinctively male, even if I couldn't yet be sure that it belonged to Dr. F.) "And unless I was the one in charge of the brakes, I didn't like it."

"Brakes aren't really an option here."

"Maybe not to you!" I countered, trying—and failing again—not to raise my voice.

My concerns didn't quite seem to be the same as his. "You'll learn to deal with it," he told me. "If you'd just give it a chance, I'm sure you'll like it here."

I heard my voice grow even louder as I continued. "Where exactly am I? And speaking of options, where's the exit?"

"It's too soon to start telling you about **hubs** and **routers** and **packets** and such. How about if you just close your eyes for a minute?"

"How is that going to help me?"

"Do you always worry this much? No, don't answer that."

At that moment, I felt that squish thing again.

"There," I heard the disembodied voice continue before I had time to get concerned about what was squishing me and why. "That address change should get you hung up in the name server long enough for me to get you back to what I now see should have been step one."

"Am I going to be home in time to eat?" I asked.

Okay, so you may not think that question should have been a priority at a time like that, but I'm a teenage boy. If I'm not thinking about my computer, I'm thinking about girls. And whenever I'm doing any type of thinking I'm usually eating, or thinking about eating. It takes a lot of calories to fuel this mind!

"Here's some fuel for thought...."

Is that guy psychic or what? "Ah," I interrupted him. "Are you Dr. F?"

"Of course I am, Beta," Dr. Franklin replied. "Who else would I be?"

"I'm not entirely sure at this point."

"Try to stay on topic here." I could almost imagine Dr. F. pacing for a bit before he continued with what I was certain was about to be another lecture. "It's obvious your mind needs time to adjust to TDM. What better place to slow down the pace than back in the PC, which is where we should have started in the first place."

"I seem to recall I *did* start at the PC."

"Not *at* the PC," Dr. F. said, a bit of irritation obvious in his tone. "I said *in* the PC. There's a big difference. You need to learn to stay focused. Pay attention."

"*In* the PC?"

"Exactly!"

That really clears things up, I thought. *Maybe I should try a different approach.* "How is it that my thoughts no longer seem to be coming to me in multiplex-style quadra-phonic anymore?" I asked.

"Because you're in the name server and not at a hub connection," Dr. F. replied (a bit too impatiently in my opinion), using his any-idiot-should-know-that tone of voice. What Dr. F. has in intelligence, he sometimes lacks in sensitivity.

"But," he continued. "We don't have time to discuss the details of when a packet arrives at one **port** and how it's copied to all of the other ports, thus enabling all seg-ments of the LAN to see—or, as in your case, seemingly hear—all packets at once. You may recall that I asked you to stay focused."

"LAN?"

"Focus, BT!"

"On what?"

"Close your eyes."

Port

A **port** is a connec-tion point in the computer allowing you to attach a peripheral to the computer for communication between the two. A **port** can be serial (information travels only one way at a time) or parallel (information can travel both ways simultaneously) between the computer and the peripheral.

"Isn't that a contradiction?" I asked. "How am I to focus on something with my eyes closed?"

"Now you're being silly. You need to direct your intelligence. For that, we need to get you into the PC so your mind can acclimate itself to the TDM. It's obvious to me now that Time Division Multiplexing is an acquired skill and we need to ensure that you acquire it."

"But why *in* the PC?"

"You can't begin your Journey to the Center of the Internet from outside of one, can you?"

"No, but...."

"Just close your eyes!"

I closed my eyes. Then I felt a squish here and a squish there. Next even my heart rate seemed to slow down. I could almost sense things moving at a much slower pace, despite remaining obedient and keeping my eyes closed. Maybe I was too scared to open my eyes and risk that squishes-to-the-pit-of-my-stomach-like-I'm-on-a-rollercoaster-headed-downhill feeling again. As it was, Dr. F. gave me further instructions before I had much time to dwell on my options.

"You'll need to keep your eyes closed a bit longer," he told me. "Let's get your mind headed in the correct direction. What can you tell me about a PC?"

"A personal computer?"

"Exactly!" he said, with the enthusiasm and sparkle I prefer back in his voice. Now I just needed to try to keep up with him so that I could keep it there.

"Well," I said, somewhat stalling for time while I gathered my thoughts. "A personal computer is a general purpose tool. It's built around a CPU, which is also known as a microprocessor. It has an assortment of parts that all work together."

"Why would you consider it 'general purpose'?"

"Because it can perform more than one task. I'm not just talking about **multitasking**—performing several functions or running several programs simultaneously— I mean that you can do all sorts of things with a PC, like

Multitasking

Multitasking is the computer's ability to run two or more programs simultaneously. This ability depends on the computer's operating system, amount of memory, CPU capability, etc.

play games, type up your homework, and connect to the Internet."

"Good job!"

Despite myself, I felt a smile form on my lips. It was nice getting Dr. F.'s approval. I still didn't understand why exactly we were back to a Computers 101 course, but that didn't seem important at the time.

"Keep your eyes closed, pretend you're looking at your computer on your desk at home, and tell me what you see," Dr. Franklin instructed.

"I see a keyboard, a mouse, a tower, a monitor, some speakers, and my external peripherals, like my printer and scanner."

"Thinking of your PC as a general-purpose information-tion processing device, how does it receive information to process from a person?"

"Directly from a person, I guess. Through the keyboard and mouse."

"Exactly!"

I still didn't know where all of this was headed, but at least it was easy so far.

"How does a PC receive information to process from a device?" he asked.

"You mean like when it receives information from the hard drive or floppy disk or CD?"

"Exactly! How about from a network?"

"That'd be through a **modem** or a **network card**."

"After your computer processes the information, how does it show you the results?"

"On the monitor."

"You've just summed up the basics of connections. You see, it doesn't matter how powerful the components inside your computer are if you don't have a way to interact with them. This interaction is called input/output (I/O)."

Just when I thought Dr. F. was done asking questions, he fired this one at me: "Once the computer processes information, where does it store what it's processed?"

Modems and NICs

Modem is short for **MOdulator/DEModulator**. This device takes digital signals, converts them to analog signals (for phone line use), and reconverts them to digital signals once it reaches another computer.

A **Network Interface Card (NIC)** also called a network adapter, regulates the information flowing between clients and servers within a network.

Central Processing Unit (CPU)

The **CPU** is a small chip inserted into a microprocessor which rests on the motherboard of a computer. It is responsible for coordinating everything done by the computer. The speed of the **CPU**, known as **clock speed**, determines the speed at which the computer as a whole will operate. **Clock Speed** is measured in either **megahertz (MHz)**, **gigahertz (GHz)**, or **millions of instructions per second (MIPS)**, all of which are a measure of how fast the **CPU** can handle instructions.

"Most commonly on the hard drive, although there can be exceptions to that."

"That's good enough for our needs now."

I could almost imagine the wheels turning in Dr. F.'s brain as he was deciding what to ask me next. As far as oral quizzes go, this one had been pretty easy so far.

"Okay, we've established that a PC is a general-purpose computer. Can you give me examples of some specific-or special-purpose computers?"

"I imagine that would be something like a game machine or any computer that's designed to only handle a specific task, like one you might find in a car or an alarm system or a kitchen appliance."

"Exactly," Dr. F. said, repeating what was seemingly becoming his favorite word. "A special-purpose computer is designed to do one thing. In the case of a PC, it's the **CPU** that enables it to do all of the general-purpose tasks you want it to accomplish. What can you tell me about a CPU?"

"CPU stands for **Central Processing Unit**, the control that coordinates everything done by the computer. It's the heart of the computer, pumping information as it performs its function as a complete computation engine fabricated on a single chip." I felt pretty confident about this topic. I'd even swapped chips in my own computer, which was one way to say that I'd updated my CPU. "A CPU is a basically a piece formed out of a metallic substance with a tiny microchip in it. It's designed to be nested in the computer's **motherboard**. It determines the speed of the computer. The speed of a CPU is known as the **clock speed**. Until recently, that speed was gauged in **megahertz (MHz)**. A **hertz** is a cycle; one megahertz represents one million cycles per second. Each computer instruction requires a fixed number of cycles, so the clock speed is one of the factors that determines how many instructions per second the CPU can handle. Newer chips have speeds calculated in **gigahertz (GHz)**, or one billion hertz. **MIPS**, which stands for **millions of**

instructions per second, is another acronym you'll see referring to processor speed. The first CPUs for personal computers could only handle 1 instruction per 15 clock cycles, or 0.03 MIPS; today's can handle 2 instructions per cycle. In other words, even though CPUs for personal computers have been around for 20 years and they still handle information in basically the same way they did back then, they do it a whopping 5,000 times faster!"

I took a breath and heard Dr. F. say, "You can open your eyes now." And so I did.

Imagine my surprise to find myself inside a computer tower, standing next to the motherboard, looking over at a CPU nested snug and secure within its socket.

The motherboard is the main circuit board to which all of the other internal components connect. The CPU and **memory** are usually on the motherboard, while other components, such as the sound card, can be built into the motherboard or connected through PCI that we'll discuss in a little bit. Now that I had a chance to look around, I could see lots of things that until then I'd just taken for granted.

"You doing okay in there?" Dr. F. asked.

"Yep."

"Okay," he said. "Take your time and look around. Just holler if you need me."

I liked being able to do things at my own pace for awhile.

Next I checked out the computer memory, which are the types of fast storage used to hold data. Memory has to be fast because it's directly connected to the microprocessor. Actually, there are several different types of memory in a computer.

The one with which most people are familiar is known as **random-access memory** or **RAM**. The computer uses it as temporary storage for information with which the computer is currently working. Most computers sold today come with a certain amount of RAM in megabytes (MB), which is 1,048,576—or 2 to the 20th

> **Motherboard**
> The motherboard is the main circuit board in a computer to which all of the other internal components connect.

power—bytes. Common RAM configurations run at 64MB, 128MB, 256MB, and so on.

Read-only memory (ROM) is the permanent memory storage used by the computer for essential data that doesn't change.

Basic input/output system (BIOS) typically comes on a ROM chip, sometimes called the **ROM BIOS**. The BIOS has the built-in software that determines what a computer can do without accessing programs from a disk, including, but not limited to, booting up. Boot-up instructions are the basic communications between the chip and the computer when it is first turned on. Because the BIOS is on a chip, it's always available and not subject to disk failures.

Caching, which is pronounced *cashing*, is the storage of frequently used data, usually in extremely fast RAM connected directly to the CPU. **SRAM** is the chip usually used for the cache, while slower **DRAM** is used for RAM.

To take a look at the other kind of memory, I took a temporary detour over to the **hard drive**. That's where the **virtual memory** used as another type of temporary data storage is housed; it's swapped in and out of RAM as needed.

Over here is another essential type of memory: the hard drive. In fact, many people often confuse their hard drive capacity with their computer memory. It's important to remember that RAM is the temporary memory storage, and is generally what is meant by computer memory. It's the amount of space the computer has

available in which to run programs. The hard drive is a large-capacity permanent storage device used to hold information such as programs and documents. The hard drive capacity refers to the size of the hard drive, such as 40 gigabytes. Another term with which you'll need to be familiar is your available hard drive space. That's the amount of free space left on the hard drive into which you can save data or install programs.

The hard drive is sometimes referred to as the brain of the computer because it stores and remembers all the information given to it—permanently, which means it stays there until you perform a specific action to delete that information and send it to the trash can.

There are two parts to the hard drive: the drive itself, which records and reads the information, and a spinning metal disk, called the hard disk, onto which the computer puts the actual information.

Like a brain, the hard disk remembers information until the computer needs to use it. When the computer needs that information, it reads it from the hard disk using RAM. As the name Random Access Memory implies, the computer doesn't have to read everything from the hard drive into its memory. It reads only those specific pieces of information that it needs. In this way, the hard disk then works like a book. Pretend you read a Jules Verne novel and want to share a really exciting part that came in the middle of the book with your friend. Instead of reading every word in the book until you get to that part, you can just open to the page that part is on and read only those sentences or paragraphs you wish to share. The computer can access the hard drive in much the same way, turning only to that "page"—or sector and track within a specific cluster on the hard drive from which it needs to find and retrieve the data.

The hard drive interfaces with the computer via either an Integrated Drive Electronics (IDE) or Small Computer System Interface (SCSI—pronounced "skuzzy") Controller. These controllers can also be used as the

Memory

There are several types of **memory** in a computer, each with its own unique role to play in the operations of the computer.

◎ **Random-access memory (RAM)** is the one with which most people are familiar. The computer uses **RAM** as temporary storage for information with which the computer is currently working. Most computers sold today come with a certain amount of **RAM** in megabytes (MB).

◎ **Read-only memory (ROM)** is the permanent memory storage, usually contained on a chip, used by the computer for essential data that doesn't change, such as the **BIOS**.

Continued

- **Caching**, which is pronounced cashing, is the storage of frequently used data, usually in extremely fast RAM connected directly to the CPU. **SRAM** is the chip usually used for the cache, while slower **DRAM** is used for RAM.
- **Virtual memory** is another type of temporary data storage; it's swapped in and out of RAM as needed.
- The **hard drive** is a large-capacity permanent storage device used to hold information such as programs and documents. The hard drive capacity refers to the size of the hard drive, such as **40 gigabytes**.

method of adding additional devices, such as an additional hard drive, a scanner, or a CD-ROM drive, to the computer.

The Peripheral Component Interconnect (PCI) and Industry Standard Architecture (ISA) buses are two of the ways to connect additional components to the computer. On a computer, a bus is a collection of wires through which data is transmitted from one part of a computer to another, a sort of local highway on which data travels within a computer. When it comes to those used within personal computers, the term bus usually refers to internal bus, or the connection between all of the internal computer components to the CPU and main memory. There's also an expansion bus that enables expansion boards to access the CPU and memory.

All buses have two parts: an address bus and a data bus.

The Accelerated Graphics Port (AGP) is a very high-speed connection by which the graphics card interfaces with the computer.

The computer uses its sound card to convert analog sound into digital information and back again, thus enabling it to record and play audio.

The graphics card translates image data from the computer into a format that can be displayed by the monitor. Image data is just a fancy way of saying "pictures."

Coming into the back of the tower is the power supply. That one's pretty self-explanatory. Elementary as it may be though, it's essential because it's the electrical transformer that regulates the electricity used by the computer.

"I bet you seldom stop to think about all of the stuff that's going on inside of your computer, do you?" I heard Dr. F. ask.

"Not really, sir." I'd begun to think that maybe Dr. F. had forgotten about me.

"You getting along okay in there?"

"Just fine, sir. I do have a question though." Now that I'd had a chance to stop and think about some things, I did have one worry other than when I'd get to eat again.

"Well, then. What are you waiting for? If you don't ask it, I can't very well answer it, can I?"

"Is there any chance I'll get fried while I'm in here stepping around all of these electrical components?"

Dr. Franklin actually laughed out loud. "No, Beta. Not at all. And the computer is just as safe from static electricity generated by you as you are from getting zapped by it. In fact, if we had time, you could jump on the hard disk and lit-erally take it for a spin. Unfortunately, we need to wrap things up in here."

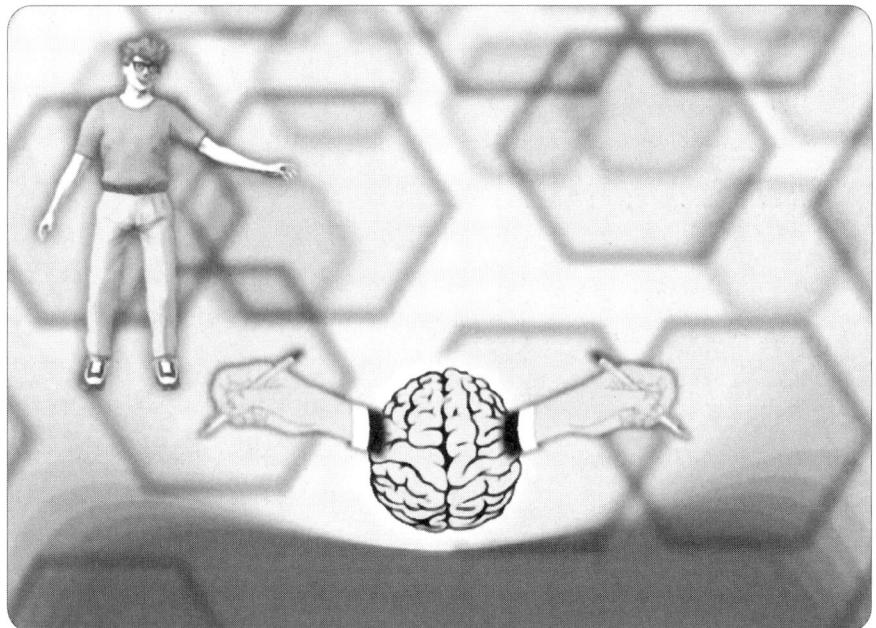

I was almost afraid to think where Dr. F. would send me next. Things inside the computer did seem to be occurring at a much slower pace. That had to be in part because my brain must have been finally wrapping itself around the whole Time Division Multiplexing concept. After all, the computer isn't exactly a slouch when it comes to moving data, so my ability to watch it do just that had to mean that TDM was working.

There wasn't much more to check out inside the computer anyhow. Aside from the parallel port com-monly used to connect a printer and the serial port typi-cally used to connect an external modem, that about wrapped things up. Which should have been my clue that I was about to receive another Dr. F. infodump lec-ture. (I say that without any disrespect. You know how it

> ## Broadband and Baseband
>
> **Broadband** is a connection that holds several channels, each of which can send information.
> **Baseband** is a connection that has only one channel.
> **Broadband** usually has a lot of bandwidth, and can send information much faster than a **baseband** connection.

> ## Network
>
> A **network** consists of two or more computers that are connected to one another and can communicate with each other's hard drives.

is sometimes when you're around somebody who just loves to share knowledge!)

"Now that you understand a bit about hard drives, my young Beta Test," Dr. Franklin began, "it may interest you to know that the Internet is really nothing much more than a whole bunch of computers reading information stored on the hard disks of other computers—computers that are often hundreds, or thousands, of miles apart. When you view a Web page, you are actually reading information on the hard disk in a computer at one of those locations. Sometimes, this information is read very slowly because the connection between the computers can't send data very quickly. I like to think of the connection as a garden hose. The bigger the hose, the more water that can go through it at once. Connections are like that, too. Some Internet connections can transmit a little information at a time; others can send a *lot* of information all at once. Other connections can only handle a small trickle of data. The amount of data that can be transmitted over the connection at once is called bandwidth. The more bandwidth, the faster the information can be sent. Of course, with a water hose, you can increase the pressure and get the water to go faster; you can't do that with data, but you get the idea.

"Not every connection works exactly the same way. In fact, there are two different kinds of connections: **broadband** and **baseband**. Broadband allows the same wire to carry multiple channels, while baseband only allows one channel. What that means is broadband is like a hose with a bunch of smaller hoses inside it; each smaller hose carries a different set of information. Baseband only has the one hose. What's interesting about broadband, though, is that each of the channels inside it can usually carry as much or more information as a single baseband connection. This means that broadband usually can transmit information faster than baseband because it can carry all those different channels at once.

"A network is like the Internet on a smaller scale. A computer network is where two or more computers are connected to each other and communicate with each other's hard drives. You can set up a network in your home if you have two computers, but most networks are in offices or colleges where all the computers need to talk to each other.

"There are two types of networks: **LAN**s and **WAN**s. LAN is short for **Local Area Network**—a network that is in a small area. Usually this means that all the computers are in the same building or in buildings close to each other. WAN stands for **Wide Area Network**. WANs include computers in locations far apart from each other and use a private connection to link them. The important thing to keep in mind about networks is that they can allow computers to talk to each other without necessarily using an Internet connection. Unless the network is also connected to the Internet, no computer outside of the network can talk to computers inside the network.

"If a computer is part of a network it needs to have an **NIC** or **Network Interface Card**. This electronic card is put into a computer so a cable or wire can connect the computer to the network. Without an NIC, a computer can't connect to a network. The NIC is sort of like the telephone of the computer world. This is very important for the Internet because, as you'll see later, some Internet connections, like cable Internet, are really just big networks with links to the Internet."

As I pondered what Dr. F. had just told me, I wondered where I'd be off to next.

LANs and WANs

A **LAN**, short for **Local Area Network**, is a group of computers connected to one another in one physical location, usually within the same building or in buildings close to each other. A **WAN**, short for **Wide Area Network**, is a group of computers connected to one another by a private connection but located in different physical locations, often many miles apart. Computers in a particular **LAN** or **WAN** can communicate with other computers in their respective network without needing to be connected to the Internet. Unless the network is also connected to the Internet, no computer outside of the network can talk to computers inside the network.

Chapter 2

History of the Internet

I didn't like having too much time to think, so I decided to ask Dr. F. a question. "Is it safe to say that the Internet is primarily another communications tool?"

"Yes, Beta," Dr. F. replied. "That'd be one way of putting it, assuming that your assumptions about *communication* and *tool* are correct ones."

I heard what sounded like the shuffling of some papers, followed by some scratching noises that I certainly hoped were made from chalk moving across a blackboard—or blueboard, in Dr. F's case. I'd hate to think that there were mice inside this computer along with the one connected on the outside of it!

"How many times have I told you that if you only take the time to listen to it, your subconscious will help you arrive at the answers that are best for you?"

"Well..."

Dr. F. interrupted before I could continue. "That was a rhetorical question, Beta. It was also an acknowledgement that you've inadvertently helped me see exactly where your journey should proceed next." I heard more of those scratching noises, and then he continued. "I had to make some modifications to the map, you know."

I wasn't sure that I did know, but at this point I figured it was safer to accept him at his word and let him continue. I figured the quicker Dr. F. got his map modifications out of the way, the quicker I'd be able to go get something to eat.

"Throughout history, what do you suppose have been some of the other *communication tools* to revolutionize the ways people exchange information?"

I pondered the question for a moment. "Well," I began, "I suppose originally man had to come up with ways in which to communicate in the first place. They probably started out using hand gestures—pointing at things and making noises to add emphasis. We know from cave drawings and hieroglyphics on the pyramids that some used pictures as a way to record information." I paused for a moment to wonder if hieroglyphic writers

got any more respect than Jack Kirby, Peter David, or other comic book creators. I figured probably the first kid to draw cave paintings was sent outside to play by his mom. Then I realized that Dr. F. was doing that nose-breathing thing he does when he's impatient. "While I'd need to do some research to know in what order things evolved from there, I imagine early man figured out ways to develop a language that provided the means to discuss simple everyday ideas like what to have for dinner or where to hunt for wooly mammoths, and from there language advanced to where it could be used to explain concepts like counting."

I paused again to take a breath and Dr. F. interrupted. "Move ahead, Beta. What are the early ways people transmitted information from person to person across great distances?"

"I suppose the earliest ways would have been by shouting."

"Further ahead."

"Smoke signals?"

"You're getting closer, but move a bit further ahead than that."

"Letters?"

"Even faster ways."

"You mean like the more recent means, from a historical standpoint, like the telegraph and Morse Code, then the telephone, and later the radio?"

"Exactly! Now, without getting too technical and forgetting about radio waves and whatnot for a moment, what do these forms of communications have in common?"

"I remember reading about how they strung wires across the ocean for the telegraph and I suppose early telephone lines would have been a type of wire, too, right?"

"Wires it is! When we think of communications wires today, we most often associate that component with cables."

Knowing that Dr. F. had told me that I couldn't get fried by any of these components inside this computer, I decided to lean back and sit down on one of the chips nestled in the motherboard. If I scrunched my shoulders just so, it wasn't too uncomfortable. I figured it'd be better than standing through what I assumed was going to be another one of the doctor's lectures. A series of questions was usually the signal that another lecture was about to begin.

"Don't get too comfy there, Beta."

I jumped back up, hitting my head on an adjoining chip as I did so. As I worked to loosen some strands of my hair that had gotten tangled up in the works, I heard Dr. F. mumble something about "every good map should allow for a detour."

I heard some more of those scratching noises, followed by the sound of Dr. F. sneezing. He ignored my "gesundheit" and said, "Remind me to come up with a way to make chalk that creates less dust."

"I'll make a note of it." I almost rolled my eyes, then I remembered I didn't know how closely Dr. F. was viewing my actions at any given time, and despite how impatient I was feeling at the moment, or how hungry, I didn't want to hurt his feelings.

I didn't have much time to worry about his feelings after that. I felt a squish, then a jolt, and then I heard Dr. F. talking through that backwards megaphone again. "Let's do a quick test of TDM...." (You may recall from the introduction that *TDM* is the acronym for what Dr. F calls *Time Division Multiplexing*. *TDM* and *MRTTR* are the terms that Dr. Franklin uses to explain the ability to observe nanosecond operations using one's real time senses.)

Dr. F.'s voice trailed off as I felt myself zoom out to where I appeared to be looking down on the earth from somewhere out in space. Just as quickly I felt that squishy feeling in the pit of my stomach, although I must admit that it was less squishy this time, and my line of

vision seemed to travel back toward earth where I saw a boy pulling a wagon along what looked like a lane leading back to a farm. There were several cars, each with fancy taillight housings that I seem to recall are called tailfins, parked close to the farmhouse. I noticed a tractor moving slowly across an adjoining field. The guy driving it actually appeared to be sitting on a wide seat, out in the open, without any way that I could see for the air conditioning to be doing much good. I thought those things had enclosed cabs or something for that.

I didn't get much chance to ponder that before, feeling the sun on my back, I veered at an angle and zoomed in on what, judging from the number of cherry blossoms in evidence, I could only assume was Washington, D.C. I blinked to adjust my line of vision, and the Washington Monument came into view, confirming my suspicions. Next my gaze fell on the Pentagon, and I couldn't help but wonder if at that moment the Department of Defense might have a way to pick me up on radar or something.

"Will I even be able to see a stealth bomber before it shoots me down?" I asked out loud.

No sooner were my words spoken then I felt another squish, followed by another jolt, and found myself back standing next to the computer motherboard.

"How are you feeling?" Dr. F. asked.

"Hungry."

"Good!"

"I'm serious," I told him.

"So am I," he said. "If you're hungry, that means your brain has adapted to TDM and we don't have to worry about any motion sickness now. You're ready to continue with your Journey to the Center of the Internet."

"Or to eat," I mumbled, knowing that he would be in another one of his preoccupied states and therefore ignore anything I said until he asked me my next question.

"Beta," he finally said.

I waited for more. Evidently something other than the state of my stomach had his attention.

"It's obvious you need to know where things have been before you can adequately know where you're going."

"Okay," I said, not really knowing what he meant. I figured he'd just tell me "everything in its own time" if I asked for clarification anyhow.

"Just how much do you know about how the Internet came to be?"

"I know there was some controversy during the presidential election about whether or not Al Gore invented it," I replied.

"Beta," he began, followed by an obvious harrumph. "Al Gore was part of a congressional initiative to fund the further development of the Internet intended to broaden its scope. Whether or not he was vague or used politician-speak in the way he stated his involvement or downright lied is open to interpretation based on which side of the political spectrum those doing the debating happen to fall upon. We certainly don't have time to ponder such matters."

I heard what sounded like more scratches, so I waited for what I'd begun to accept as his updates to that elusive map I kept hearing about.

"All debates aside, I suppose Al Gore is as good a place as any to start the next leg of your Journey to the

Center of the Internet," he said. "It'll help add perspective to MRTTR and the time-line calendar."

I leaned my elbow against the motherboard, blinked, and when I opened my eyes, I found myself back at the farm I had seen earlier, leaning against a cow that actually seemed to turn its head and smile at me.

"Checking the calendar that will always appear to your upper left will help you maintain your Modified Real/Time Theory of Relativity perspective in this part of the journey."

I was hearing Dr. F.'s voice, but I swear it was that cow that was moving her lips.

"What year do you see on that calendar?"

"1958," I replied.

"Exactly," said Dr. F., starring in his new role as the talking cow. "In 1958, when Al Gore was 10 years old and living on this farm in Tennessee, and back when cars were cars –(you only have to look at that '57 Chevy parked over there to see what I mean) and your grandma was in grade school, probably wearing a poodle skirt and saddle shoes, the United States government formed the Advanced Research Projects Agency (ARPA)."

I looked around for a milking stool or somewhere to sit down. It was obvious that Dr. F., in whatever form or wherever he might be, was entering into another one of his infodump lectures. I had to settle for leaning against the cow again. After all, it seemed friendly enough. I was finding it disconcerting to look into her eyes while she spoke anyhow. Despite the distinctively male voice, I didn't want to even begin to ponder the possibility that I might be that close to a bull. I've heard they can be fierce, and I didn't have a red cape with me.

"ARPA was, and is, a segment of the Department of Defense charged with ensuring U.S. leadership in science and technology with regard to military applications. In other words, that agency was formed and given the responsibility for overseeing the direction and perform-ance of advanced research and development projects designated by the Secretary of Defense. The name was later changed to the **Defense Advanced Research Projects Agency (DARPA)** in 1972, reverted back to ARPA in 1990, and then became DARPA again in 1996. But we're getting ahead of ourselves. DARPA maintains a Web site at www.darpa.mil if you want to find out more about them."

The calendar was having fits keeping up with the con-versation. I finally noticed it settled on 1962 and appeared to be ready to stay there, for the time being at least.

"The first recorded descriptions of what would become the Internet were a series of memos about the social interactions that could be enabled through net-working. These memos were written by J.C.R. Licklider, of MIT, in August, 1962."

I couldn't help myself. I laughed. "Licklider?" I asked. I'd certainly never heard a name like that before.

"Beta, pay attention," Dr. F. said. "In these memos, Licklider discussed his concept for a 'Galactic Network.' As the first head of the computer research program at DARPA, Licklider was instrumental in convincing others of the importance of this networking concept."

I heard a subtle shuffling sound and saw the calendar flip to yet another year.

"In 1969, which you may recall was the year Neil Armstrong walked on the moon and the hippies in San Francisco were becoming known as 'Flower Children,' ARPA established the **Advanced Research Projects Agency Network (ARPANET).** ARPANET was the forerunner of the Internet.

Defense Advanced Research Projects Agency (DARPA)

Founded in 1958, the Defense Advanced Research Projects Agency is a segment of the Department of Defense. Its goal is ensuring U.S. leader-ship in science and technology with regard to military applica-tions, and it is responsible for over-seeing the direction and performance of advanced research and development projects. Originally named simply the Advanced Research Projects Agency, its name has changed several times, and since 1996 it has been known as the **Defense Advanced Research Projects Agency.**

Advanced Research Projects Agency Network (ARPANET)

Created by the **Advanced Research Projects Agency** in 1969, the **Advanced Research Projects Agency Network** was an early forerunner of the Internet as we know it today.

Originally connecting computers at four universities in the United States of America, it evolved into a network connecting government, academic, and industrial sites around the world.

"ARPANET originally was a network that connected major computers at the University of California at Los Angeles, the University of California at Santa Barbara, Stanford Research Institute, and the University of Utah. It evolved from that early beginning of linking four locations to eventually linking government sites, academic research sites, and industrial sites around the world."

The calendar movement I had come to accept. Imagine my surprise, however, when I looked down and discovered I was now dressed in bell-bottom jeans and wearing a tie-dyed T-shirt with love beads and a peace symbol around my neck. I discovered the peace symbol when I had to get it untangled from my hair, which now flowed past my shoulders. I found myself hoping that this was Dr. F.'s idea of getting me in character and not evidence of MRTTR gone wrong, turning me into a JTCI-stranded Rip Van Winkle. I didn't have time to find out, because the Doctor's info narrative continued.

"More computers were added to the ARPANET network during the ensuing years, while work was underway to complete a Host-to-Host protocol and other network software. In December 1970, the Network Working Group (NWG) completed the initial ARPANET Host-to-Host protocol, called the Network Control Protocol (NCP). A protocol is a format standard for transmitting data between two devices, which we will talk more about later. This meant that for the first time, network users could begin to develop network applications. In 1972, the first application was the introduction of a new feature known as 'electronic mail.'

"All this was taking place at the height of the Cold War. In anticipation of the threat of nuclear attack, ARPANET created a design that allowed for continued communications between its networked sites, even if any of those networked sites were destroyed. At this point, ARPANET only linked the military personnel, computer professionals, engineers, and scientists who knew their way around its complex workings."

I heard the now-familiar shuffling sound and the calendar changed yet again. During the calendar shift, my wardrobe switched from a white disco-style suit and platform shoes to a neon pink T-shirt with a surfboard logo, shorts that came down almost to my ankles, and a jean jacket covered with buttons displaying various catch phrases.

"1984, the year Molly Ringwald appeared in *Sixteen Candles*." Dr. F. paused, and I swear I heard him sigh. I found myself wondering who this Molly person was.

Dr. F. coughed, apparently to compose himself, then continued, "In 1984, as a security measure in anticipation of the expansion of the network, the military communications part of ARPANET split off and was named MILNET. What remained of ARPANET at that time were those research networks that eventually became the testing ground and then the original backbone of the Internet.

"At this point, most users were still only affiliated with universities, although libraries began to connect their catalogs to the Internet as well. This expansion came about because the Internet was based on the idea that there could be multiple independent networks, embodying the key underlying technical concept that they would operate with packet switching and **open-architecture networking**. Open-architecture networking meant that the individual networks could each have their own unique interface; that foundation principal is why today you can connect to the Internet regardless of which operating system your computer uses.

"Under NCP, the key components of the packet switches called Interface Message Processors (IMP) did not have the ability to address networks (and machines) further downstream than the destination IMP. This meant that if any packets were lost, the protocol (and presumably any applications it supported) would come to a grinding halt. Bob Kahn rectified this problem by creating what is known today as Transmission Control

> **Open-architecture Networking**
>
> One of the key underlying technical concepts of the Internet, **open-architecture networking** allows independent networks to use their own unique interfaces, making it possible for them to connect to the internet regardless of which operating system they are using.

Protocol/Internet Protocol (TCP/IP). TCP/IP is a term you'll encounter often on your journey, Beta. We'll also talk more about packets later."

I could swear I heard a disembodied gulp that led me to assume that Dr. F. had just taken a drink of water, then the info continued.

"Widespread development of LANs, the home PC revolution, and workstations in the 1980s allowed the budding Internet to flourish. As the early computer-to-computer, modem-linked communication medium of Bulletin Board Systems (BBS) popped up between home computer users, the further need for linked communications became evident. Although a BBS required that you dial directly to the site instead of connecting to an interlaced network of sites, it was still an important development. The first real 'hacker' movie, *War Games,* dealt with this development.

"In addition to using 'home brew' BBS communications, people from Computer User Groups began to meet online using services like Delphi, CompuServe, GEnie, and others. In fact, Delphi Forums still exist today. The most popular online service these days is AOL.

"Developers eventually created Archie, the Wide Area Information Server (WAIS), and other indices to help keep track of the rapidly growing amount of information on what was becoming the Internet. In anticipation of more users joining the network, developers recognized the need for a friendly, easy-to-use interface with which to work. BBS-type communication was the model for

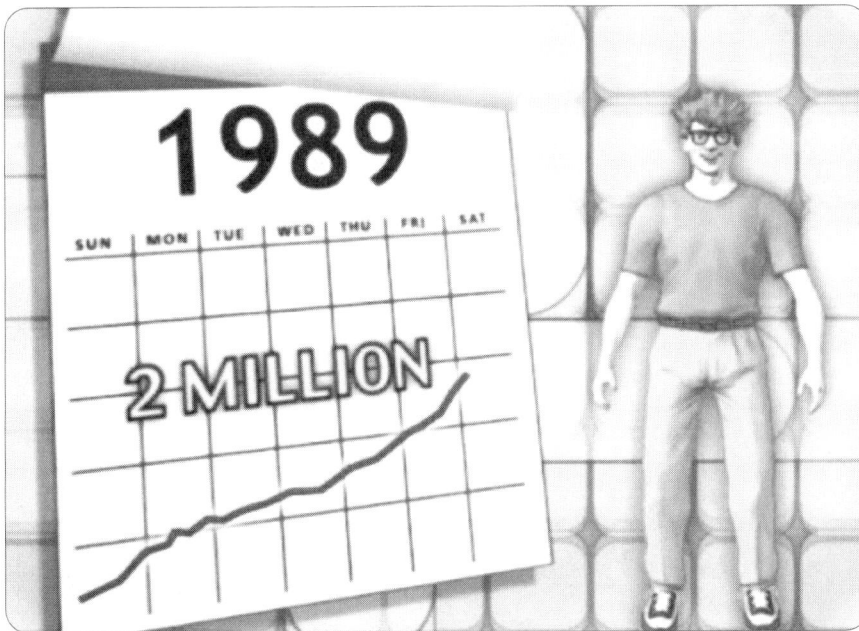

how the infant Internet organized and allowed access to information. In 1991, the University of Minnesota created Gopher, a simple menu system for accessing files.

"All of this paved the way for Tim Berners-Lee's role in the 'birth' of the World Wide Web and the development of the World Wide Web Consortium, all of which you'll learn about soon enough."

With that, the cow hit me with her tail.

"It's time to moooooooooove on, son."

Chapter 3

Bones, Backbones, and More Bones

"Mooooooooooove" would be an understatement. Faster than I could say "Yikes!" I was on top of what looked like the skeleton of an enormous dinosaur. Let me tell you something: until you've ridden on the back of a lumbering bag of bones, you won't appreciate how much I wished I had more padding in the seat of my pants.

I decided not to stick around waiting for this set of bones to develop wings and take off, so while I heard Dr. F. begin another lecture, I started climbing down each disk of the backbone, one by one.

"Another way to think of the Internet is as the skeleton of a big monster," Dr. F. told me.

This was a comparison I could agree with, because I liked monster movies, like those old *Godzilla* movies where he fights the big dragon. At least I liked those monsters as long as I wasn't riding on the back of one!

"The Internet is big and monstrous, too. Fortunately, it's a big *friendly* monster if you know about it, and it isn't going to rampage through Tokyo and destroy everything."

Dr. F. had more to explain. "Like the skeleton of any other animal, there is one really important part: it needs to have a backbone to hold it all together. The backbone of the Internet is called **Very high-speed Backbone Network Service**, or **vBNS**."

'Very high-speed Backbone Network Service' sounded like a silly combination of words to me. Fortunately, Dr. F. likes to use those acronyms, so I

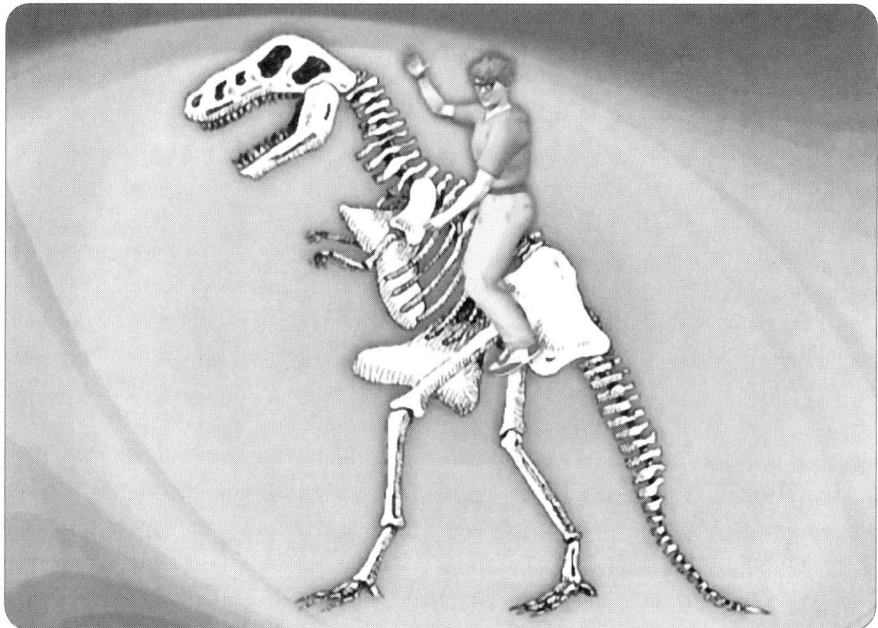

expected to hear vBNS a lot more often than that big jumble of words.

"A **Backbone Network Service**, or **BNS**, is a fast set of wires that stretches for long distances—all the way across the country, for example. This serves as the main connection to the computers that want to interact with the Internet. That's what makes it the backbone; it's like the spine in your body. Your spine takes signals from the brain to the farthest parts of your body and back again. A BNS does the same thing for the Internet. The **vBNS** connects supercomputer centers around the world and has a lot of bandwidth (which means it can carry a lot of information at once). The vBNS has a bandwidth of 2.4Gbps. That means it can send over 2.5 billion little pieces of information a second. That's fast!"

"So who runs everything on the Internet?" I asked, stepping down from the last vertebrae of that enormous backbone. I figured, so long as we were comparing it to a monster, it should have a brain that controls everything. Boy, was I was wrong.

"Well, no one really," Dr. F. explained. Then, after a pause, he added, "At least no one has control over all of it, although there is a hierarchy for deciding how things should work. At the top of the hierarchy is something called the Internet Society. The Internet Society may sound like the name of a computer club at school, but it's really a non-profit organization that tries to maintain and enhance the Internet. The Internet Society develops and defines the standards and methods that the Internet uses to run.

"There are two main branches of the Internet Society. One is the Internet Advisory Board, or IAB, which helps run everything in the Internet Society. (The IAB is also sometimes referred to as The Internet Architecture Board, or The Internet Activities Board.) The IAB is an administrative body that runs the organization. The other branch is the Internet Engineering Task Force, or IETF."

Backbone Network Service (BNS)

A **Backbone Network Service** is a set of wires stretching long distances that connect different computers together. The **Very high-speed Backbone Network Service (vBNS)** serves as the main connection for the Internet as we know it today. Connecting supercomputer centers around the world, the **vBNS** carries information at a bandwidth of 2.4 Gbps.

I was beginning to realize something: sometimes it seems like there are more abbreviations on the Internet than there are in Washington, D.C.

"The IETF is a division of the Internet Advisory Board. It's in charge of documenting all of the standards and protocols for the Internet."

"Now, if they make up all these standards, they have to write them down somewhere, right Dr. F.?" I asked.

I suddenly thought about the many blueboards in Dr. F.'s lab, and I couldn't help but hope that all the technical data wasn't written out in chalk. "Where do they keep it?" I asked hesitantly.

"There really isn't one organized manual. Everyone who has comments or suggestions about the procedures or the protocols on how the Internet works (or should work) can submit a **Request For Comments**, or **RFC**. They call it a Request for Comments because when the Internet Society reviews the information, all members review the submission and make comments about it. They give each request a number and decide on which ones to publish. Some RFCs are so popular or so well done that they eventually become standards that determine how the whole Internet runs.

"I've written several that have become standards," Dr. F. confided. He sounded pretty proud of himself.

I used to think that there was some sort of governing body running the Internet. You know, a group of guys all seated around tables in a place that looks like the floor of Congress or the United Nations General Assembly. I was beginning to see just how wrong my assumption had been.

"Another organization that helps control the Internet is the **Internet Network Information Center**, or **InterNIC**. AT&T and a company called Network Solutions, Inc. got together, with support from the National Science Foundation, so they could run services to support Internet users. They perform several important tasks. They run and publish a "phone book" of publicly

> ## Request For Comment (RFC)
>
> These documents are recommendations for changes to and enhancements needed for the Internet. Each **RFC** concerns itself with a particularly technology used within the Internet. Groups like the IETF use **RFCs** on a continuing basis.

available databases, and manage domain name registration and IP Address assignment. We'll talk about those later. They also provide education and information services, and run news services that report on Internet-related events.

"Registration of domain names is important. A domain is a part of the Internet. Domains like syngress.com, ricehahn.com, and saintehlers.com are places you can go to view Web pages on the Internet. You can't just make up a name and decide that you want people to come to your site when they type in that name. The name has to be registered so that all the computers on the Internet will know about it. The biggest registrar is Network Solutions, Inc. In fact, they used to be the only registrar you could use. These days, however, there are many registrars available with varying prices and levels of customer service.

"Once domains are registered, they are stored and maintained by an **Internet Registry**. There is a registry for each top-level domain. There are several top level domains, and you can tell which top level domain any address is in by looking at the letters that come at the end of its Internet address. You are probably already familiar with some of the more common top-level domains like .com or .net. This is something we'll discuss in more detail later. The important thing to remember is that the Internet Registry stores all the information for every domain under each top-level domain heading, along with the Internet address to find that domain."

I was starting to get a headache. Some pizza or some Chinese food really would have helped me process all this information faster.

"So, all of this is stuff about how the Internet is organized, but how do you get in contact with all of it? I mean, you've told me about some groups that set things up, but I don't know how it really works yet."

> ## Internet Network Information Center (InterNIC)
>
> This organization is responsible for registering the domain names. If you go to the **InterNIC** Web site, you can usually determine who owns a particular domain name. If no one owns the name yet, you can purchase it.

There was a pause while Dr. F. blew his nose. Evidently the chalk dust must still be bothering him.

"Good question, Beta! Let's start talking about that. To do so, you have to start with another acronym."

No wonder Dr. F. loves the Internet so much, I thought.

"You contact the Internet with the help of your ISP," Dr. F. continued. "An **ISP** is an **Internet Service Provider**—probably one of the easiest terms to remember and understand because it's one you'll encounter often.

"An ISP runs a small segment of the Internet and sells customers connections to the Internet. They also provide access to a search engine to find items of interest on the web, and an e-mail address. In other words, they provide you with basic Internet services.

"ISPs sometimes are in the form of an Online Service. The biggest Online Service is probably AOL. These services allow you to have all sorts of convenient services without having to tell your computer where to look for them. Usually these services are things like instant messaging, online shopping, and space to use for your own Web page. Most of the time these features also come with a lot of advertising. Which ISP or Online Service a user chooses to connect to the Internet with is a matter of personal taste and work habits. Some people don't like using the proprietary methods of an Online Service; they prefer to choose their own online applications and have control of their online choices. Others like the convenience of having those

> ### Internet Registry
> An **Internet Registry** stores all of the information for every domain under a particular top-level domain heading, along with the Internet address for each domain. There is a separate registry for each top-level domain.

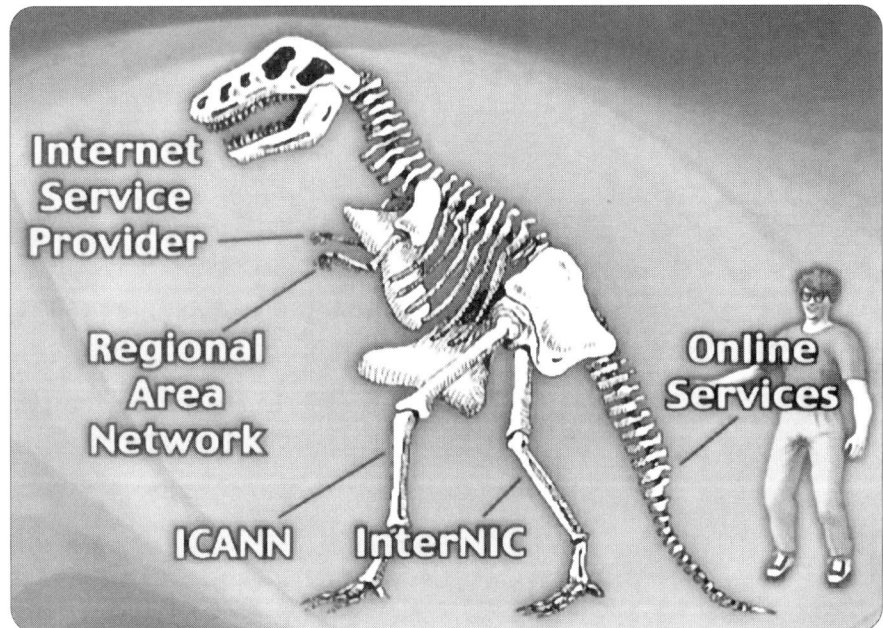

Internet Service Provider

Regional Area Network

ICANN   InterNIC

Online Services

decisions made for them, and don't mind paying to get additional features along with the advertising.

"ISPs are usually part of a regional network. Regional networks are another way of organizing how the Internet is accessed and run or, to make it simple, how computers talk to each other. We discussed LANs and WANs earlier. A regional network is really just the same thing: a group of computers all linked together. The big difference is that a regional network controls and maintains access to the Internet in a certain geographical area. Often, regional networks are made up of smaller networks and organizations (like ISPs) that work together to improve their access to the Internet and their performance."

"Most online services allow you to install other programs if you prefer, don't they?" I asked. "Like your choice of browser?"

"Yes," Dr. F. replied. "There are sometimes restrictions, and making those types of changes is usually a little more difficult than doing so with a regular ISP account, but there is information online on how to do it, if you're willing to look.

"So, Beta, do you think that you can define for me what exactly the Internet is?" Dr. F. suddenly asked. "I'll give you a hint: the Internet is all the coordinated operations with the backbone. Can you tell me what that means, Beta?"

I bet that Dr. F. didn't think I could. But I was grinning, because I already knew this, so I told him. "That's just a fancy way of saying that any information that travels over the backbone and network of wires and cables and phone lines is part of the Internet. Anything that gets sent using that system is part of the Internet. It includes the WWW, IRC, FTP, Telnet, P2P, and a bunch of other alphabet stew names, and all the computers and wires and routers, too."

Dr. F. paused. I thought I heard a sniff, and I swear I could hear the rustle of a tissue that indicated he was also drying tears. "Yes, Beta," he said. He cleared his

Internet Service Provider (ISP)

The **ISP** is the company that connects you and your computer to the Internet. This company provides service to the Internet.

throat, using a cough to disguise his efforts to get his voice back under control. I'd distinctly heard the slight hesitation that indicated he was indeed a bit choked up. "I'm so proud of you. There's one thing you mentioned in that alphabet stew of names and acronyms on which we need to focus next. You mentioned the WWW, which is an acronym for the World Wide Web. Can you tell me what exactly the World Wide Web is?"

I was feeling a bit uncomfortable with this display of affection, and I just happened to know a little bit about the World Wide Web from my own reading, so I quickly answered his question. "It's what most people think of when they talk about the Internet. It's a bunch of special computers that can display and send out documents that are written in a code called **Hypertext Markup Language**, but most people just call it **HTML**. Documents written with HTML allow you to connect to other documents through the use of links—or hypertext—look at pictures, listen to music, or even see moving video. Almost all of the Web pages you see online are written using HTML code, or something very similar to it."

Dr. F. must have thought I was talking too much because he interrupted and continued his lecture.

So much for being proud of me, I thought. *Either Dr. F. has a short attention span or he's a bit embarrassed, too.*

"Yes, and those HTML-written pages are seen using special programs called **web browsers** that make it

> **Hypertext Markup Language (HTML)**
>
> **HTML** is a programming language used to design a Web site. This language helps a programmer/designer mark the site and hyperlinks in it.

easier to use the World Wide Web. The two most popular browsers are Internet Explorer, made by Microsoft, and Netscape Navigator. These programs are usually free and allow you to do a lot of things like remember where Web pages are located, make minor tweaks such as changing the appearance or size of the text, as well as a variety of other options."

I remembered my own Favorites and Bookmark lists. I have a lot of neat comic strips like "Sluggy Freelance" and "Calvin and Hobbes" marked so I don't have to type in the address every time; I can just click the mouse a few times and be there.

Dr. F. kept talking, apparently realizing that I was getting ahead of the JTCI agenda he had mapped out. "We'll discuss browsers in more details later," he said. "For now, it's important to know that the World Wide Web is the fastest growing part of the Internet, probably because it appeals to so many different types of people. It has more than just information or files you can download. Using HTML, you can present information in interesting ways. Because of all the things you can do with it, artists, designers, and writers use the World Wide Web to get their ideas across in their own creative ways. Businesses can use it to conduct meetings, sell products, or advertise. It's a wonderful medium that affects, influences, and brings together millions of people throughout the world."

Just as Dr. F. was getting excited, he changed direction and started talking about organizations again. *Definitely an attention span problem with the old Doctor*, I thought.

"The World Wide Web also has an organization that helps keep everything running smoothly and makes sure the standards in place are consistently met. It's called the **World Wide Web Consortium**, but since computer folk like to use short names, they usually call it the **W3C**. Initially led from MIT's Laboratory for Computer Science by Tim Berners-Lee (the inventor of the World

---

Web Browser

A web browser is a program that allows the user to see pages written in Hypertext Markup Language. Usually free, these programs also allow users to make a note of favorite Web page locations, and change the appearance and size of the text that is displayed on their screen.

Wide Web) and Al Vezza, the W3C keeps track of everything that HTML can do and how to do it. In other words, they're the ones responsible for setting those standards. They also keep track of other languages, like JavaScript, and other kinds of documents and protocols, like accessibility standards, that can be used to make Web pages.

"While it's something we'll discuss in more detail later, you should also know a little bit about Internet security now, too. For whatever reason, there are some people out there who want to steal information, especially secret and useful information like credit card or social security numbers. Sometimes, it can be relatively easy for someone who knows how to do it to tap a line (like a spy from a James Bond thriller) and steal any information that comes through that line. Usually, Web sites that use or collect sensitive information like that can protect the data. They encrypt the data with a secret code that makes the information unreadable unless you have a special program that will change the information back to its original form. This way, people buying things or using a password on the Internet don't have to worry about complete strangers having access to their personal information."

With that said, I soon recognized the telltale sign that Dr. F. was about to change lecture directions. Once again my vision blurred, and the next thing I knew I was back atop the huge dinosaur skeleton. As what I was beginning to think of as the Webosaurus galloped off into the circuit-fired sunset, I couldn't help but feel grateful that, even though I was moving on to the next leg of my JTCI, I was still wearing my own clothes.

> ## World Wide Web Consortium (W3C)
>
> The World Wide Web Consortium (W3C) is an organization responsible for setting the standards for the World Wide Web and making sure those standards are consistently met. The **W3C** also keeps track of all of the possibilities that HTML offers, as well as the possibilities offered by other kinds of languages, documents, and protocols.

Chapter 4

How a Net Connection Works

One minute my fanny was getting sore from sitting atop that monstrous backbone. The next minute, with a squish and a whoosh, I was back inside a computer again.

"Now we need to talk about some of the hardware in your computer that has to do with the Internet," I heard the disembodied voice of Dr. F. tell me. I looked around the inside of the computer tower case and tried to decide if I'd be around long enough to bother to sit down.

If nothing else, I thought, as I once again took my now-familiar seat on the motherboard, *at least the acoustics are great in here.*

"There has to be some way for the computer to talk to other computers," Dr. F. said, "and that's done with wires and cables."

Dr. F. seemed to assume an almost wistful tone to his voice when he added, "It'd be nice if you could just tell your computer to connect to another computer and it would automatically do so."

Something told me that this was probably exactly how Dr. F.'s computer connected. I've yet to see him do anything else using conventional methods, so it wouldn't surprise me. Regardless, I decided to settle back and get as comfortable as I could, sitting on a motherboard, and listen to what he had to say.

"However," he said, "a computer needs somewhere for the information to come and go, like an airport of sorts. Just like you can't plug a lamp into any hole in the wall, you can't just plug a phone line into any hole in your computer to make it connect to the Internet. This is where a modem comes in. Or goes out. Let me explain.

"A modem is a piece of computer equipment that enables information to come into and leave your computer. It's the airport of your computer. Everything has to go through that point. A modem uses your phone lines to access the Internet, and those phone wires run from the wall into your modem.

"Do you like movies from the 1980's, Beta?" Dr. F. asked suddenly.

I was caught off guard. I hoped he wasn't going to ask me about that Molly Ringwald person he'd mentioned earlier. Regardless of my fears, I figured I'd better say something. "Well, I haven't seen many, so I guess I don't really know."

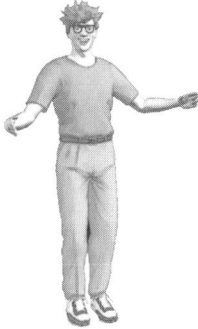

I heard a tsk-tsk of condemnation from Dr. F. "If you had seen some of the fine movies from that era—like *War Games*, for example—you would already know that years ago, modems were very big. You had to actually pick up the telephone receiver and place it on a bulky piece of equipment that would essentially use the phone like a person would, receiving through the earpiece and "talking" in a computer language into the mouthpiece. Those old modems were slow, chunky, and suffered from data loss. However, they did *look* pretty nifty... or, at least they did at the time. They were decidedly high tech for their era.

"Fortunately, modem transmissions, if not their appearance, have improved. You can plug the wires right into the modem now instead of having to use the phone receiver whenever you want to get information to or from the Internet. The equipment is also a lot smaller. You can still get modems that sit on the desk, with lots of wonderful flashing lights, but most modems now look like green plastic rectangular cards with lots of electronic things sticking off of them. These cards sit inside your computer and the only part that you see is a shiny chrome socket on the back of your computer for the phone cord to plug into. It's pretty slick."

I was starting to take mental notes of anything Dr. F. said. "Slick, right," I mumbled, trying to figure out what *War Games* had to do with computers. He'd mentioned that film earlier, so I guess Dr. F. must think it's special. I was about to ask him if *War Games* was some old Julie Andrews or Barbra Streisand musical or something, but—as usual—Dr. F. didn't stop for any confusion on my part.

"Whatever your modem looks like, they all work the same. A **modem** takes the digital information your computer has and transforms it into an analog signal that the phone lines can transmit. They then take the analog information that comes in from the Internet and change it into digital data that your computer can understand. If you want to know the difference between analog and digital, look at your CDs and your cassette tapes. CDs are recorded with a digital code. This code doesn't ever get corrupted or damaged unless you physically scratch or crack the CD. It's easy to replicate and tends to preserve quality and data integrity very well. Cassette tapes, on the other hand, are analog recordings. These recordings lose quality over time as they age. An analog recording is also nowhere near as clear and crisp sounding as a digital recording."

"So why do the phone companies use analog signals so much?" I asked. "I mean, if digital is really much better than analog—like how CDs are better than tapes—shouldn't everything use the digital signals?"

Dr. F. sighed with impatience. "Because for a long time the only wires that went all the way across the country were phone wires, and phone wires don't understand digital signals. For that reason, the Internet standard was **Plain Old Telephone Service**, or **POTS**. POTS was the only way to do stuff for years and years. Which is why new developments are called **Pretty Amazing New Stuff**, or **PANS**. I'll tell you more about POTS and PANS in a minute.

"How fast your modem can send information over the Internet depends on the modem. Early modems used to connect at speeds that ranged from 300 bps to around 1400 bps. Do you know what bps stands for?"

There was a pause until I realized that Dr. F. was asking me a question. "Oh yeah!" I finally said. "Bits per second. The higher the number, the more bits of data

> **Modem**
> A **Modem** is a piece of computer equipment that enables information to come into and leave your computer through phone lines, allowing access to the information available on the Internet. A **modem** changes the digital information that a computer uses into analog form so that it can be sent across phone lines. It also changes analog information received over those same phone lines into digital form so that your computer can work with it.

can zip through the wires, thus they travel at a faster speed."

Plain Old Telephone Service (POTS)

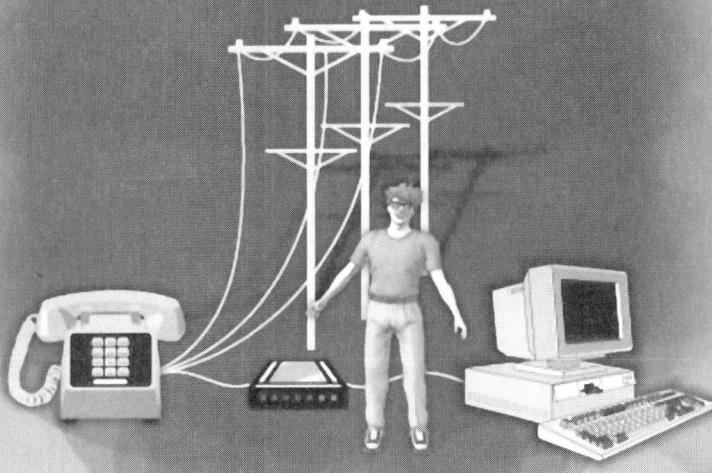

"Very good, Beta." Finally some more praise from Dr. F. "These days," he continued, "the speed has really improved, and the slowest modem you're likely to see anymore is 28,800 bps, which is usually called a 28.8 modem, although there are still some 14.4 modems out there. Most modems are now 56 K or 56,000 bps.

"Such modems only run on POTS services, but there are a lot of PANS out there now, too. And you should at least know something about them. Even though 75 percent of Internet users still use modems, a lot of people are starting to use other faster, more efficient, and more reliable methods of connecting to and using the Internet.

"One of these methods actually still uses the telephone lines. It's called **Integrated Services Digital Network**, but most people just say **ISDN**. ISDN uses telephone lines that can send both analog voice and digital data signals at the same time, so you don't even have to hang up the phone to use the Internet! What's even better is ISDN can send up to 128 Kbps: twice as fast as the fastest modem! ISDN also loses less data and stays connected better than modems. The phone company will probably be who sells you an ISDN connection—if you can get one, since they aren't available in all areas. Where ISDN is available, it's a big improvement over POTS.

"There's also the **Asymmetric Digital Subscriber Line**, or **ADSL**."

POTS and PANS

POTS stands for **Plain Old Telephone Service**, and refers to the use of ordinary phone lines to transmit data. **PANS** stands for **Pretty Amazing New Stuff**, and refers to several new technologies that allow for data to be transmitted at a faster rate than is possible with **POTS. ISDN, ADSL**, and **T-1** connections are **PANS**.

I was beginning to understand why a lot of acronyms are used to describe Internet technology: Who wants to say "Asymmetric Digital Subscriber Line" all the time? It was a mouthful, for sure.

Dr. F. continued to explain ADSL to me, and I pinched myself so that I'd pay attention. I was sure he could hear my stomach growling, too, but he obviously chose to ignore that.

Integrated Service Digital Network Lines (ISDN)

"ADSL uses regular copper telephone lines, too. But it uses special technology to send more data over the lines than a modem can. You can usually get information from the Internet at 1.5 to 9 Mbps—or megabytes per second—and send it at 16 to 640 Kbps. It's faster than a modem either way, but it sure does work a lot faster when you're trying to get information than when you're trying to send it.

"This is a good time to talk about copper wires and fiber-optic cable. Do you know what fiber-optic cable is, Beta?"

"Isn't that wire that use lasers instead of electricity?" I asked, nervous that I'd gotten it wrong.

I heard another sigh. "Well, I guess that's close enough. Not very technical though."

'Close enough' is better than being wrong, I thought. I also couldn't help but think that Dr. F. could certainly be picky and exacting at times.

"Regular phone lines use copper wire, which sends an electronic signal. Most phone companies use this sort of wire to route calls and information where they should

Integrated Services Digital Network (ISDN)

Integrated Services Digital Network, or ISDN, uses telephone lines that can send both analog and digital data signals at the same time. This allows users to talk on the phone and connect to the Internet at the same time. ISDN is also twice as fast as a 56K modem, sending data at a rate of 128 Kbps.

Asymetrical Digital Subscriber Line (ADSL)

An **Asymetrical Digital Subscriber Line**, or **ADSL**, uses regular copper telephone lines, but uses a special technology to send more data over the lines than a standard modem can. An **ADSL** can receive information from the Internet 1.5 to 9 Mbps and send information out at 16 to 640 Kbps. For this reason, it is much faster to receive information through an **ADSL** than to send it out.

go. Some more advanced lines are made of fiber-optic cable. And yes, fiber-optic cable uses lasers to send the information. Because of this, they can send information much faster and the lines are more difficult to tap. Simply put, fiber-optic cables don't use an electronic signal that can be accessed with a remote listening device.

"You should be aware of one more type of PANS connection. The T-1. A **T-1** is a very fast connection."

He paused for a moment. I guessed he was thinking about how to explain what he would say next. Maybe the pause was for emphasis. Maybe he liked hearing the sound of my stomach growling and didn't want to miss it. Regardless, Dr. F. soon resumed his lecture.

"Actually, a T-1 has twenty-four connection channels. Each of these channels inside the connection support data speeds of up to 64 Kbps. That means you can receive or send 1.544 million bits per second, or Mbps. If the numbers are too much to figure out in your head, just trust me that it's *very* fast."

I wonder if I should be insulted that Dr. F. doesn't think I can mentally perform complex equations, I thought. *At least I don't carry around and use a slide rule like he does!*

"There are faster connections, but not many groups have connections better than a T-1. Many companies have a T-1 line to their building if they have a lot of traffic on their network. You'll sometimes hear this referred to as a dedicated line, although that can also mean a phone line used specifically for Internet access purposes."

I distinctly heard Dr. F. pause to take a drink. The gulp, glub-glub sounds were magnified by whatever speech transmission method he was using.

Dr. F. cleared his throat. "Well, Beta," he said. "I think you've been sitting there on that motherboard long enough."

Finally, I thought, *he's going to at least give me a break.* Boy was I wrong!

"It's time you saw some of this stuff up close and personal," he continued.

Those—or any other words that hinted at another JTCI—weren't exactly the ones I wanted to hear. I began to hope that I would be able to remain focused and that I wouldn't start hallucinating and seeing mirages of pizza parlors and Chinese restaurants. Even a salad was beginning to sound good!

I felt that now-familiar squish and the next thing I knew, I had my arms extended in front of me like some sort of inner-hyperspace flying Superman. Flying is exactly how it felt to be whooshing my way through the decidedly claustrophobic cylindrical chamber that I suddenly found myself in. At least the place was shiny.

"You're inside a copper telephone line, Beta," Dr. F. told me, his voice coming from somewhere behind me and over my right shoulder.

I wonder if traveling this way helps prevent arthritis, I thought, remembering the copper bracelet my great-grandmother used to wear to help hers.

"You're traveling at 56 Kbps, my boy," Dr. F. said. "Just like the rest of that 75 percent of Internet users. You're just experiencing it a bit—pardon the pun—more up close and personal than most people do."

So this is what a POTS feels like, I thought as I sped along in short bursts, occasionally being pitched upwards, bumped up and over what I assumed was the top of a telephone pole, and then plunged back down before continuing on another short horizontal path. *I guess they haven't updated to buried phone lines in this area.*

I'd formed that thought too soon!

My "flight" pitched downward and I plunged down what felt like the most dramatic roller coaster descent in the world. Then, never even guessing that my body was capable of doing ninety-degree contortions, I moved in a way that I was sure couldn't be too good for my back before continuing on another level stretch of travel.

> **T-1**
>
> A **T-1** is a very fast connection that consists of twenty-four connection channels. Each of these channels can support data speeds of up to 64 Kbps, allowing the **T-1** to receive or send 1.544 million bits per second, or Mbps.

Within moments, I felt another contortion. Then I passed through one of the modems in a line of them maintained by my ISP before I began a vertical ascent as I reached the long-distance provider for the telephone company hosting the ISP services and was pitched forward and bounced off a satellite dish. *I wonder how they choose their long distance service,* I thought. *I bet they don't do it by making a decision while answering pesky phone calls that interrupt their dinners!*

I began my descent and traveled somewhat faster as I passed through a T-1 connection, then landed in the roomy—and far less claustrophobic—fiber-optic cable of the Internet backbone.

I only had a split second to stretch before the temporary IP address I'd been given by my ISP's Web server software was accepted and I sped along wondering where my JTCI would take me next.

If I get a moment, I thought, noticing that my arms were still extended in front of me, *I'll have to check to see if I'm wearing a cape.*

Chapter 5

Getting Your Computer Onto the Internet

Suddenly I had a feeling that seemed almost as if I was suspended in mid-air. Except I didn't even know if there was any air inside the cables and things I'd been traveling through. I didn't seem to be gasping for breath or anything, but for all I knew I was existing in a vacuum.

"Ahhhhhhhhh," I began as I tried to gather my wits about me and form a question. "What exactly is happening here?"

"Patience isn't really your virtue, is it, B?"

Great, I thought. *Now Dr. F. is going to go all need-to-know-basis with me and develop an attitude.* Of course, I knew patience was easier for Dr. F. After all, he wasn't the one suspended in mid-air with his arms still stretched out in front of him trying not to think about the fact that his nose had just started to itch.

"Well," I said, after taking a breath to do my best to make sure my voice didn't sound like *I* was the one with the attitude. "I am the one doing the traveling here, and you're the one with the map. That can be a bit disconcerting at times."

"Are you trying to tell me that you're the stop-and-ask-for-directions type?" Dr. F. asked.

"Are you trying to change the subject?"

Dr. F. chuckled. "There's nothing nebulous going on here, Beta," he said. "In fact, I felt that I should explain some things about that map, as you called it, before you continued on your JTCI."

"I'm not about to trespass anywhere, am I?" I couldn't help it. Whooshing through these Internet inner spaces—not to mention those occasional squishes—was making me develop what I preferred to think of as a healthy amount of paranoia.

Dr. F. sighed. I guess I must get more impatient when I'm hungry, because by then his sighs were really starting to get on my nerves. And I'd thought that I'd long ago learned how to cope with Dr. F's idiosyncrasies.

"As long as we keep you on the Internet proper," Dr. F. replied, "you can't trespass."

"Why is that?" I asked.

"It's obvious we should do a little review here," he said, which still wasn't an answer and had me worried that I was in for an even bigger delay than I'd expected.

Dr. F. continued. "If you recall, the Internet proper is a global connection of networks. In fact, the name Internet was derived from the concept of **inter**connected **net**works. No one actually owns the Internet—thus, no worries about trespassing when you enter the network."

"Then why is there a need for passwords and such?" I asked.

"Think of the Internet as the moon and stars," Dr. F. said. "The Internet is like the heavens above us or outer space. No one person or corporation owns that. That changes the closer you get to earth. First you have air space over certain geographical areas, or countries. Those entities can have some say in what can and cannot take place in that air space. The closer you get to earth individual property ownership determines what can occur on the air space closer to the ground.

"For example, let's say you and the neighbor on the other side of my property want to start hanging up your clothes to dry them. Let's also say that you're embarrassed to have your underwear out there flapping in the breeze for everybody to see, so you come up with a way that you think will allow you to dry your underwear but keep the actual underwear ownership a secret.

"You build a pole on your property and my other neighbor builds one on hers. You have a cross bar on each pole so that you can have your line and she can have hers. You construct a series of pulleys so that you can move the line once you attach the clothes to it so that they're suspended over my property when the clothes—which include that embarrassing underwear—are actually drying.

"Now, it doesn't matter if you hadn't actually set foot on my property during the construction of your clothesline set-up. Even if you threw the ropes across my property lasso-style to attach the cords from one pole to the other, your clothes that you hang out to dry would still be invading, so to speak, my space, so you'd in essence be trespassing.

"In other words, the only way you could use my air space to dry your clothes would be if I granted you the right to do so. Such agreements that apply to real estate are called conveyances if I assign you ownership of that space. In this case, I just want to grant you that use on a temporary basis, so another option would be if I granted you an easement. We'll just call it a waiver; that isn't the official real estate term, but it serves our purpose because it essentially means that I'd waive the rights to the air space your drying clothes occupy and legally look the other way while your clothes are on the line.

"The Internet is like the heavens. **Regional networks** are akin to little countries. Individual networks are like individual properties, like the lot on which your house is built. Nobody owns the Internet, but any number of different people or corporations can own—and therefore control—the networks. A password in essence grants you a waiver that lets you enter onto the network, subject to the terms of the waiver agreement.

"That's a very basic explanation, of course. In fact, we'll be discussing passwords when we go over security and other issues you'll encounter on your JTCI."

"Okay," I said. "That explains the function of passwords, but it still doesn't explain why I'm just kind of hanging here."

Regional network
A regional network, covering more area than an ISP, controls and maintains access to the Internet in a predetermined area.

I couldn't help myself; I needed to know when I'd be moving on. Again, I figured the sooner I moved, the sooner I'd be done with this JTCI and the sooner I could eat. As long as I was moving, things were fascinating. I loved the JTCI itself; that's why I'm telling you about it. I just didn't like—and never do like—letting my tummy get too empty.

"You're hanging there, as you so eloquently put it," he said, "because I felt you should know a little bit about Network Access Points."

"Oh," I said. I still wasn't clear as to why I was hanging in mid-air, but I knew from experience that that kind of vague answer from Dr. F. usually held the promise that the discussion was about to take a more linear direction. I equated linear with the hope that I'd soon start moving again, so I decided to stop asking questions for awhile and just listen.

"I'm sure you recall that we've talked about the backbone of the Internet," Dr. F. said. "Well, you can kind of look at the Internet as a big, friendly monster with lots of arms and legs."

You may recall that I'd actually come to think of it as more of a Webosaurus rather than a monster, but I decided not to interrupt Dr. F. to tell him that.

"But, here's the thing: a monster with arms and legs has to have joints with connecting tissues to attach those limbs to him. On the Internet monster, we call those joints **Network Access Points**, or **NAP**s. A Network Access Point is a facility where a bunch of regional networks or ISPs connect with each other to make a gateway to the Internet. Usually the NAP has a very fast connection.

"The connections for Network Access Points are most often **dedicated lines**. Dedicated lines are cables or wires that serve only one purpose: to transfer data from one place to another. No one ever uses them to make phone calls and they always stay connected to one computer—as does a router at a Network Access Point.

Network Access Point (NAP)

A Network Access Point, or **NAP**, is a facility where several regional networks or ISPs connect with each other to make a gateway to the Internet. Usually the **NAP** has a very fast connection.

They don't change computers and they don't do anything else. Because they're so specialized, dedicated lines generally do what they're supposed to do very well. In this case, that means doing what they do very fast.

"One really fast dedicated line we looked at earlier was the T-1. Remember that a T-1 has a net connection speed of over 1.5 Mbps.

"There's also a T-3 line option. You might think that a T-3 is three times as fast as a T-1, but you'd be wrong. A T-3 line has 672 channels contained in it, which you can visualize as something like a huge hose with 672 different hoses within it. Each of these channels can carry 64 Kbps; that means the total speed for a T-3 Line is nearly 45 Mbps!"

"Whoa! I wish I had one of those for my room!"

"Ahem."

It was obvious that Dr. F. wasn't in the mood to be interrupted, even if the interruption was, in my opinion, something said out of appreciation for something he'd just said.

"Sometimes T-1 and T-3 lines are referred to as T-1 or T-3 Carriers," he said, continuing what was obviously another one-sided discussion. "Many Internet Service Providers use T-3 lines to connect to the Internet backbone.

"There are actually a few faster lines as well. Optical Carrier, or OC, terms are used to describe the speed of fiber optic networks meeting certain standards.

"So you can better understand what I'm about to explain, let's get you in a position to see a table showing the various speeds of OC connections."

With a squish and a jolt, I felt myself on the move again. This time I didn't travel far. I soon had a view of one of the blueboards in Dr. F's lab.

"As you can see from the picture being sent from the Web cam in my lab, Optical Carriers offer tremendous speeds."

> **Dedicated Lines**
> A **Dedicated Line** is a cable or wire that serves only one purpose: to transfer data from one place to another. A **Dedicated Line** stays connected to one computer, and generally is a very fast connection such as a T-1 or a T-3.

OC-1 = 51.85 Mbps

OC-3 = 155.52 Mbps

OC-12 = 622.08 Mbps

OC-24 = 1.244 Gbps

OC-48 = 2.488 Gbps

OC-192 = 9.952 Gbps

Regional Network Routers

Regional Network Routers examine packets of data to see where they are supposed to be directed. By directing this packet traffic between LANs they create regional networks.

"In fact," Dr. F. continued, "an OC-192 connection could transfer the entire contents of your computers' hard drive, which is probably somewhere between ten and forty gigabytes in size, in just a few seconds. By comparison, transferring a one-megabyte MP3 file takes anywhere from twenty minutes to an hour using a 56K dial-up connection; transmission would be much faster on a cable connection, but it'd still take a minute or two."

Forget the T-3 line for my room, I thought. This time I kept my thoughts to myself, but I was already dreaming about the size of the music collection I could amass if I had an OC-192 instead. In fact, I decided that when I got back home, one of the first things I'd do after I ate was calculate the average size of a 100-gigabyte MP3 playlist.

"We talked earlier about regional networks. Regional networks are controlled by **Regional Network Routers**. The routers that connect the networks act like the traffic cops of the Internet. These routers direct the traffic by examining the packets of data to see where they are supposed to be directed. They don't filter information or anything else; they just direct traffic between LANs to create regional networks. They figure out what the best path between two computers will be when they connect the network to the Internet backbone.

"High-speed backbones also connect these regional networks to each other. When one regional network needs to send data to another regional network, it does so by first transmitting the information to a Network Access Point, or NAP. The NAP routes the data to the appropriate backbone necessary to pass that information on to the destination regional network."

Suddenly I felt that now-familiar squish. With that, and with my arms still stretched out in front of me, my JTCI took me from one network to the next within a regional network. My path wasn't necessarily a circular one, but it wasn't in a straight line either. I guess it was based on something on that map Dr. F. had yet to show me.

Then, just as suddenly, I felt myself leaving the by now familiar regional network I'd almost begun to think of as home and I crossed over a Network Access Point that directed my JTCI as I ventured out to parts unknown.

Darn, I thought. *While I was stopped, I forgot to check to see if I'm wearing a cape!*

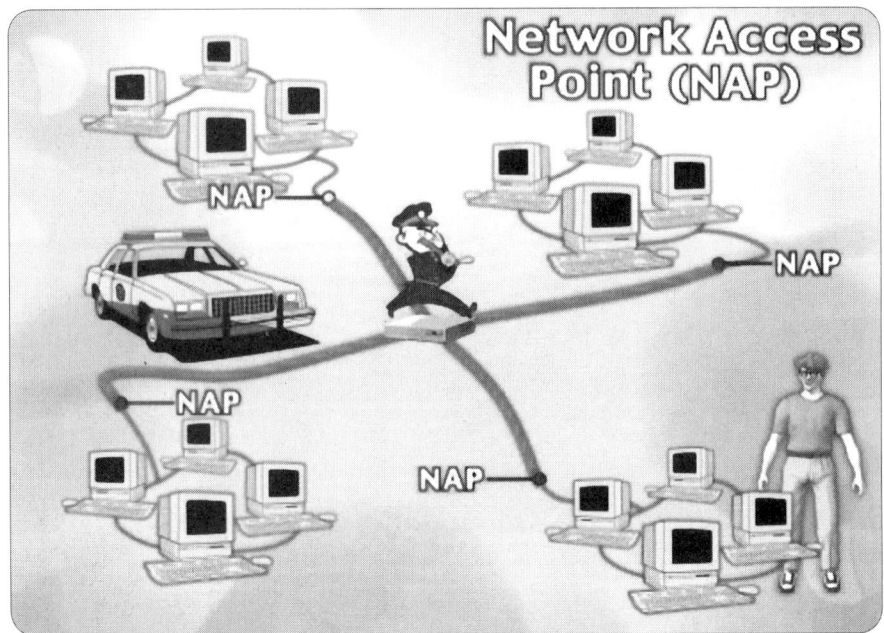

Chapter 6

How Information Moves Over the Internet

No sooner had I crossed over that Network Access Point and begun to think my JTCI was on its way again, then I just as suddenly seemed to once again be suspended in mid-air.

This gives new meaning to 'doing the limbo,' I thought.

"Ok, Beta," Dr. F. called my attention back to business. "Time for a movie question: Have you seen *Charlie and the Chocolate Factory*?"

I was wondering what this had to do with the Internet, but usually Dr. F. managed to keep on track, so I played along. You may have noticed that playing along with Dr. F. is most often easier than questioning him. "Yeah," I said, answering his question. "I think I saw it when I was a kid."

"Tell me about how Willy Wonka says television works."

Even more confused, I decided I still better follow his lead. "Well, as I said, it's been awhile since I saw the film, but doesn't he say that someone takes a picture, and then they break it into a million tiny pieces and send them into the air and the television puts them back together again so that you see the picture on your television?"

"Correct, Beta," Dr. F. told me. "And it's a terribly inaccurate description of television, but it is a good way to explain how **packets** work!"

"Packets? You've mentioned them a couple of times already." I suddenly had visions floating in my head of small packages of candy corn from last Halloween stuffed into a backpack. Crazy how the mind works sometimes, isn't it?

"Yes, packets." Dr. F. started on what I was sure was to be his next infodump lecture.

"You see, most network configurations use a method of communication called **packet switching**. In packet switching, the information is broken into little parts of data called packets. Each packet contains a little piece of the data, as well as a header that explains where it came

Packets and Packet Switching

Packet switching refers to the process of breaking information into little parts of data known as **packets**. Each **packet** contains a little piece of the data, as well as a header that explains where it came from, where it's going, and a code to tell the computer it arrives at how to figure out if the data has been corrupted.

from, where it's going, and a code to tell the computer it arrives at how to figure out if the data has been corrupted.

"The header works a lot like an envelope for a letter. On a letter's envelope you can see the address (where it's going to) and the return address (where it came from). The actual information you want to read is held inside. The difference, of course, is that you usually put an entire message in one letter, you'll recall that I just said that packets only have a small part of the message.

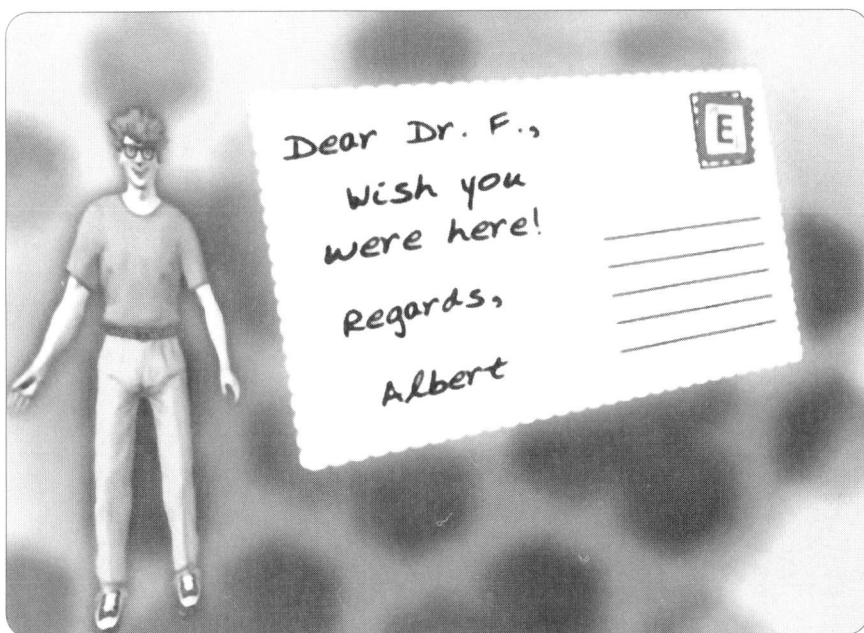

"Oh look! Here come some now."

Suddenly a whole bunch of shiny pieces of something swarmed around me and then continued down the cable. On the next cable over I saw lots more. On closer inspection they looked like tiny little back-packs, each with cute little shuffling feet. I was beginning to believe Dr. F. could read my mind.

"You're referring to those shiny, shuffling, backpack-looking things?" I asked.

"Yep," he replied. "Clever gimmick on my part to make them look like little backpacks with feet, wasn't it?"

I decided not to acknowledge his last question. It was probably another rhetorical one anyhow. Instead, I asked one of my own. "Was I looking at more than one message?"

"Nope," Dr. F. told me. "That other cable has part of the same message as the packets that swarmed around you."

"Why are they traveling along different cables?" I asked.

"Not all of the packets follow the same path to get to their destination. Some may go through one router and some through another one. Continuing the letter analogy, some of the letters may go from Salt Lake City to Houston on their way to get to Washington, D.C., while other letters may go through Chicago instead. All the packets wind up where they're supposed to, however, and the computer that receives them then checks the code. If all seems to be well—if none of the data that arrived is corrupted—it then puts them all back together so it can look at the complete file."

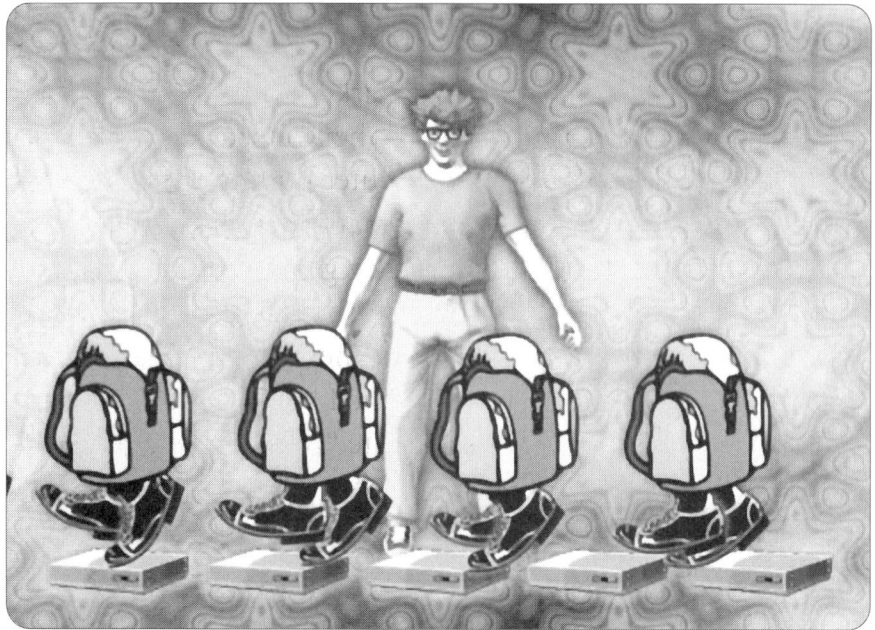

"Cool," I said. And I wasn't lying. That was pretty neat that all that information could get taken apart and put back together again. It was just like Willy Wonka said! "What about this error-detection thing—the code—that you said every packet has?"

"That," he said, "is called **checksum**."

"What kind of a word is that?" Okay, I admit it was a stupid question. After all, most words used to talk about the Internet are a little weird.

But Dr. F. got a little testy about my question; I didn't think it was that far off base to warrant one of his harrumphs. "It makes perfect sense, Beta," he said, adding another harrumph for emphasis, I guess, "which you would know if you would pay attention."

After that I heard what sounded like Dr. F. inhaling and exhaling a few deep breaths, evidently to calm

Checksum

When a document or other piece of information is broken down in packet switching, each packet is marked with the original size of the data. When the packets arrive at their destination, the computer **checks** the **sum** of the original data to make sure all of the data is present and that none of it got lost or mixed up. This process is known as **checksum**.

himself down, and then he continued. "You see, when the packets are made from the original information, they are marked with the size of the original document. That way, when the packets arrive and are reassembled, the computer putting them together can *check* the *sum* of the information to make sure it didn't get mixed up and that nothing got lost. See? Checksum is a very good word for it. You should really learn about things before making fun of them." I could almost hear him gloating while I imagined him using his finger to write a "1" in the air to indicate "score one for the home team."

"But moving right along, let's talk about **protocols**," Dr. F. continued.

Finally, a movie reference I understood! Finally, something I could get excited about! "Like C-3PO!" I shouted. "He was a protocol droid!"

"No! No! No!" Dr. F. sounded furious. But then I heard a few more of those now-familiar scratches as he evidently wrote something in chalk on one of the blueboards and, judging from his voice as he continued, he'd settled down. Settled down probably doesn't adequately describe it; he seemed enthusiastic again.

"You know, Beta," he said, "I think you've hit on something there. In *Star Wars*, the protocol droid C-3PO spoke millions of languages; he served as a translator between people who couldn't otherwise understand each other. He even managed to speak to computers that other computers couldn't understand. That's kind of what a protocol does. It is an established pattern of arranging data to communicate between two machines. The machines must each have this protocol to understand what the other is sending to it.

"One of the most common protocols for communicating over networks and the Internet is called **Transmission Control Protocol/Internet Protocol**."

"Is it all right if I just say TCP-slash-IP?" I asked.

Protocol

A **protocol** is an established pattern of arranging data to communicate between two machines. The machines must each have the same **protocol** to understand what the other is sending to it.

"That's what most people do. Only, while the 'slash' appears when the term is written, it isn't spoken. It's said as just 'T-C-P-I-P.'"

"At any rate, **TCP/IP** is actually a group of protocols put together, but the most important of these protocols are TCP and IP.

"The TCP part is what establishes the connection and makes sure the computers can send information to each other. Its job in a packet switching setup is to guarantee the packets get where they belong and that they get there in order.

"However, TCP only knows how to do that because of the IP part. The IP part makes sure the packets are addressed, how big they are, and what format they come in. Without IP, the computers can't figure out where to send anything. Without the TCP part, they'd be unable to do the actual transmission.

"Now, the IP has to address each packet, just like you address a letter. How do you think it does this, Beta?"

I felt on the spot, so I just guessed. "With URLs?"

"No!" I could almost hear a vein bursting in Dr. F's skull. "Don't you know that computers don't use the words like we do? They use numbers! The numbers are called **IP addresses** because they're the addresses that IP uses for the packets. IP addresses are always one hundred percent unique and are formed by 4 groups of numbers between 0 and 255. Like 128.121.123.98 or 255.0.0.1 or even 64.210.13.248. You can type this IP address into your web browser instead of the URL and you'll see the same thing."

"That doesn't sound much more difficult to remember than a phone number," I said. "Why do you we use URLs if the computer is just going to look at that IP address number anyhow?"

"Because IP addresses on the same server tend to have very similar numbers. For example, 64.210.13.230, 64.210.13.226, and 64.210.13.248 are all IP addresses on the same server. Would you rather remember those few

---

Transmission Control Protocol/Internet Protocol (TCP/IP)

TCP/IP is one of the most common protocols for communicating over networks and the Internet. The TCP part is what establishes the connection and makes sure the computers can send information to each other. Its job in a packet switching setup is to guarantee the packets get where they belong and that they get there in order. The IP part addresses each packet with a number, known as an IP address.

Internet Protocol (IP) address

An **IP** address is the Internet address for a Web site or page. This address is a series of four numbers (from 0 to 255) separated by three periods. Since most people have trouble remembering numbers, we changed the number sequence to a written address, such as www.syngress.com, which is also known as the URL. An analogy would be dialing your friend by using his or her name instead of phone number.

digits that are different in each IP address? Or is it easier to remember the URLs ricehahn.com, webosaurus.net, and writers-group.org? Those are the corresponding domains for the IP address numbers I mentioned."

He didn't wait for an answer. "Now, every computer and domain on a network or on the Internet has to have an IP address that is completely different than every other IP address that is out there.

"There are two kinds of IP addresses, and they have to do with the way that the IP addresses are given. The first is a static IP address. That means that the IP address is given to that computer or domain and it won't ever change. This makes serving Web sites easier and improves security for computers on the Internet.

"Most personal computers or workstations use dynamic IP addresses, however. Dynamic IP addresses are assigned by a server, which is usually the ISP that controls the connection being used when the computer connects to the Internet. That way the ISP doesn't have to have a unique IP address for every single one of the people who use that ISP. This is mostly a practical approach, because it is very expensive to own the rights to using an IP address.

"So now I'll bet you're wondering how that IP Address is located when you type in a domain name."

I wasn't, but now that he'd mentioned it, I was starting to get a little curious. Fortunately, I didn't have long to wait, because Dr. F. was in lecture mode.

"When someone registers a domain they have to specify a Domain Name Service, or DNS. The Domain Name Service is a program on a computer that tells what IP Address goes with domains associated with it. It's that simple.

"So that's how the packet gets addressed and knows where to go. But there's still the problem of getting there. How do you suppose a packet finds the way to get to the address it's sent to?"

"By using the address?" I thought that one was a no-brainer, but apparently I was suffering from some sort of assumption delusions again.

"Beta," Dr. F. said crossly, "if I asked you to deliver something to 42 Answer Way in PoDunk Junction, Ohio, would you know how to get there? You have the address."

"Uh... no. I guess not," I admitted sheepishly. "I guess I'd need to get some directions."

"Right! You'd need a **router**!"

"A router?"

"Yes, a router. A router is a machine that figures out how to get a packet to the address it's headed for. It figures out the best path based on hops, the queue length, and other factors."

My head was spinning again. I thought only two things would fix my situation: a good pizza and an explanation of some terms. I wasn't going to get the first, but I was betting Dr. F. was already willing to give me the second in spades, so I listened.

"The first factor a router uses to calculate the best path is the number of hops it needs to get to the destination. A hop is a journey between computers. The more computers that a packet has to pass through to get to the receiving computer, the more hops, and hence, the longer the journey. A router tries to use the path with the fewest hops, because each packet's header says how many hops the packet can take on its journey. But remember, there are other factors involved in the calculation."

Router

A router is a device designed to send data (or packets of data) from one network or area to another. **Routers** decide what is the most efficient way of sending information much as when a delivery person must decide which streets to drive on to save the most amount of time.

I can only imagine that at this point Dr. F. had some sort of compulsion to stress his point, because I felt myself leave my mid-air suspended animation state and take off on another part of my JTCI. I only had time to emit the "Wh…" part of my thoughts aloud before I found that having one's size checked to determine its checksum is somewhat like getting another squish. That done, I felt myself break into a bunch of—I could only assume at this point, despite the knowledge that assumptions had gotten me into thus far—predetermined sizes, which then bounced between routers. Something told me I was experiencing the packets making that hop process.

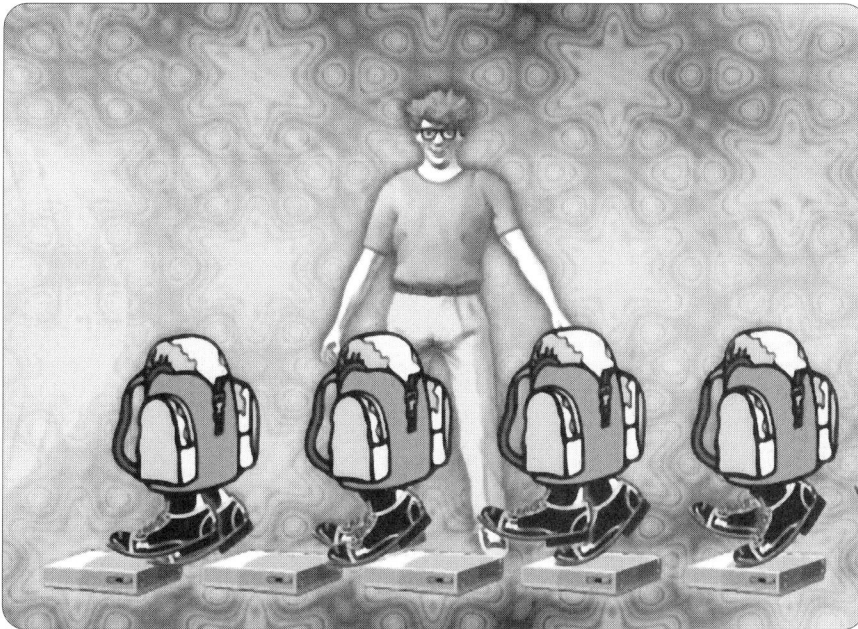

I didn't really have time to have any "Hey! I'm dismembered!" concerns, but I can still tell you that it was very odd flying about like that. My head was in one computer, my fingers in another, and I think my feet were somewhere near Little Rock, Arkansas. Every little bit of me was being read, and my elbows were waiting in line in some computer in St. Louis. My parts kept shifting around and around, moving steadily in one direction.

This is definitely not a linear journey, I thought. As if to add emphasis to my thoughts, a squish and shuffle later I was finally able to finish my earlier thought as my body was reassembled in a computer in San Diego, and I shouted, "Whoa!"

I found myself pointed back facing in the direction I'd been in before I did all those hops. In other words, I was doing the mid-air limbo again.

"As you've now learned firsthand," Dr. F. continued, "each computer the packet will travel through will be another router, so this process will be repeated for each hop. This process is quite logically called the routing process, and it's handled by a software procedure within the router.

"When a router receives a packet, it reads the header. It looks at the target address of the packet and the number of hops it will take. It then compares this information to the routing table. The routing table is a collection of data about where to send the packets next based on the IP address.

"Sometimes, packets come into a router faster than the router is able to handle them. Some computers—and some people—just stop working when there is too much to do. But not a router! A router doesn't just drop tasks when it has more than it can do. Instead, it lines up all the packets in order and remembers them. It writes itself a sort of virtual to-do list. That is, it stores the packets in RAM until it can deal with them. This waiting line of packets is called the input queue. A queue, by the way, is a word the English use to mean 'line.' Another logical name for it because the first packets that are sent from the input queue are the first ones dealt with. A router is very professional and responsible, and precise.

"However, each router only has so much RAM to use to remember and keep track of the packets. Because of this, each router also has a **queue length**. Once the queue length is full, it can't accept any more packets. Its queue length is kind of like the maximum capacity limit at a theater or concert. Except at a theater or concert, you only get turned away. When a router's queue length is full, packets can get lost. But routers are responsible about the packets they send as well. If a packet looks like it may get lost, the router that just sent it will use the TCP protocol to send it again.

"Each router sends the packet on to another router closer to the destination until the packet finally arrives

> ## Queue length
> The amount of memory/data the queue can hold. If the queue length in a router is full, it cannot accept any more packets of information until the router has processed what it already has.

where it's intended to go. Once this happens, the packets are all reassembled in order again.

"Isn't it great how this technology works, Beta?"

Again, Dr. F. didn't wait for an answer. I braced myself expecting to feel another squish at any moment, but Dr. F. just continued his talk.

"Most people think they just type in the words and what they want appears suddenly. But as you can see, a lot happens in between those two things. Routers and packets and the whole Internet is working very hard and doing many tasks just to make sure you can see a Web site or get your email. Isn't it wonderful?"

Oh, yeah, I thought, but I knew better than to express my sarcasm out loud. I figured matching Dr. F.'s enthusiasm might bring me closer to the end of this JTCI and the chance to eat. As fascinating as I was finding all this newfound knowledge, I couldn't seem to get past the feeling that it'd be just as compelling if I could view a Dr. F.-narrated video or something. At least then I could sit back and munch on some popcorn at the same time.

"Absolutely!" I answered. "There's a lot more that goes on behind the Internet scene than meets the eye, isn't there?"

"That's true for most people," Dr. F. replied. I swear I heard him choke back a chuckle as he added, "but we've determined that you're not like most people, haven't we?"

I decided that question was another rhetorical one and remained silent. Instead I flexed my arms and legs a bit as I realized that this mid-air limbo stuff didn't feel all that different from floating on water. Granted, I wasn't getting wet, so that wasn't a totally accurate analogy, but I also didn't seem to be covering a lot of physical distance at the moment either, which therefore made it a comparison that was close enough for me.

Chapter 7

How Everybody Knows Your (Domain) Name

I was about ready to see if I could roll over on my back and do a super-limbo back float when Dr. F. interrupted my reverie.

"Bert, earlier I told you about the **Domain Name System**. Will you summarize what it is for me, please?"

I was beginning to feel like I was in class at school. In fact, I felt like I was in the class that comes right before lunch period. But, because I could recall what I'd learned about the Domain Name System from his lecture, I answered in the hope it would speed up the arrival of my lunchtime.

"A Domain Name System is in place so that we can use a set of easily remembered letters or words instead of a numeric address for Web sites. The words we use are called **Uniform Resource Locators**, or **URLs**. The numbers that are the real address are called IP addresses. A Domain Name Service finds the IP address that belongs with the URL you type in and uses that IP address to find the Web page for you."

"Close enough, BT," Dr. F. responded.

Close enough? I thought that was pretty good. But I knew it'd only take longer if I argued about it, so I let Dr. F. continue.

"The point, my dear Beta, is that E-mail works the same way."

"What?" I hadn't realized that we were talking about E-mail. But then that often happens when I'm talking to Dr. F. Things seem to jump from topic to topic, seemingly without any sort of transition.

Domain Name System (DNS)

This software keeps a domain name database (collection of data) to make it easier for us to find a specific URL instead of using the IP address' numbering system.

syngress.com

Domain Name

"E-mail, B. What is so difficult about that? The packets that make up an E-mail message follow the exact same routes as do Web pages. They get broken up and sent through routers and then put together again at the far end."

No sooner had Dr. F. shared that information then I suddenly felt another series of all-too-familiar squishes as E-mail headers were applied to each part of me that broke off into its own packet. *Transponder time again*, I thought as my packets passed through the internal router on my network. It soon became obvious that I was being sent somewhere outside of the network as I was maneuvered through the steps necessary for me to pass through a firewall that directly preceded my trip to the Internet router. The Internet router then examined each packet to determine its address, and once it learned where I—the human cannonball of messages—was to be sent, I spurted forward until I landed at the gateway of the network meant to receive me, the human E-mail message. That gateway filtered me through its TCP, which reassembled my packets so that I once again resembled myself—or at least myself as I'd look if I were an E-mail message. This transmogrifying was getting to be a bit disconcerting!

"You understand a bit better now how an E-mail can reach its destination so fast?" Dr. F. asked, his voice again sounding like he was talking through that megaphone held backwards.

He didn't wait for my answer. I felt another series of squishes as I turned to face the direction from which I'd come and felt myself break into packets again and begin what ended up being another short JTCI as I got emailed back—as what I assumed was a reply to the earlier message of me. I passed through all the steps again and got reassembled, and then a squish later, felt myself become myself again back in my now familiar in-limbo position. The only difference was that this time Dr. F. evidently decided he needed some comic relief, because now I was

---

Uniform Resource Locator (URL)

Uniform Resource Locators are the computer/electronic addresses of Web sites. An example of a URL is www.washingtonpost.com, which is the URL for the Washington Post newspaper.

dressed in a familiar red, white, and blue costume. And, I *did* have a cape!

This guy is so close to psychic it's eerie, I thought. I didn't have time to ponder the fact I wasn't exactly sure how I was able to get from Point A to B and then back again, or what parts of me knew what went where or the server knew what to send where. In fact, I'm embarrassed to admit that as ridiculous as I probably looked in that cape and costume, I figured I probably still looked better than I do in those jeans that make my rear-end look big. Of all the pants to wear and of all the days to wear them, on the day of my JTCI I chose the jeans that were a part of my failed bleaching experiment. I probably couldn't duplicate the experiment again if I tried. All I know is I threw a pair of dark jeans and this bright-enough-to-make-you-go-blind yellow sweatshirt my grandmother had gotten me for Christmas into the same load and added extra bleach. My goal was to end up with lighter blue jeans and a light yellow sweatshirt. Instead I got bleached Brussels sprouts green. Not exactly the fashion statement I'd wanted to make, especially not what I'd purposely pick out to wear had I known ahead of time that I'd be starring in some videos. Life can be cruel at times.

"Welcome back, B."

Leave it to Dr. F. to interrupt me during some serious thinking. Ah well, it was probably better for my state of mind that I now needed to listen to him continue his lecture anyhow.

"You've probably noticed that E-mail addresses look similar to URLs in a lot of ways. They all have a domain name attached to them. This is because E-mail is controlled and delivered by the domain name. Before we talk about delivery, however, we should look at how an E-mail address is formed. That will help in understanding how E-mail works. We'll use the example bert@webosaurus.net.

"The first part of an E-mail address is the **username** of the person who belongs to the E-mail address."

I found it was funny that, to Dr. F., people belonged to an E-mail address rather than the other way around. (You'd think he would have stopped to explain to me some specifics about my most-recent JTCI. I soon learned that it'd be up to me to figure things out from the context of his one-sided conversation.)

"The first part designates a specific person, in this case, the person with the username *Bert* who uses the server that provides the E-mail address."

Once I realized the logistics of the E-mail address to which Dr. F. was referring, I suddenly got the impression that this discussion was about to become very personal.

"The username is usually the same as the login name. When you tell a server you want to send a message or collect the messages you have, it demands you identify yourself. It's not going to let just anyone collect your E-mail. You have to say who you are and, as an extra precaution, you have to tell it your secret password. If you can prove that the username and password are yours, therefore proving that you are who you say you are the server will let you send or receive E-mail.

"The next part— the part in the middle of an E-mail address— is known as the **at sign**."

A picture of an at sign appeared before me. It looked like an "a" with a circle around it. I'd seen it before. It was the @ in bert@webosaurus.net. I hadn't known what it was called

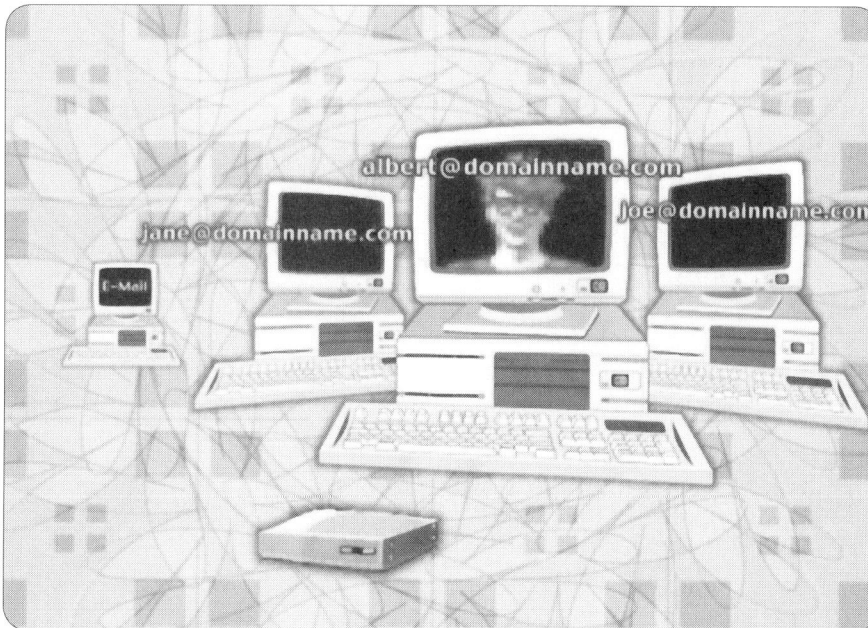

before, but I didn't tell Dr. F. that. In fact, I got momentarily sidetracked with a visual image of how funny a pair of those slinky eyeball glasses would look with slinky at signs instead—especially if they had a big nose and Groucho mustache attached, too.

"The @ symbol is what separates the username from the domain name—or distinguishes which user on a given domain should get the E-mail. How many people named Bert do you think use the Internet, B?"

"Huh?" These questions were really starting to catch me off guard. I blamed hunger. "I guess there are probably hundreds. Maybe thousands."

"So you can't just send a message to Bert and hope it will get there?

This was another rhetorical question, and I knew it, so I kept quiet.

"See, this is why E-mail addresses have a domain as the last part of the E-mail address. The domains make sure they each only have one user called Bert; anyone else on that domain that has the name Bert will have to select a different username—like Bert2 or something. The domain makes sure servers can identify the Bert that belongs to a certain domain. When you send a letter, you address it in a way that says you want to send it to the Bert who lives at a specific location. The domain in an E-mail address does the same thing. It's basically telling the server, 'This email is going to go to this user of this domain,' or this username *at* this domain.

"So the last part is the domain. The domain is what helps the routers find where the email message goes. That domain is turned into an IP address using DNS just like it is with a URL. But once the E-mail arrives at the server, instead of returning a document it looks at the username. The server that holds the domain then has the responsibility of putting the document in the correct mailbox. The routers get the E-mail message to the right place, but getting it to the right user is the server's job. Once the message gets that far, though, it's a simple job

At (@) sign
We use the @ symbol to separate the username from the ISP in an e-mail address.

from there because there can only be one user for each username on a domain, so it's pretty easy to find to whom the message belongs.

"The server also has the responsibility of making sure the user looks at the right mailbox when he logs in. By that I mean the server makes sure that the user only receives and views the E-mail that was meant for him and not that which was meant for someone else. The server does this when the E-mail recipient's client (we'll talk about that in a minute) logs into the server. This works a lot like getting your mail from a post office box. First, the client has to make a connection to the server. The server then acts almost like a guard blocking access to the virtual mailboxes and asks who the client represents. In other words, it digitally asks, 'Which user's messages do you want, client?' The E-mail client then tells the server which user by showing the username. But, like I said before, the server still needs proof. If you wanted to pick up a packet at the post office, you'd have to show the clerk something that proves you're who you say you are. Therefore, at the post office, you'd show your driver's license or student ID card. A server can't see those things, so it asks for a secret password. When the server has checked that the username and the password match up, it sends all the messages to the client. Once again, the messages get broken up into little packets for the journey, and they get reassembled once they get back to the client."

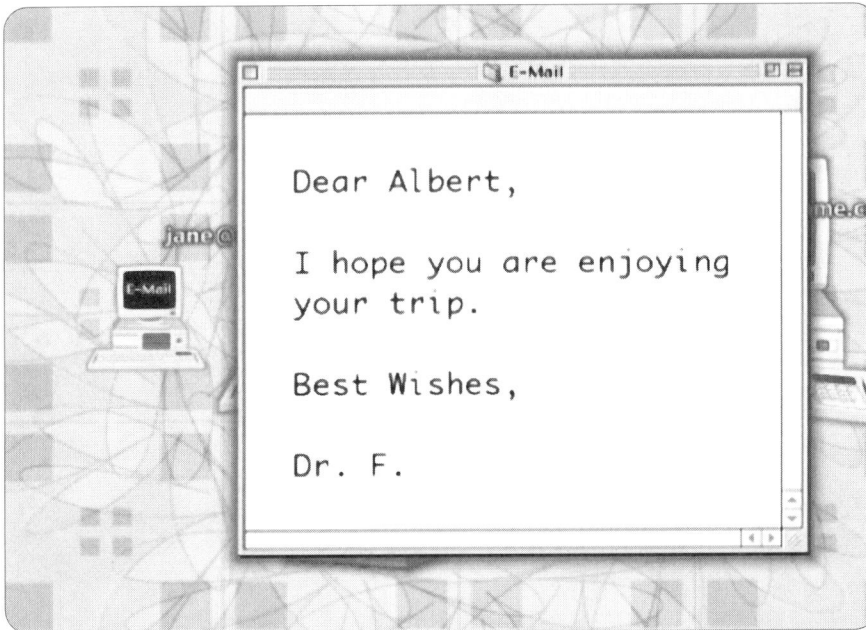

Dear Albert,

I hope you are enjoying your trip.

Best Wishes,

Dr. F.

"What's this 'client' thing you keep talking about?" I asked.

"You are always so impatient, Beta. I guess I can excuse some impatience when it shows that you're curious and want to learn more."

I thought Dr. F's impatience observation was a bit ironic, considering Dr. F. was impatient most of the time and never hesitated to let me know when I was too slow. I guess it really wasn't anything to get stressed about, though, especially considering he'd acknowledged my curiosity in almost the same breath.

"A **client** can be a program, but for this part of our discussion, a client refers to a computer on a network (or the Internet) that requests information, files, or services."

"So, that means any computer is a client."

"Close, Beta. But not every single computer is a client. Just most of them are. Your computer is a client, and my computer is a client. In fact, most computers perform client functions at one time or another. But there are also servers. Before we talk about them though, let's go a little bit more into clients, servers, and services.

"For general pur-

> ### Client
> In a network, the **client** is the computer/workstation that connects to the network to request files, information or services. The **client** connects to the server, which is the computer(s) that controls the network.

poses, let's think of a client as a computer that accesses the Internet. A client goes out and asks the server to view Web pages or for E-mail, or asks for the server to send E-mail, or asks for printing on a network, or tries to log in to the server. Basically, the client computer is the computer than needs to get something done.

"Sometimes, a specific program that uses network or Internet services is also called a client. That's why I mentioned 'a client can be a program' earlier. So, for example, the program you use to read and send E-mail can be called an E-mail client. A client can be a program for E-mail, Web browsing, file transfers, chatting, instant messaging, telnet, and anything else you would do on the Internet. We'll talk about how most of those things work later. Right now you just need to know that 'client' can either refer to a computer that needs Internet services or to the specific program that asks for the services."

"Right," I said, making mental notes again. "The client wants something done."

"Services are, well, services. They're things that a computer needs to get done. Whether that is authenticating a log-in, sending a message, or downloading a file. Services can be simple, like those I mentioned, or they can be more complex, like updating databases or generating new information. Anything that is done on the Internet is called a service.

> **Server**
> A server is a computer used by other computers in a network to provide a variety of services.

File Server

stores and provides access to files

"That leaves us with **servers**, but I guess that you have already figured out what servers are. Servers are the computers that serve, or provide services. You can have an E-mail server, a Web server, a database server, and many other kinds of server. Each server performs specific kinds of jobs, depending on what it was programmed to do. The server is what does the job that the client needs done."

"So the server serves the client," I made another note. Apparently Dr. F. didn't hear me because he barely even stopped for breath.

"Just like clients, 'server' can also apply to a specific piece of software. What this means is that a server computer usually doesn't perform just one job or service. The reason why server computers are often called hosts is to distinguish between the computer and the software. A host may have a POP3 server, an SMTP server, a Web server, and several other kinds of servers that run on it all at the same time. I'll explain more about specific servers and how they work later, but often in the cases of file transfer servers, Web servers, and E-mail servers, each of these pieces of software will have a different URL in the same domain, like ftp.webosaurus.net or smtp.webosaurus.net, even though they all point to the same computer."

Print Server manages and allows equal access to one or more printers

That was a lot of information, but I guess by now I was used to Dr. F. and his acuity for information dumps. I decided, however, that I had better repeat all that just to make sure I got it.

"So," I started slowly, thinking it through as I went, "there are client computers on the Internet, and they're called clients because of the client software they run. Client computers are like customers, because they want to have something done for them. Is that right?"

"Yes B!" Dr. F. sounded really excited. "That's a great way to explain it. Clients are like customers who want services performed for them. Those services are performed by servers!"

I was kind of miffed, because that was what I was going to say next. I just hoped Dr. F. remembered that was my idea if he ever used it again. More importantly, I hoped he remembered how I understood it the next time he thought I was learning too slowly—or not paying attention. Most importantly, I hoped this meant there was a reward at the end of all this that came in the form of consumable items. Then Dr. F. could perform a service for *me* by getting pizza delivered. I made myself another mental note to suggest that once I got the chance, then finished the explanation. "So the term 'client' can refer either to the computer or the specific program that wants a service, and the term 'server' can refer either to the computer or the specific program that gives the service, right?"

"Exactly, B. Let's move on now," he said with typical impatience.

As I hung here in my mid-air limbo, wiggling my arms and legs occasionally to keep my circulation moving, I couldn't help but wonder if Dr. F. meant 'let's move on now' in the literal or figurative sense.

Chapter 8

Ways to Connect to the Internet

I could hear those scratching noises in the background again, so I figured Dr. F. must be doing some more of his writing on the blueboards.

I needed something to do myself. I had to take my mind off of my empty stomach somehow. The leg and arm flutters had seemed to help improve my circulation, but that got boring fast. Suddenly, inspired in a way that I imagine any astronaut first experiencing weightlessness must feel, I decided to get creative.

I rolled over on my right side. Whether the feeling was accurate or not, this gave me the impression that I'd just turned my back on Dr. F. This wasn't meant to be a symbolic gesture or anything; it just seemed like the best way to get started. I rested my head on my elbow and started doing scissor kicks, lifting my right leg as high as I could get it to go in the same way I'd seen those people do on the yoga shows my mom watches. (Of course, in mom's case, I've yet to see her actually do any of the exercises. I think it's a mind over matter experiment she does, optimistic that those visual efforts will help improve her appearance before she switches to the food network. I obviously inherited my fascination with food.)

I was well on my way to getting my mind cleared enough to stop thinking about eating and start feeling really inspired when I felt a dunce cap appear on my head. Don't ask me how I knew it was a dunce cap. I just knew. I don't recall looking at myself in some sort of virtual mirror or anything. I just felt it there and automatically knew what it was.

Then I heard Dr. Franklin speak.

"DT," he said.

"Don't you mean BT?" I asked.

"I *always* mean what I say," Dr. F. said with one of his infamous harrumphs. That guy can get so touchy when he's questioned. "DT is what I said and DT is what I meant. Any idea why?"

"Errrrrr, no."

Dumb Terminal (DT)

This monitor (display capabilities only) has no ability to process information. It merely displays the information. An example of a DT could be an Automated Teller Machine (ATM), which can do nothing unless attached to its network.

"Think, B! We've laid the groundwork for your understanding of how things—and you in your JTCI—move across the Internet. Don't you think it's time we discussed some of the ways you can actually connect *to* the Internet? After all, you have to connect before you can get anything moving across it."

"I understand the connection part. I'm still a little unclear about the 'DT' part though."

"**Dumb Terminal**," Dr. F. said, with another harrumph. "You, Bert, are now a **DT**."

That guy's lucky my parents instilled in me a healthy level of self worth, I thought. Otherwise I would have been feeling absolutely devastated right then. As it was, I only felt very insulted.

"Terminal, as in computer terminal?" I asked.

"You only look like a computer at this point, B," Dr. F. answered. "An intuitive one, maybe, though. I will grant you that. Those yoga exercises you were doing to clear your mind were the perfect ones for getting ready for this role. Who knew I had a method actor on my hands? A Dumb Terminal is a display monitor that has no processing capabilities and devices that can only enter and accept data. Alone, it's an empty vessel like your mind right now. It relies on the network to which it's connected to do its thinking for it.

"You'll recall that when you connect to the Internet, your computer becomes a part of a network—in the case of the Internet, a worldwide one. In fact, every computer that connects to the Internet becomes a part of that worldwide network."

I settled back and listened to another one of Dr. F's infodump lectures, feeling a little bit like the Scarecrow in *The Wizard of Oz*. At least sitting there without a brain meant that I didn't have the capacity to worry about how stiff I'd feel if the lecture went on for very long before Dr. F. got me moving on another JTCI.

"You already know that you may use a modem and dial a local number to connect to an Internet Service Provider, or ISP—or, at least you knew that back when you had a brain, inefficient as it was."

I swear I heard him chuckle at that point. Dr. F. evidently loves to laugh at his own private jokes.

"Dumb terminals used to be common on workplace networks," Dr. F. said, "but because computers are now so inexpensive, that isn't as prevalent as it once was— although there are times when an older computer is dummied down to perform like a dumb terminal of sorts. In other words, a dumb terminal of that nature then doesn't have to rely on the speed of its processor to process data because the network performs that function.

"Technically, however, a dumb terminal is one that is basically just a work station with the means to view data—on a monitor, usually, although older ones like the teletype terminals once used in law enforcement or newswire services sent information directly to a printer for display, using a terminal emulation program. That's

another term you'll eventually encounter, so it's good to know. A terminal emulation program is a program that allows a personal computer to access a mainframe computer or bulletin board service.

"While a computer on a network can connect to other computers on that network via modem, many business networks connect directly to the Internet via a Local Area Network, or LAN. When that's the case, they don't use an ISP. They can use a dedicated line to connect, or a dial-up. Regardless of which method they use to connect, however, in each region there is what is known as the local **Point of Presence**, or **POP**.

"As I've mentioned several times, regardless of whether or not you're a part of a network before you connect, once you're on the Internet, you become a part of that network. This is most commonly your ISP's network, which in turn belongs to a regional network, which in turn connects to the combined network of networks we know as the Internet.

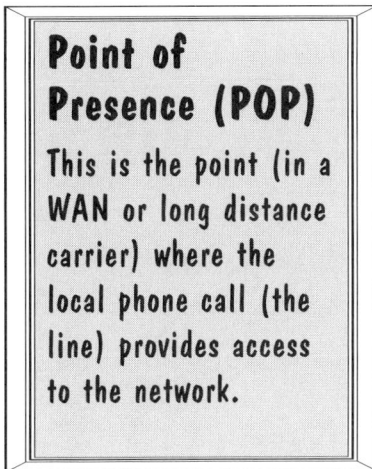

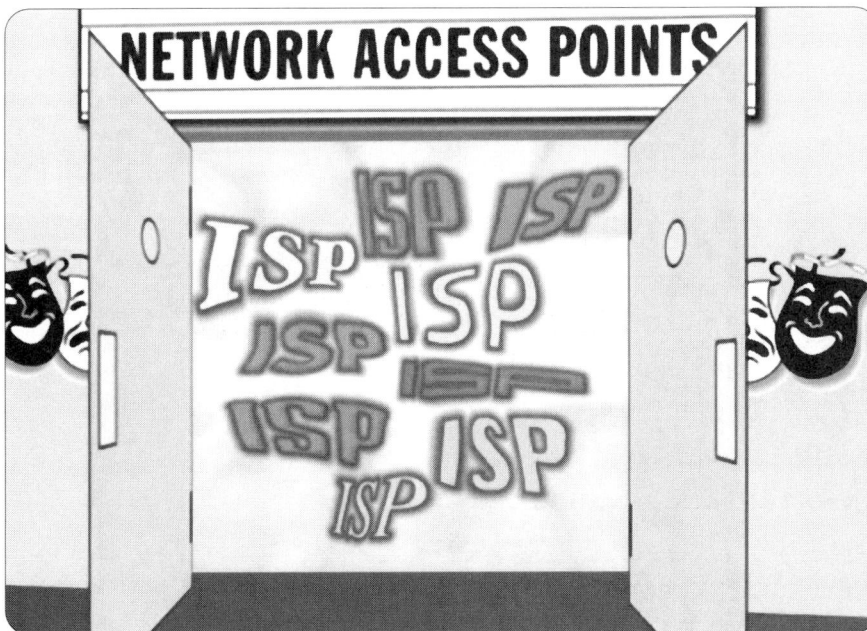

> ## Point of Presence (POP)
>
> This is the point (in a WAN or long distance carrier) where the local phone call (the line) provides access to the network.

"The fact to keep in mind is that there is no overall controlling network for the Internet. Instead, there are several high-level networks connecting to each other through Network Access Points, or NAPs."

"If a dumb terminal isn't the most common input component on a network anymore, why do you have me sitting here acting like one?"

I felt a squish that made me worry at first that Dr. F. didn't like my question. I know, I know. You'd think I'd have learned by now that the doctor doesn't appreciate when I question his methods. But all of this in-limbo with my stomach growling stuff was making me irrational.

"I've shut down the rest of your network, so now I want you to attempt to work on something."

"Like what?"

"Whatever you like."

It's kind of difficult to make those kinds of decisions when you don't have a brain, I thought. "Okay," I said, feeling rebellious. "I'll play a game."

"Fine," Dr. F. said. "Whatever you like."

That was easier than I thought it'd be. Maybe Dr. F. is about ready to let me take a break.

I decided I'd take advantage of the situation and try to break my record on minesweeper. I moved the mouse. Nada. I tried using keystrokes to call up the program. Still nothing. "What gives?" I asked.

"I wanted you to get the true feeling of what it's like to attempt to operate without a brain."

"I'm not trying to do brain surgery here," I grumbled. "I'm just trying to play minesweeper."

"Doesn't matter," Dr. F. replied. "Without the network, you can't do anything—regardless of how simple or complex the task. You're a dumb terminal, remember?"

"So, for a dumb terminal, when the network goes down, it's sort of like how it is when your ISP goes down and won't let you dial up?" I may not have phrased that question in the best manner—after all, I was working here without a brain, but I did raise my voice inflection so Dr. F. would know I meant it to be a question.

"Good comparison," he said. "The only difference is that when you're using your home computer to attempt to connect to your ISP, even if the ISP isn't currently available to let you get online, you can still use your computer for other tasks—like for minesweeper or to run one of your other programs.

"On the other hand, when you're a dumb terminal on a network," he continued, "if the network is down, your desktop usefulness drops to that of a paperweight."

"Does that mean I don't get to play minesweeper?" I tried not to whine, but geez! Did I have to suffer such extreme disappointment just so Dr. F. could make a point? It just didn't seem fair!

"So, as you can see, there is more than one way to connect to the Internet."

I guess Dr. F. decided to ignore my last question. I suppose that was better than listening to another harrumph or sarcasm.

"Right now you're experiencing one of the least popular connection methods," Dr. F. said.

"When you use a terminal emulation program that makes your computer act like a dumb terminal, Internet software doesn't actually run on your computer; it's run on the computer to which you've connected. That means what you see on your screen is filtered through that other computer, so you only see what's happening there. It also limits your access options. In most cases, when you connect using a dumb terminal, you can't view graphics. Text-only browsing can get boring once you're used to seeing all the fancy stuff normally available on the World Wide Web.

"One difference between actually being a dumb terminal on a network and using terminal emulation software to connect is that when you use the software you still connect via a phone line; however, you'll use what is known as a shell account for your actual browsing, which is why you're limited to viewing text only.

"The most popular is still a dial-up," Dr. F. continued. "That's how you got online for your JTCI, when you were routed through an ISP.

"Of course, I have a direct connection in the lab, but that would have been a boring way to start your journey. A direct connection has a definite speed advantage over a dial-up because a T-1 or T-3 line transmits and receives

data much faster than what you can do using a modem.
It's also a much more expensive way to connect, though,
so it's outside the budget of most home users.

"There are other ways to connect that provide the
advantage of increased speed at affordable fees. We'll go
into more detail about some of those options later—like
cable, ASDL, and ISDN connections."

I felt a squish and suddenly my dunce cap was
gone—thank goodness! I found myself back in my in-
limbo, floating-through-hyperspace stance, which I guess
was an improvement.

"Dr. Franklin?" I asked.

"Yes," he replied. "I see you have your brain back."

He chuckled again. Geek humor, I guess. I'd hoped to
ask him a question about our agenda, but he was back to
continuing his lecture before I had the chance.

"You already know that you can't get on the Internet
just by plugging into the phone jack in the wall. You
have to establish a relationship with an online service
like AOL or arrange to connect via an Internet Service
Provider, or ISP. The online service or ISP then connects
you to Network Access Points that allow people to connect to the information on the Internet.

"When you connect to the Internet through an ISP or
an online service, you do so in one of two ways.

"**Serial Line Internet Protocol**, or **SLIP**, is now the
least popular way to connect. It's not as reliable or stable
as the other method, so it's falling from favor for those
obvious reasons.

"**Point-to-Point Protocol**, or **PPP**, is now the
method of choice. One main reason for that is that PPP
has the ability to retransmit garbled packets, an important consideration because line noise can play havoc with
packets transmitted over telephone lines. Without the
ability to send them again, garbled packets are lost,
which means the entire transmission is lost.
Reassembling packets isn't like viewing a jigsaw puzzle

Serial Line Internet Protocol (SLIP)

This is one of two protocols for dial-up access to the Internet. The other is PPP. **SLIP** aids in gaining access to the Internet via dial-up access, especially to TCP/IP networks. This protocol defines the transport of data packets through a telephone line and allows non-LAN computer connections to the Internet. **SLIP** is less expensive than PPP but does not perform as well.

Point-to-Point Protocol (PPP)

This is one of two protocols for dial-up access to the Internet. The other is SLIP. **PPP** performs better but is more expensive than SLIP. For instance, **PPP** can retransmit garbled data packets, which SLIP cannot do.

with one piece missing; it requires all packets to be in place before the transmission can be complete."

"You mean to tell me that each of those times I broke up into packets to be transmitted from place to place that if I'd have gone out using SLIP, and if a part of me had gotten garbled, I might have lost that part and never been able to recover it?"

"Makes you appreciate how much I'm looking out for your well-being by making sure we used PPP, doesn't it, B?"

Great! I thought. *I'm freaking out here and Dr. F. answers my question with a question.* I took a mental inventory of all my parts, suddenly aware that with one wrong move I could have been missing more than just lunch!

Chapter 9

How Alternative Connection Methods Work

It's scary sometimes how one thought can lead to another. One minute I was worrying about whether or not I was missing one or more of my pieces. The next thing I knew, I had visions of what could happen if, through some Internet transmission fluke, I had an extra part added!

"Ah, Dr. F.?" I asked, once I'd found myself thinking more and more of the changes that occurred to that guy in the film *The Fly*. "I now know from what you've told me about PPP and checksum that safety measures are in place to ensure that all packets arrive unaltered at a destination before a transmission is reassembled. Does that system also make sure that one packet isn't dropped and other is picked up and used to replace the dropped packet by mistake?"

"Don't get hung up on unjustified paranoia, B," Dr. F. replied, his voice a bit too stern in my opinion, considering. After all, *he* wasn't the one being broken apart and reassembled after traveling all over all sorts of virtual spaces. "We're not dealing in Wiley E. Coyote-style experiments here. Of course none are added."

I'm sure Dr. Franklin meant that to be reassuring, but to me that still didn't seem like an answer. In my worried state, the fact that he kept his answers to short sentences instead of going into great detail about why no wrong packets could be added seemed like he was holding something back. Part of my mind told me that surely the checksum measures would prevent that wrong-part-added mistake from occurring; the other part just wanted to continue worrying.

"Besides," Dr. F. continued, "sometimes life *is* just an illusion, Bert."

Now what's that supposed to mean? I thought. I didn't have time to ponder for long before Dr. F. asked me another question.

"I think you've been in limbo long enough, don't you?"

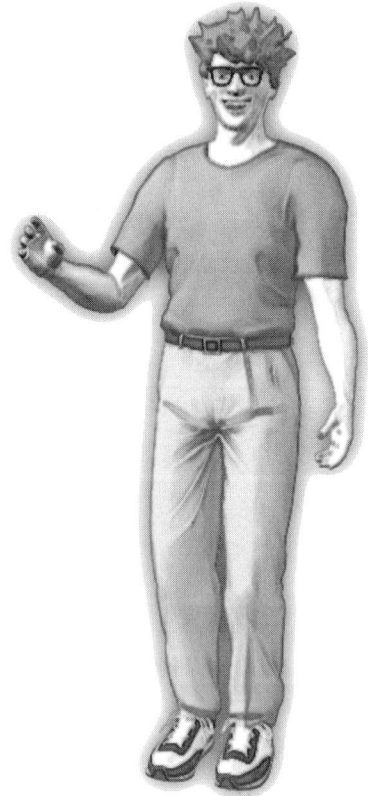

Great! I thought. Maybe Dr. F. is hungry, too, and is going to bring me back so we can get something to eat.

The bad thing about having an over-active imagination—and a food-deprivation-altered mind—is that it caused me to miss my window of opportunity to make a suggestion. Because I thought my JTCI was about to come to an end, I got lost in a few thoughts about what I'd get to eat and before I knew it, Dr. F. continued his part of the conversation without waiting for my answer.

"I think it's time your JTCI got a bit more interactive," he said.

I felt a squish and before I knew it, I was transported to inside another computer. *Don't panic,* I thought, suddenly wishing I'd brought my towel. But it wasn't the time to recall any of my *Hitchhiker's Guide to the Galaxy* trivia; I had to get acclimated to my new surroundings.

At least I'm getting better at steering myself in different directions, I thought as I maneuvered my way out of the tower and into the monitor. I pressed my face against the inside of the computer screen and took a look around.

I was in a computer that appeared to be in somebody's bedroom. Somebody's high-tech bedroom, in fact. Somebody's high-tech bedroom that definitely could use some help from an interior decorator.

"Tell me what you see, B," Dr. F. said.

"Well," I began, "it appears that I'm now trespassing in somebody's bedroom. Did you get permission or anything for me to be here?"

"That's *my* bedroom, Bert," Dr. F. said. "And, because I know your look around is somewhat limited, you have my permission to take in all that you can see."

I peered out through the screen and began to do just that. I never thought of Dr. F. as the type to be concerned with his appearance, but he evidently occasionally takes a look at himself as he gets ready for the day. Across from the monitor stood one of those full-length mirrors in a wooden frame. In it I saw the reflection of a huge dark wood four-poster bed straight out of one of those historical-type movies—or the pages of my mom's favorite magazine. It was neatly made with military precision corners that looked so tight I wished I had a coin to bounce off the covers. The design on his bedspread definitely didn't match the period of the furniture: it looked like a motherboard. One pillow was shaped like a stuffed computer tower and the other one was a computer monitor with huge letters spelling out "JTCI" in the center. *He's evidently been dreaming about this trip I'm on for a long time*, I thought.

On one side of the bed sat a marble-topped antique table that evidently served as his nightstand, judging from the digital alarm clock, lamp, books, and phone sitting on top of it. On the other side of the bed, the computer and monitor were housed in what appeared to be a custom-converted antique armoire.

"What do you see, Bert?"

I knew I had to think of a way to be diplomatic about how I'd answer. I didn't think it'd be in my best interest to say something like what I was thinking: *If this room is any indication of your overall decorating style, I can see your home will never be featured in an issue of Architectural Digest.* (My mom loves that magazine. Because of all the stuff she shows me each time she gets a new issue, I know far more about decorating than I'd ever admit to my friends.)

I cleared my throat and replied. "I see you have a computer in your bedroom."

"That goes without saying, B. I have one in every room of my house."

Silly me, I thought. *Like I should automatically know he'd have computers everywhere.* "Want to give me a hint about what I should be looking for?"

I hoped my voice sounded nice and everything. I was trying hard not to, but it was difficult to avoid not being a little jealous of one guy with that many computers.

"What do you see on the wall opposite you?"

Splitter

A splitter is a device which splits a signal so it can travel along two cables simultaneously.

"You mean on that bright royal blue wall?" That wall did stand out. The rest of the walls were painted blue, too, but at least they were done in a pastel tone.

"Oops," Dr. F. said. "Silly me."

I don't know about you, but as for myself, "oops" was about the last thing I wanted to hear the guy directing my JTCI say.

I heard some clicks. "Look now."

"Wow! How do you decide which screen to watch?"

"Like my TV set-up?" he asked, ignoring my question.

I couldn't ignore the sight in front of me. I'd never seen such an impressive bank of television screens. One large screen in the middle was tuned to a news channel, while more screens than I had time to count displayed programming ranging from the Cartoon Network to a science fiction channel to sports and *Baywatch* to vintage and current movies to weather maps and to what even looked like it must be the NASAvision channel or something.

I heard another click and a whir and then the baseboard slid back and a panel near the floor opened up to reveal some snaking cables and stuff.

"I installed a cable modem in this room for your journey," Dr. F. said. "If you'll notice the box nearest the bank of television monitors, you'll see that it's a cable TV converter. Of course, I tweaked mine a bit to allow for enhanced digital television viewing, but you get the idea. The cable that runs from that box and away from the screens connects to a **splitter**. The wire running from the splitter connects to a cable modem, which is also sometimes referred to as a broadband modem.

"The cable modem is attached to an Ethernet network card inside the computer. You'll have to take my word on some of that because those wires run under the floorboards in this room."

Dr. F. was right about that. From my line of vision, I couldn't see the flooring directly in front of what I'd

come to think of as my computer, now that I appeared to be living in it. I looked over at the mirror and I could see some of the flooring though. I wasn't surprised to find that Dr. F. had had the wooden floor finished in a navy blue stain.

"Now for the interactive part," Dr. F. said as I felt a squish, which suddenly took me away and out of my newfound home.

I felt myself following wires that dipped and then leveled out for a bit. The smooth travel didn't last long before I felt myself do a few loop-de-loops and then make a sharp right turn and come to a halt.

"You've made your way from the computer and through the cable modem. You're now at the splitter."

I bet I won't be here for long, I thought. It wasn't exactly a prophetic insight on my part. Knowing Dr. F. was sending me off on another JTCI, I knew I'd be on a longer move than the distance I'd traveled thus far. I felt another squish and knew things (with "things" being "me") were moving along (pardon my pun) exactly as I'd predicted they would.

"You've left the splitter and are traveling through the Internet data portion of the coaxial cable. The other portion of the cable carries the television transmissions, but we've not concerned with that right now, other than to be aware that both types of signals travel through the coaxial cables simultaneously.

"The computer sends signals within the broadband spectrum on a 6 MHz channel on the coaxial cable.

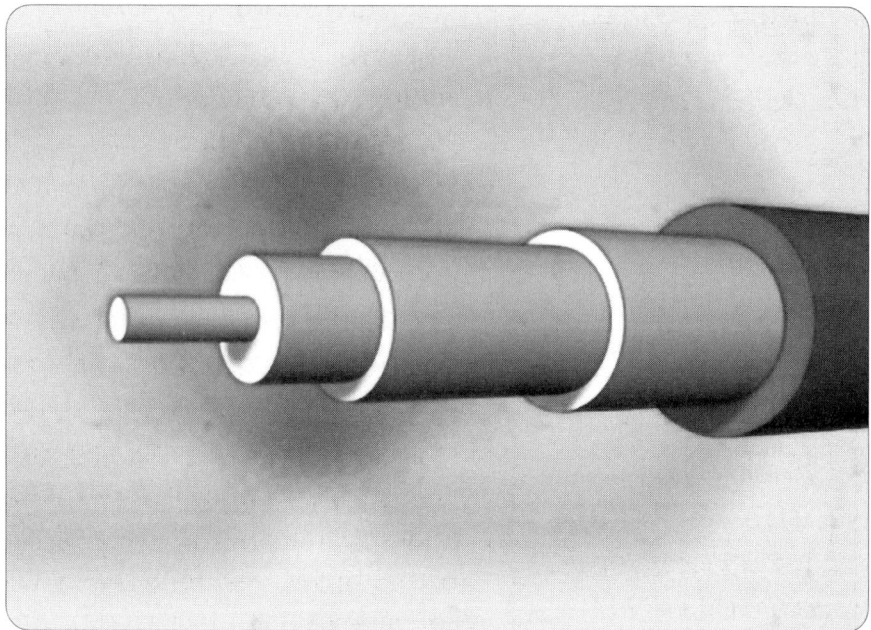

Those signals headed back to your computer from the Internet follow the same path you traveled on your way out. They're fed into the splitter and from there go through the cable modem to your computer where they are routed through the network card.

"We need you to learn how they get from the Internet to the splitter, so that's what you're about to discover up close."

Arms out in front of me again, I was back to wondering if I was wearing a cape as I sped through the cable as Dr. F. continued his talk.

"Cable companies divide their service areas into single local area networks known as **nodes**. Both Internet and television data travel to and from the homes within that network on the coaxial cables connected between those homes and their local node. Cable modems can receive data at speeds up to 1.5 million bits per second and can transmit data at up to 300,000 bps, so Internet access is much faster than what you experience using a standard dial-up connection. Those speeds can decrease according to the number of users within each node who are accessing the Internet at the same time, but even when things slow down a bit because of that simultaneous access, they're still most often much faster than using a dial-up. Each channel only takes about six megahertz, so there's plenty of space to use to connect to the Internet.

"From the node cable transmissions travel to the cable company's **head end**, which has its own high-speed Internet servers: a newsgroup server for access to Usenet, a proxy server for caching frequently accessed Web sites, and a mail server for handling E-mail.

"You notice any difference in the scenery, Bert?"

As usual, Dr. F. didn't give me time to reply as I continued to zip in and out of servers and back to the computer, then back out to the Internet again in a dizzying frenzy of high-speed travel.

Node

A **node** is a junction within a network. A **node** is found wherever lines meet and join, e.g., a workstation, in a network.

Head end

This is often the beginning point of the transmission just before reaching you. Two examples are the computer that runs the network or the satellite dish that receives the transmission that goes to your television.

"Once you reach the node, your JTCI switches from travel on a coaxial cable to a high-speed fiber-optic cable. High-speed fiber-optic cables connect the lines leaving from the nodes to the head end. From the head end, signals are sent out to the local Network Access Point."

"Fascinating," I said, as I felt myself jolt to a stop. I noticed I was back in the computer from which I'd started that leg of my journey. I hoped that meant we were done and I was going to get to eat. I thought maybe I'd have ice cream and started mentally running through the flavors that I hoped Dr. F. kept on hand.

"Now we need to get you to the computer I have hooked up to use Integrated Services Digital Network service."

NAP

Any hopes for ice cream any time soon were dashed as I felt another squish before I literally dashed across the lines that networked the computers in Dr. F's house. This time I landed in a computer set up in the kitchen. A center island with a shiny dark blue marble top gave evidence that the doctor must like to sit down while he chops vegetables. It was far too low for him to stand up and work at comfortably.

Next came a torturous observation. I never pictured Dr. F. as the "decorates with baskets" type, but at one of the counter sat one basket filled with veggies. At the other end stood the real temptation: a basket full of bananas, apples, grapes, and oranges.

I needed to divert my attention away from all that food, so I looked at the rest of the kitchen. All around the center workstation were other surfaces reflecting the industrial stainless steel efficiency of the room. I almost expected to see a robot amble into the room at any moment and whip up some sort of Jetsons'-style meal. In fact, I'd have welcomed that sight, assuming I could figure out how to exit this thing and eat some of it!

"As we've talked about, Integrated Services Digital Network, or ISDN, uses existing copper telephone wires for digital high-speed Internet connection and transmissions. In those areas where the telephone company has ISDN digital switches installed, no additional phone lines are needed. You can connect to the Internet and talk on the phone simultaneously, using the same line."

Evidently Dr. F. didn't appreciate the torture I was going through. Listening to a lecture while stuck in a computer in his kitchen—with so much bounty so close but yet not within reach. Looking at the refrigerator only a few paces away, I felt like I was in a desert and seeing a mirage. He was obviously oblivious to my condition. He just continued to talk, confident that I'd continue to listen—at least to what I could hear over the sounds of my rumbling stomach.

"While you connect to the Internet using an ISDN modem, that name is a misnomer because it actually performs more like a terminal adapter. You see, because ISDN transmits and receives information in digital format, there's no need to convert the signal. (You may recall that one of the functions of a dial-up modem is to convert digital signals from your computer to analog so that they can be transmitted over standard telephone lines.)

"The phone lines are split to separate the data into different channels. **Bearer channels**, or B channels, can carry voice or data information. They are capable of data transfers of 64 Kbps. The Data channel, or D channel, transfers at 16 Kbps and sends signal or routing information. This gives a total of 128 Kbps when the signal is in-band using Multilink PPP or MP, and 112 Kbps if the signal is out-of-band.

"While there are other variations of ISDN, the one used most often is known as **Basic Rate Interface**, or **BRI**, which has three logical channels, one of which is a D channel for data and two that are B channels. Because B channels can be used for voice and data, one can be being used for the Internet while another is used for voice communication. The D channel routes the data that is being transmitted over the B channels.

"Other than that, I think things are straightforward enough that you don't really need a JTCI to understand ISDN. What do you want to do next, B?"

You know how I planned to answer that question. I didn't get the chance.

"There is one more thing!"

"What's that?" I asked, trying to keep any food-craving-induced disappointment out of my voice.

"We didn't discuss power."

"Power?"

"As in electrical power," Dr. F. said. Standard telephone lines receive power from the phone company. That's why they're often not disrupted during a power outage.

"That isn't the case with ISDN lines. They require power from an outside source. You'd probably think of it more like an inside source though, because you plug your ISDN modem into an outlet in your home."

I suddenly became grateful that I hadn't taken an ISDN-version JTCI. I shuddered to think what could

> **Bearer channel (B channel)**
>
> This communications channel can send/ receive voice and data information at 64 Kbps when using an ISDN.

> **Basic Rate Interface (BRI)**
>
> BRI is two 64-Kbps B channels, used for data or voice, and one 16-Kbps D channel, used by the carrier for control and signaling. Each B channel can make a second connection, or you can use the channels together.

have happened to me, had the power gone out during the wrong point in my trip. I imagine Dr. F. has a generator backup power system for his residence and lab. Regardless, that wasn't the kind of chance I wanted to take voluntarily. That's why I was especially jumpy when I felt the next squish.

"Next we'll discuss another popular way to connect to the Internet: **Digital Subscriber Line** or Digital Subscriber Loop, which is also referred to as **DSL**."

I found myself in yet another computer in yet another room in Dr. Franklin's house. *This place is evidently bigger than it looks like from the outside*, I thought. This time as I peered out through the monitor screen, I couldn't help but notice that this room was tastefully decorated. There was a massive stone fireplace at one end of the room, the flames from which reflected off the highly polished surfaces of the wood-paneled walls and dark wood floors. A rich deep brown leather sofa flanked one side of an area rug—the pattern in those familiar shades of blue. Two chairs sat across from the sofa. The only window visible had a leather-cushioned seat with recessed bookcases on each side of it. Floor-to-ceiling bookcases took up the remaining space along that wall.

Evidently the prior owners liked blue, too, I thought. I couldn't imagine Dr. F. doing the decorating for this room after I'd seen the choices he'd made for his bedroom furnishings. The only personal touches in the room were the framed pictures of old movie stars like Molly Ringwald and Farrah Fawcett sitting among the books. (I couldn't tell for sure, but they actually looked like they were autographed. Maybe the geezer doesn't spend all of his time in the lab!)

"DSL technology requires that your connection be located within a limited distance from the telephone company office, which is why the service is seldom available in rural areas. The distance from the phone company determines the type and speed of the DSL service available.

Digital Subscriber Line (DSL)

DSL is a technology that brings high-speed connections to homes and small businesses using standard phone lines. **DSL** allows you to make a phone call and connect the computer to the Web on the same phone line at the same time. **DSL** is also sometimes called **Digital Subscriber Loop.**

"All DSL technologies work on the same principal. DSL also allows for simultaneous Internet activity and voice communications across the same line. For our discussion today, we'll limit ourselves to **Asymmetric Digital Subscriber Line**, which is also sometimes called Asymmetric Digital Subscriber Loop, or **ADSL**.

"ADSL refers to the type of equipment you use to connect to the Internet, not to the lines themselves. As is the case with ISDN service, ADSL connection equipment are often referred to as modems even though they don't convert signals from analog to digital and vice versa. ADSL receives and transmits data in its native digital form.

"An ADSL 'modem' is required at both ends—one at the connection point and another at the phone company. ADSL is possible because analog voice transmissions over phone lines only use a portion of the available bandwidth.

"Similar to how ISDN operates, ADSL also divides the phone line into three channels. In this case, however, there is one channel for sending data, another for receiving data and another for voice. ADSL can receive data at speeds ranging from 1.5 Mbps to more than 8 Mbps and transmit at 640 Kbps."

I thought I heard Dr. F. making scratching sounds like he was writing on a blueboard, which was usually a signal that he was contemplating what to do next.

I took that as my cue for a chance to relax. I rolled over onto my left side and rested my head on my arm.

Asymmetrical Digital Subscriber Line (ADSL)

This technology uses twisted copper wire pairs to support broadband transmission. **ADSL** does not transmit information as quickly as Symmetric DSL but can transmit farther distances. However, **ADSL** can receive information more quickly than Symmetric ADSL if you are using the Very-high-bit-rate DSL (VDSL) variety. **ADSL** is also sometimes called **Asymmetric Digital Subscriber Loop.**

Chapter 10

URLs 101

I didn't get to relax for long. Dr. F. soon had more questions for me. It's difficult to think on an empty stomach! I figured that meant I'd just have to try harder, then, so I resigned myself to the tasks ahead of me on this part of my JTCI.

"Bert, tell me about how a Web page is retrieved to a Web browser. We've already talked about it, so you should be able to do so."

Right, I thought, *that's assuming I can remember my mental notes*. "You mean how a Web page can be seen once someone types in the address?" I asked.

"Yes, please start from the point where the user types in the address and hits enter."

"Ok, well, let's see...."

This shouldn't be too difficult, I thought. *Just take it a step at a time.*

"You type in the address or click a link, and then the browser sends a request to a name server. The name server looks up the IP address that corresponds with the domain and tells the Web browser what that IP address is. The Web browser then sends a request to the server at that address for the page. If the page exists on that server like it should, the document is broken up into packets, which go through a bunch of routers until they show up in the Web browser that asked for them."

"Very good, Beta, but what if that Web page has pictures in it?"

"Uh," I felt sure this was a trick question. "They come with the page, too."

"Please be more specific, B. We're trying to learn something here."

"What if we just want lunch?" I wanted to ask, but I bit my tongue. Instead I said, "They get broken up into packets, too."

"Yes, they do, but are the pictures part of the document?" Dr. F. pushed.

"Well, yes, aren't they?"

"No, B, they aren't. Pictures and Web page documents are different files. The Web page has special tags in the HTML that tell the browser what picture to display there. You may have noticed when you wait for a Web page to display that you see all the text first and sometimes see little placeholder icons for the pictures. That's because the Web browser has the document but hasn't received the pictures yet."

That was interesting, but so what? I decided to ask, "So what?"

"So what?" Dr. F. was getting upset again. I guess I sounded more flippant than I'd intended. "So that is very important. It means that the Web browser has to request the pictures, too. It means that each picture in the page makes the total time it will take to get all the information longer, because it needs more information to know what to show."

Oh. I guess that did make a difference. "Is that why my Web comics sometimes take a long time to download?"

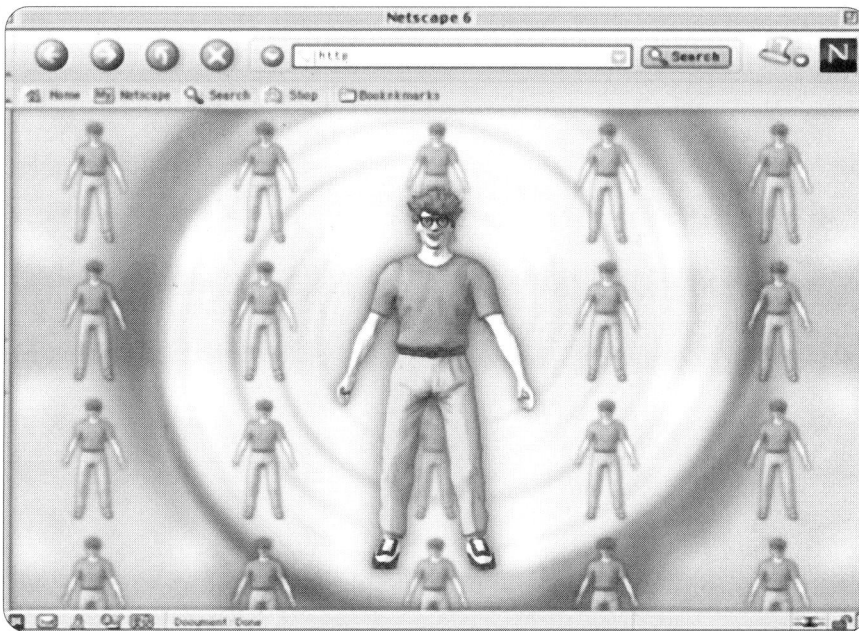

"Yes, B," Dr. F. confirmed. "Web comics tend to have a lot of graphics and pictures on them, so they'll have a higher total size, making it a longer wait for all that information to get to your computer." He paused. "Unless you have a really fast connection like I do. Then you don't notice it."

I wondered if he was trying to make me jealous on purpose. I decided to believe that he was probably just trying to make another point. After all, Dr. F. tends to deal more in facts than feelings.

Dr. F. moved on. "The same thing applies to any sound files or movies or other extras included on a Web page, like Flash animations or games. We'll talk more about these kinds of files a little bit later."

I almost sighed at this point. That meant that this wasn't going to be the last thing we talked about before I got my food. That flash thing had made me think of a really cool Japanese restaurant I ate at once, where the chef prepared the food at our table and had set some oil on fire on the stove before cooking, but I decided I better keep listening to keep Dr. F. from getting off-topic or angry. He was still talking.

"For now," he said, "all you need to remember about file types is that anything that ends with .htm or .html is a normal Web page. There are a few other file extensions that indicate Web pages like .php and .asp, but this will do for now.

"Now, we already talked about the makeup of an E-mail address. Would you like to try your hand at explaining the different parts of a Web page URL, Bert?"

Actually, I really didn't want to, because I was sure I would miss something. "No thanks," I said politely.

"Discretion is the better part of valor, eh, Beta?" I got the feeling he was laughing at me privately. "I'll explain it to you then," he said. "Let's use the example *http://www.Webosaurus.net/index.html*, then. The first part of this address is the 'http' part. What do you suppose that means?"

HyperText Transfer Protocol (HTTP)

HyperText Transfer Protocol is a set of standards or protocols. As parties exchange information on the World Wide Web, HTTP ensures the information arrives to the receiver in the same condition it left the sender.

I didn't know. That's why I didn't want to explain it. I shrugged, assuming he could see me even though I couldn't see him.

Whether he saw me or not, he answered his own question. "HTTP stands for **HyperText Transfer Protocol**. We talked a little bit about what protocols are when I explained TCP/IP. The HTTP explains that the address is going to use this particular protocol to view the document the browser is requesting. Other protocols that can be used are HTTPS (which is a more secure version of HTTP) or ftp. Most browsers use HTTP by default if you don't type that part in.

"The protocol that is used determines what responses servers will take when commands are given. It also defines the format that that information takes when it travels.

"Now, the 'colon, slash, slash' part is mostly to separate the protocol from the domain. So let's talk about the domain now. B, do you know how much of this address is the domain?"

http://www.webosaurus.net

Well, he'd said it was next, and I knew that 'www' wasn't the domain. So I took a stab at it. "Everything through 'Webosaurus' I think."

"Well, you need to think again."

That comment made me feel a little defensive. I felt he could at least be nice about how he told me I was wrong.

Dr. F. evidently didn't have time to stop and consider my feelings. "The whole domain in our example is www.Webosaurus.net. You can see that it's easily split into three parts, separated by periods, which are pronounced 'dot.' These different parts get more specific about the location they specify the further left they are. We're going to look at it backwards, because it's easier to understand that way.

"Every domain has an extension like .net or .com. I'll talk about those different types later, too. For now, it'll help your understanding to know that those are called extensions and they designate what's called a **Top Level Domain**, or **TLD**. A TLD is the broadest category domains can have. Everything else is kind of a subdivision of a TLD. Like I said, I'm going to explain more about that later, so I'll move on.

"'Webosaurus' is what most people think of when they think of domains. Well, not 'Webosaurus' specifically, but the part of the domain that goes where 'Webosaurus' is in our example. This is the part that usually defines specific Web sites. If you go to register a private domain, like we talked about briefly before, you actually register something.com or whatever.net. You don't ever register a Top Level Domain.

"The www part is the most interesting to me. Did you know that for most sites you don't actually have to type 'www' in the address line when you want to retrieve a Web site?"

I did. One of my Web comics actually didn't ever display the 'www' when it was advertised. So I nodded.

"The 'www' is what's called a sub-domain. When you type in the address *www.Webosaurus.net*, the browser actually asks the name server about the Webosaurus.net part. The name server, if it has never heard of Webosaurus.net, then finds the listed name server for that domain—when you register a domain, you have to say what the name servers for that domain will be—and asks it about the sub-domain. Each sub-domain will have a different IP address.

"The administrator of a domain can determine what sub-domains will exist for that domain. Sub-domains

> ## Top Level Domain (TLD)
>
> Within a URL, the **Top Level Domain** is the most important or largest category in the Internet naming system. We designate **TLD**s with .com, .org, .net, etc.

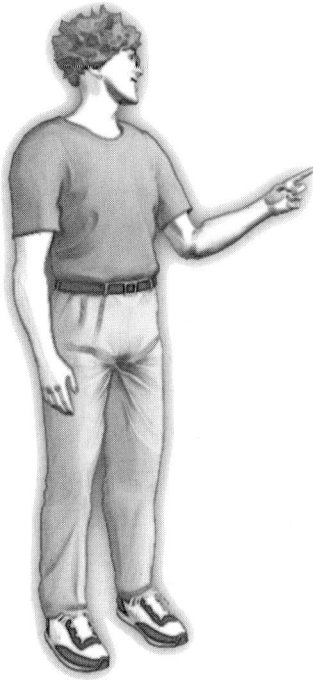

can go many layers deep. For example, in addition to www.Webosaurus.net, the administrator can specify sub-domains like ftp.Webosaurus.net, friendly.Webosaurus.net, scary.Webosaurus.net, or very.scary.but.friendly.Webosaurus.net. If the administrator had set things up correctly, each of these would look for a specific location designated by an IP address.

"After the Top Level Domain, you'll see a slash. That slash separates the domain, which is used to find the actual computer where the Web site is located, and the specific file and path for the document requested. In our example, the document is *index.html*. Usually, you don't have to type in anything that's called index.whatever. The index file is the file that the server automatically displays when that folder is opened in a Web browser. The administrator running the server chooses what the file is, and can choose to have many of them listed, giving preferential order if there are several files that meet the description on this list. Usually, the list has .html or .htm files called index or default.

"Like I said, you can have a 'path' in this part of a URL. Path is the word used to describe the location of a file on the computer hosting the Web page, and it gets more specific as you read from left to right. In other words, if you were looking at the page with the URL http://www.Webosaurus.net/books/jtci/index.html, then once the computer found the right server by IP address, it would look for the folder called 'books.' Then it would look for the folder 'jtci' inside the 'books' folder. Finally, inside the 'jtci' folder, it would look for the document called 'index.html.' If you just typed in *http://www.Webosaurus.net/books/jtci*, then once the computer was found it would look for the 'jtci' folder inside the 'books' folder. Once it found the 'jtci' folder, it would display the document that the administrator determined should be the one automatically displayed. If there is no document with a name on the list, then usually you'll see a list of all the files inside that file."

I chewed on that for a minute while Dr. F. caught his breath. It was a lot of information to assimilate. I didn't know that domains had sub-domains with different IP addresses. That was pretty neat that you could spell out phrases with sub-domains, but I suspected it wasn't done very often.

I did already know about the path of documents. You can organize documents on a Web server exactly the same way that you do on your home computer and still find them.

I was going to mention that, hoping that it would impress Dr. F., but he obviously wasn't done with his explanation, because he started talking again. "Let's go into a little bit more detail about how URLs help retrieve a Web page," he said. "The first thing that happens after the browser knows what IP address to look at is your computer uses TCP/IP to connect to the server computer's TCP/IP. That TCP/IP, if you remember, is what makes and maintains connections. This connection is made to the HTTP server on the same host computer, and the information is sent using this method.

"The information that actually arrives is the HTML document. We're going to talk more about HTML later, but the Web browser takes the information that the HTML gives it and constructs the page from that.

"This would be a good time for a little review."

I didn't know if I liked the sound of that. Sure enough, my paranoia was justified because I felt a squish and I was on the move again. Before I knew what was happening, I found myself in a browser.

"You'll recall that the browser on your computer is the client-side of any Web application," Dr. F. said as I felt myself move away from the browser. "The client uses TCP/IP to issue an HTTP request for a Web page. This time we'll request *http://www.blueroses.com/fall2000/stygs.html*, which is the URL for a document within embedded folders rather than the default index page we'd discussed earlier. That request is broken into packets..."

Here we go again, I thought as I felt another series of squishes that sent me out—literally scattered across the Internet in the form of packets.

"Those packets—or you, in this case—will eventually reach the host computer where the server software resides. The server software retrieves the information it needs to determine the request from those packets. Once it's done that, it sends the specified Web page back to the client."

I wonder if 'myselves' is the proper term, considering I was in packets and therefore plural? I'm not sure, so suffice it to say that I felt myself making a bunch of individual U-turns and I was soon back at the browser.

"Once the Web page appears in your browser, the HTTP connection between the client computer and server is broken. This is because the Web page is now displayed on the client so the server's job is done; however, your ISP still continues to maintain your TCP/IP connection to the Internet in case you need to retrieve any more information, either in the form of more information from the requested document server or from another location, such as when you click on a link for another Web site."

Apparently blue roses aren't just found in Dr. Franklin's gardens. They surrounded me on the Web page that was now displayed in the browser. I wondered if I'd get the chance to hang around long enough to stop and smell the roses—or to read the page.

Chapter 11

Understanding the Types of Domains

I didn't get to spend too much time smelling the roses. As usual, Dr. F. had other plans.

"Let's talk a little bit more about domains, shall we Beta?"

Gee, that's exactly what I felt like doing, I thought to myself sarcastically as my stomach growled. Dr. F. obviously made a lot of assumptions about the length of my attention span.

"When I say domains, we're mostly going to be talking about domains that identify a unique IP address. We'll talk a little bit about Top Level Domains too, but mostly the level right below them.

"What would you say is the reason for a domain, B?"

I really need to stop getting surprised by his questions, I thought. He asks them so often, you'd think I'd be used to them by now. "Well, they provide something that's easier to remember than an IP Address. I guess they have to be as unique as an IP address, too, or they wouldn't resolve correctly."

"Clarify what you mean by 'resolve,'" Dr. F said.

"Well, that's when the name server figures out what IP address belongs to a domain, because the server computers actually use IP addresses to find sites rather than the words and letters we use."

"So you would say that domains are used as a unique identifier for a site on the Internet that is easier for people to remember and distinguish than the numbers computers use for the same purpose?"

"Uh... yes?" I always worried that he was trying to trip me up when he gave me answers in the form of questions like that.

"Very good, B. You're learning."

I guess so, I thought. After all, it was really his own summary that he was praising.

"Now I need you to explain to me how domains are made up. How are they formed?"

http://64.210.13.248

DNS

Why do you need me to give you that? We just talked about it, I wanted to say. Instead, I just explained it. "The far right part, the part that usually ends with .com, .net, or .org is the Top Level Domain. The middle part is the domain that distinguishes the unique domain. To the left of that is a list of sub-domains. Usually the only one you see is 'www.' Each sub-domain will have an IP address."

"That's a good rudimentary explanation, B. Let's go a little bit more into it. The different parts of a domain are separated by periods that are pronounced 'dots' when you say them out loud. This is very much like an IP address. The IP address for *webosaurus.net* is 64.210.13.248. The different parts of the IP address are also separated by dots.

"The more important thing that you left out, however, is that each Top Level Domain is what determines the **registry** to which the domain belongs. Each extension has a registry associated with it."

"Is a registry where you register a domain?" Dr. F. had been talking so much about *webosaurus.net*, probably

Registry

A registry is a listing of the domains included in each Top-Level Domain.

having read my mind when I called that Internet monster-skeleton a Webosaurus (don't laugh, I'm sure he's got some gadget that can read minds!). Anyway, I'd heard him talk about it so much that I was thinking that *webosaurus.net* would be a fun domain for me to register.

"No, that's a registrar. A registry is a listing of the domains that are in each Top Level Domain. A registrar is a company that allows you to register your own domain and have it entered on the TLD registry. At first the only registrar for U.S. domains was InterNIC. If you wanted to own a domain, you had to use Network Solutions, Inc. to register it. But because this is a capitalist society, there soon arose the **Internet Corporation of Assigned Names and Numbers**, or **ICANN**.

"ICANN was created in 1998 by the late Joe Postel. This creation was in response to a policy statement issued by the United States Department of Commerce that called for the formation of a private sector, not-for-profit Internet organization to administer policy for the Internet name and address system. The initial function of ICANN was to oversee the domain-name registration system's transition from the government to private enterprise, which also involved coordinating its decentralization and integration into a global community. ICANN's five original participants were America Online Inc., The Internet Council of Registrars, France Telecom/Oleane, Melbourne IT (an Australian e-commerce company), and register.com. ICANN's goal is to establish the means to remove any limit to the number of companies that can register domains.

"They've done a pretty good job, too. There are now many companies all over the world that you can use to register a new domain name. You can find a current list of these registrars at http://www.internic.org."

"So what choices do I have if I want to get a new domain? And what, if anything, do all these endings mean? Which ones can I get and which one should I get?"

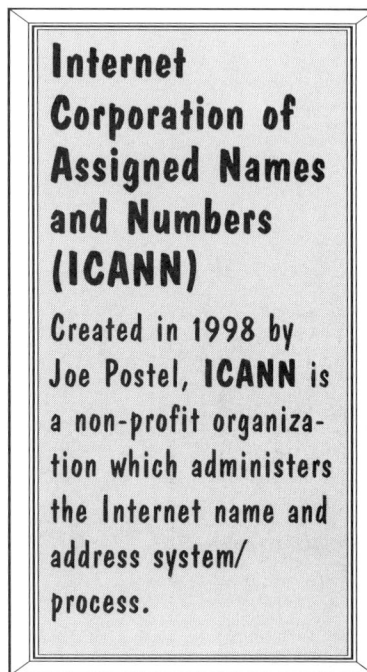

> **Internet Corporation of Assigned Names and Numbers (ICANN)**
> Created in 1998 by Joe Postel, **ICANN** is a non-profit organization which administers the Internet name and address system/process.

"There are a lot of Top Level Domains. Although you usually only see domains that end with .com, .net, and .org, you should know that every country has a Top Level Domain associated with it. These Top Level Domains are two letter combinations and include such things as .ca for Canada and .uk for the United Kingdom.

"In the U.S. there are several Top Level Domains from which you can choose. Each of them was instituted for a specific purpose, but some of those criteria have become blurred.

"The most common Top Level Domain is .com. This extension was originally intended for commercial Internet sites, but many private individuals have bought domains with this extension. Syngress.com is an example of a corporate domain, while rice-hahn.com is a private domain in the .com registry.

"Another extension is .net. This extension is supposed to be for administrative sites, but it is also commonly used for personal domains when the .com version is not available, such as is the case with webosaurus.net or thelemur.net."

I wonder if that means webosaurus.net is already taken, I thought. I made myself another one of my mental sticky notes to remember to check on that the first chance I got.

"The TLD .org was originally for non-profit organizations, but, again, because there was no restriction on

who could use it, it has become widely used by other groups or persons as well.

"The only exceptions to the adherence to the original standards are the two U.S. TLDs .gov and .mil, which are only used by the government. The former is used for general government sites, while .mil is strictly for use by the United States military.

"Educational institutions also have a restricted TLD for their own use. If you see a domain that has the .edu extension, you can bet that a college or other school runs the URL.

"Those domains are all fairly well established. But there is another crop of new extensions being released in the United States. One of these, .info, is fairly unrestricted. It's supposed to be for informational sites, but I believe it may be used for other reasons as well, such as commerce and such.

"Most of the new extensions are restricted for certain purposes. For example, those who apply for .biz domains will have to provide proof that they will use the site for legitimate commercial use. The same goes for .coop, which is reserved for use by business cooperatives, like credit unions. In this case, members of the National Cooperative Business Associations or an affiliated group can only apply for these registrations. Another extension, .museum, will be restricted for use by museums.

"Likewise, .aero is reserved for use by members of the air transportation industry, which includes airlines, airports, and the like. The .aero TLD is run by the Societe Internationale de Telecommunications Aeronautiques

SC. This organization plans to make all the third level domains the same from airport to airport. So *departures.jfk.aero* will show departures from JFK International Airport, while *departures.slc.aero* will show departures from the Salt Lake City International Airport.

"Speaking of third level domains (the part before the main domain, the third component when counting from right to left), two of the new Top Level Domains will only allow the registration of third level domains. One of these, .name, is for personal use. For example, John Doe could register john.doe.name for his own personal use. Of course, with a common name like that he'd have to act fast.

"The other TLD that only allows third level domain registration is .pro, and this extension will be restricted to professionals, such as lawyers or accountants or doctors. You have to provide professional credentials to register a .pro domain."

I thought for a moment. "So, basically, I can only register .com, .net, .org, .info, or .name domains unless I have some sort of proof that I'm the right kind of person or belong to the right organization?"

"That's right, B. It's all part of keeping the information on the Internet easier to figure out. It will be interesting to see if this sort of restriction will actually work. It's so common to see .com on every domain. It's so easily recognized that it has some sort of brand name recognition. It's almost a status symbol to own a dot-com domain. I theorize that many companies will still prefer to have a .com domain rather than .biz or something else. I suppose only time will tell, however."

"Oh," I said simply. I didn't know what else to say to that.

"Now, Bert," Dr. F. resumed. "We've already talked about the role that domain name servers have when figuring out domain names and how to find them. We also talked a little bit about sub-domains. Tell me about those sub-domains."

"Well," I said, "a sub-domain can be anything that the administrator wants. The most common sub-domain is 'www' and usually leaving out the www when typing a URL will take you to the www sub-domain anyway."

"Yes, but did you know they're hierarchical?"

"Hire-whatal?"

"Hierarchical. One of the examples I used before was very.scary.but.friendly.webosaurus.net. But, very.scary.but.friendly isn't one domain. 'Friendly' is the third level. Which makes 'but' a sub-domain of friendly, and 'scary' a sub-domain of 'but.' And so on down the chain. I told you before that as you move to the left from the Top Level Domain you get more specific, and that holds true for sub-domains. Each domain is subordinate to the domain immediately to its right. Just

http://www.webosaurus.net

DNS

like everything else on the Internet, it's all very organized and clear once you know the system."

I was learning that the "once you know" part was becoming an important part of the equation. I wondered if I'd ever learn it all.

"There's a lot more involved behind the scenes of the Internet than I ever imagined," I said. I was finding this behind-the-scenes attention to detail impressive. I hoped Dr. F. was likewise impressed that I was taking a genuine interest in the subject.

Chapter 12

Browser Basics

"Well, Bert, now that we've discussed in some detail how Web pages get to your computer, it's time to talk about what is used to look at Web pages. What do you use?"

"I prefer Internet Explorer, but my mom prefers Netscape. And my sister uses Opera," I answered.

"I was thinking something more generic," Dr. F told me. "What are all those programs called as a group?"

"Oh!" I finally understood the question. "They're **Web browsers**."

"Yes, Bert, they are a type of client software called Web browsers. Web browsers are what are used to view Web pages. Most of them will also support a File Transfer Protocol, or FTP connection if you type in the address for one.

"You'll notice that when you type in an ftp address that the part before the ://,"—he said it as "colon, slash, slash," by the way—"is not 'http' but 'ftp.' This is because a different protocol is used to transfer the information from the host to your computer. I already told you all about this information. I only bring it back up because the way the information is transferred determines how the information is displayed.

"When you connect to an ftp site, you'll often see a list of files you can transfer to your own computer or from your computer to the ftp site. These will be displayed as a simple vertical list of filenames, with no other special formatting, except for size and date or other information about the files.

> **Web browser**
>
> A web browser is a program that allows you to examine files on the Internet and/or World Wide Web, such as its pages, images, videos. **Web browsers** allow you to bookmark a site, so you can find more easily next time you want to visit it. Web browsers are often called simply **browsers**.

"When the page is delivered using http, the browser will take the file that is sent to it and interpret it using the tags that make up the page. The browser will take these tags, figure out what they are telling it to do, and will build the appearance of the page according to those meanings. It will also respond to various commands given it using scripting languages and will call on other programs to send other information, according to what programs are set as plug-ins. I'm going to talk about plug-ins and the tag languages, usually HTML, in more detail later.

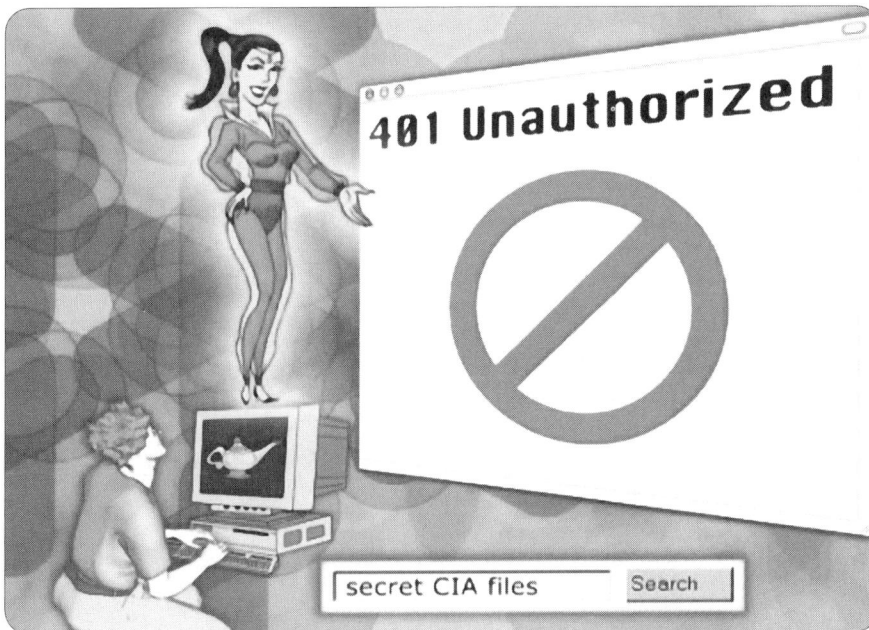

"So you see, the browser is intelligent enough to know what it should do not only with different information, but what it should do depending on how that information comes to it."

"What happens when it gets the wrong information?" I asked.

Dr. F paused. "It depends on what you mean by 'wrong information,'" he finally said. "There are quite a number of **error** messages that a browser will return if it can't display the information that you asked for.

"These errors are usually returned from the server contacted—unless, of course, the problem is that you can't contact the server. If you can't get to the server, you will either get a request from your browser to make sure you spelled things correctly, or if you use a proxy server you may get an error like 'Failed DNS Lookup.' This error means that the browser couldn't get the DNS server to say what IP Address goes with the domain name. This usually means that you typed it in wrong.

"The most common error you'll get on the Internet is when the domain has been found, the browser has connected to the server, but the server can't find the document or folder you asked for. When this happens, the server will tell your browser to display a '**404 error: file not found**' error message.

"Another common error message is '**401: Unauthorized**.' This means that the server you contacted is trying to find a special encryption key on your computer, but it can't locate it. A similar error is '**403: Forbidden Access**.' Usually this means you entered the wrong password.

"Sometimes, your computer may just have a really difficult time sending or receiving information. Often no error message will pop up when this happens; instead, your mouse cursor will just look like an hourglass, turning over and over again.

"Does that answer your question?"

Dr. F. didn't wait for an answer. (This no longer surprised me.)

"Now, let's talk some more about this HTML stuff that forms Web pages, shall we? I find it very interesting. Do you remember what HTML stands for Bert?"

"Isn't it **HyperText Markup Language**?"

"Yes, it is. Very good, my lad."

"But, what does that mean?" I asked. It was a lot of words that didn't necessarily make sense. Was the text hyperactive?

"Good question. Let's explore it." I heard some scratching that made me think Dr. F. was writing on one of his blueboards again. I was reaching the conclusion that the guy had to organize his thoughts in writing perhaps before he could verbalize them. He soon continued the explanations.

"I'll bet you think that 'hyper' means the text has too much energy, but that would be silly, wouldn't it?"

Yeah, I guess it would be. I remained silent, blushing a little bit.

Errors

There are a variety of errors you may encounter while online. Some of the more common ones include the following:

◎ **401 error**
A **401** error indicates this Web site/page has not authorized your entry.

◎ **403 error**
Similar to a **401** error, a **403** error message means the Web site/page has forbidden you access.

◎ **404 error**
A **404** error indicates that the Web site/page you want cannot be located. If this happens, either the spelling of the Web site/page is incorrect or the Web site/page has disappeared.

HyperText Markup Language (HTML)

HTML is a programming language used to design a Web site. This language helps a programmer/designer mark the site and hyperlinks in it.

"Actually, Beta, *hyper* is an old Greek prefix that means 'beyond or above.' It means that in HTML, the text is beyond normal text. It's better than normal text, because it can do more.

"The markup part is because it uses tags to surround text that needs to be modified. In other words, the tags mark up the text. The hyper text is actually what is modified, or rather, normal text is made hyper text by the markup done by the language. Does that make sense, B?"

It took me a second, but I got it. "So you're saying that the language we call HTML marks up text to make it better than normal text. But better how?"

"Another good question! Text modified this way is more functional; you can do more with it. You can also make it look different and organize it in different ways. You can insert pictures, sounds, movies, or games into the text."

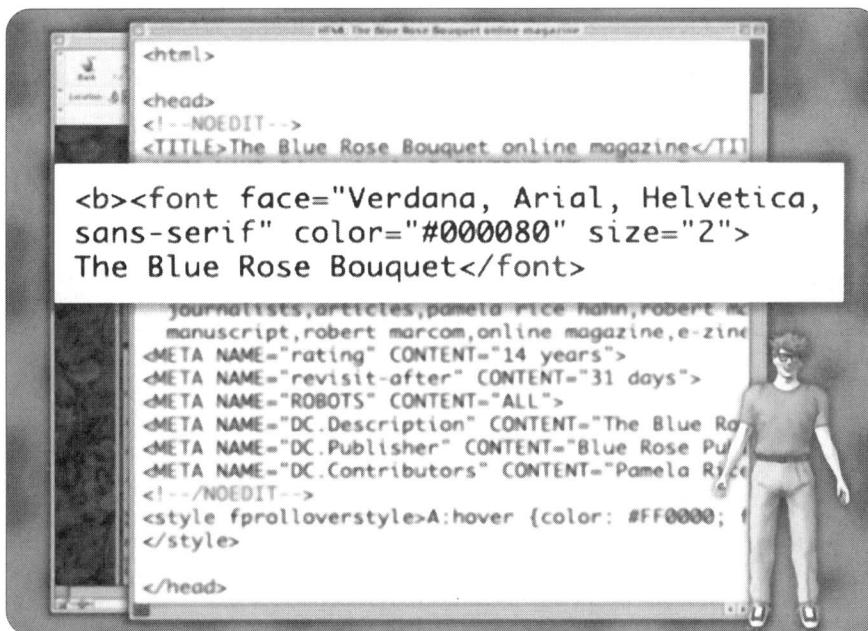

```
<html>

<head>
<!--NOEDIT-->
<TITLE>The Blue Rose Bouquet online magazine</TI
```

```
<b><font face="Verdana, Arial, Helvetica,
sans-serif" color="#000080" size="2">
The Blue Rose Bouquet</font>
```

```
journalists,articles,pamela rice hahn,robert m
   manuscript,robert marcom,online magazine,e-zine
<META NAME="rating" CONTENT="14 years">
<META NAME="revisit-after" CONTENT="31 days">
<META NAME="ROBOTS" CONTENT="ALL">
<META NAME="DC.Description" CONTENT="The Blue Ro
<META NAME="DC.Publisher" CONTENT="Blue Rose Pu
<META NAME="DC.Contributors" CONTENT="Pamela R
<!--/NOEDIT-->
<style fprolloverstyle>A:hover {color: #FF0000;
</style>

</head>
```

Dr. F. sounded very excited, so I pressed my luck and asked another question. "So what do these tags look like?"

"Tags are just words describing the function you want applied to the text surrounded by pointy, or angle, brackets. Let me show you an example."

Suddenly some characters appeared before me. They looked like this:

<FONT FACE="garamond" SIZE="+1" COLOR="blue">Hi, Beta!</FONT>

Below that, the words "Hi, Beta!" appeared in large blue letters.

Dr. F. spoke up. "The words below are what you get when you put in the information on the top row. Let's look at this tag. First, there are two parts to each tag, the element and the attributes."

"Will this be on the test?" I asked jokingly.

"Yes, B," he answered quite seriously. I got nervous suddenly and started making mental notes again. "The element is the main part of the tag. It says what aspect of the text you are going to be altering. In this case, we're going to play with the font of the text. The attributes are the specific changes to make. In this case we're changing face, size, and color. The face will be Garamond font, the size will be one size larger than normal text, and the color will be blue. You should also note that the tag surrounds the text it modifies. The tag is closed by putting a slash before the name of the element inside the brackets.

"Not all tags take attributes, however. For example, if you wanted to make a paragraph, the tags would look like this."

More characters appeared; they looked like this: <P></P>.

"Anything that was part of the paragraph would be in between the opening and closing tags. Tags can be used to make tabular data, insert images, or even create **hyperlinks**." Dr. F. said that last part in a very mysterious tone of voice.

"Hyperlinks," I whispered, feeling that they were something sacred because of the way Dr. F. spoke about them.

> **Hyperlink**
> This is a clickable icon, graphic, or word in a Web site/page/ document which takes you to another Web site/page/document. If the **hyperlink** is a word, you will see it underlined.

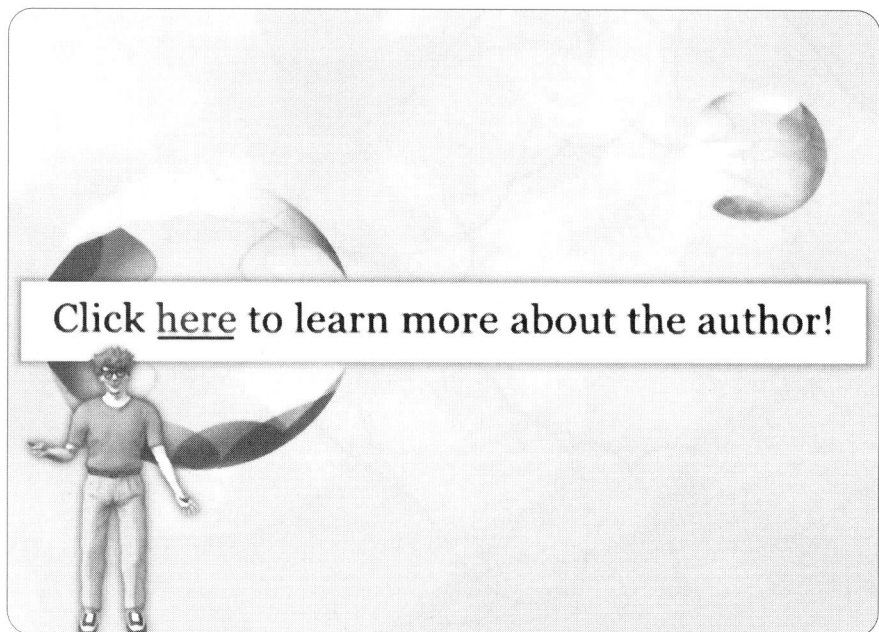

Click <u>here</u> to learn more about the author!

Hypertext Reference (HREF)

In this line of Web design code, you insert the hypertext address of the HTML document. So, after the equals sign in HREF=, you add the address you want it to take the user to.

"Hyperlinks are a magnificent development that allow interactivity and expansion on the Internet. A hyperlink is a word, phrase, or area of a Web page that the viewer can click to go to another location. Usually, the location that the viewer is taken to is relevant to the picture or word that forms the link. The link is programmed using specific HTML code and is done by the person who makes the page. The hyperlinks—links for short—are marked in a way that helps the viewer see that the link is there. Generally, making the text a different color and underlining it does this. By default, hyperlinks appear as underlined blue text, but this color and decorating scheme can be altered.

"Hyperlinks are what truly make HTML hyper text. It allows a word to have more functionality and interactivity. They are made using the anchor element with a **Hyperlink Reference** attribute. The anchor element (which is just <A> when actually written as a tag) is to specify that the text is special and will be a trigger to make something happen. The anchor tags go on either side of the text or image that will be the link. Hypertext Reference is written as 'HREF' when it appears in a tag, and it indicates the place the link will go. The link can be a completely different Web page or site, or it can be another anchor in the same document.

"When a hyperlink it clicked, it tells the browser to find the location specified in the HREF attribute and display that page. That works the same way as typing in a URL.

"There are a number of concerns about how hyperlinks should appear and how they should point at information. When you create links on a Web page, you should pay attention to how the link looks, where it actually takes the user, and that sort of thing. I'm not going to tell you how to arrange a Web page. There are many excellent sources for learning how to design Web pages that people will want to see and that function well. In fact, sometimes it helps to first view how NOT to create a page. Viewing other Web page designer's mistakes can help you learn how to recognize what to avoid on your own site. One place to start to learn how to recognize bad Web page code and design would be at WebPagesThatSuck.com.

"There are also many Web page design tutorials online, as well as books on the subject from Syngress.com. If you're serious about designing your own Web pages, there's enough information available to help you learn how to do so on your own. Of course, those who like more structure can also take classes. Some people are more comfortable learning in that type of environment, but something tells me that you're a more independent-type spirit, Bert."

How did the guy guess I was already coming up with which phrases I'd try when I did a Web search looking for HTML tutorials? I thought. I made a mental note to remember those phrases. I had a feeling that I was going to be building Web pages a lot after this journey.

Dr. F. continued, "Now that you know how hypertext works, and what a browser does, you should learn how the two most popular browsers function.

"The two most frequently used browsers are Netscape Navigator and Microsoft Internet Explorer. There are a few other browsers, some of which are text-only, meaning that they won't show images, but most everyone uses one of these two, and nearly all Web pages are designed to work best in one or the other. There's a lot of arguing among geeks about which browser is

Favorites and Bookmarks

This function, known as **Favorites** in Internet Explorer and **Bookmarks** in Netscape Navigator, allows you to mark a Web site or page to find more easily the next time you want to visit it.

better. Some people claim that Netscape doesn't show pages correctly, and others say that Internet Explorer is unstable, or some other complaint about one or the other. But when it really comes down to it, which browser you use is mostly personal preference. Which interface you like and which looks better on your computer. Both browsers have essentially the same functionality, but they use these functions in different ways.

"Internet Explorer has the customizable options in the Tools menu, which means that you use the mouse to click on the word 'Tools' at the top of the window in order to get a choice to change the program options. With these options you can tell the browser not to display pictures, to block sites, change the page that opens when you start the computer, and many other options, some of which are for security, some for appearance. This is where you'd go if you want to choose between the option of only printing the text and pictures on a Web site or choosing to include the background colors in the printout, too, for example.

"Internet Explorer has a '**Favorites**' menu as well. There are several pre-defined favorites, which are just hyperlinks that are part of the browser rather than part of a Web page. This means the hyperlinks will always be available. You can add or delete hyperlinks from the list and even rearrange their order. This makes it easier to remember a Web site you like without having to write down the URL.

"Netscape looks different than Internet Explorer. For one thing, some of the buttons look different. The tool bars are all in different places as well. Netscape also has a '**Bookmarks**' list. Bookmarks are essentially the same things as Favorites in Internet Explorer but with a different name.

"Netscape places the customizable options in a different location as well. In Netscape, these options are called 'preferences' and are located in the Edit menu.

The specific options are different too, though many of them do the same things.

"There are many things that work the same in all browsers. For example, they all have somewhere to type in an URL (although Netscape calls this area 'location' and Internet Explorer calls it 'address'), they all have a 'back' and a 'forward' button that will take you to the last page you viewed and the next page you visited (if you are not on the most recent page visited already), and they have a 'history' area that lists the titles and links to all the pages that have been viewed recently.

"Both browsers also have a **cache** (Internet Explorer calls it '**temporary Internet files**'). The cache is a folder on your computer where files that were viewed recently are stored. These files are sometimes used instead of the ones on the server where the site belongs so pages will load faster when you go back to visit pages soon after visiting them the first time. If you find out that a page has changed, but that your browser is still showing the old page, it's probably drawing the file out of your cache. You can get the updated page by requesting the new code for the page. Netscape calls this option 'reload,' while Internet Explorer calls it 'refresh'."

"That's interesting," I said, trying to mask the impatience in my voice. I already knew how to use a Web browser, but I guess nothing was going to keep Dr. F. from going into every detail about my JTCI. I did have to admit, though, that I *was* learning about details I'd overlooked before. I vowed to do my best to pay attention.

> **Cache**
> Pronounced "cash", a cache is a folder on your computer where files that were viewed recently are stored. Internet Explorer's name for the **cache** is **temporary Internet files**.

Chapter 13

Talking the Talk and Walking the Walk

It soon became obvious why I needed that focused attention span. Dr. F. was about to begin another lecture.

"Now Beta, it's time to talk about something I've mentioned many, many times. It's time to talk about protocols."

"You mean the C-3PO thing?" I remembered Dr. F. had liked that analogy.

"Yes, B, as you put it so elegantly, it's time to talk about the 'C-3PO thing.' How about we start with a quiz? Give me a better definition for Internet protocols than your *Star Wars* character."

I felt up to the challenge. "Well, a protocol is a set of procedures and formats for transmitting information or sending files over the Internet. Both the client and the server have to be using the same protocol or else they won't be able to send the information, because they won't understand each other."

"Very good, B," Dr. F. said.

This was getting eerie; Dr. F. was doing a lot more praising now than he had been earlier.

"What is the protocol used to transfer Web pages?" he asked next.

"Hyper Text Transfer Protocol, or HTTP."

"Yes, and HTTP is a stateless protocol. What do I mean when I say '**stateless protocol**'?"

"Uh…" I stuttered. I didn't know this one. I wasn't even sure if he'd ever mentioned it before. I couldn't remember.

"I knew I'd catch you with that one." I could almost hear Dr. F's smirk. "A stateless protocol is one that

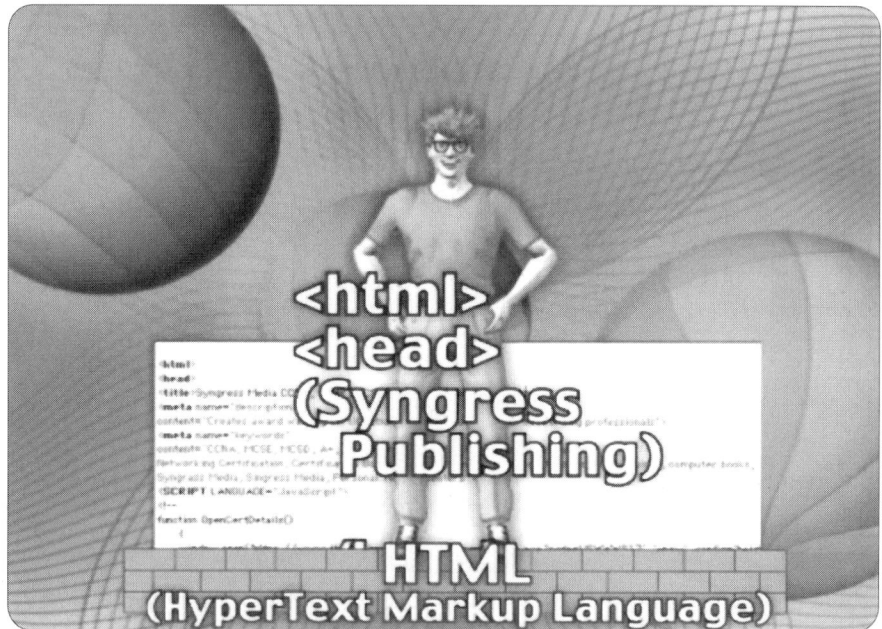

Stateless protocol

This type of protocol does not keep track of nor depends on commands already given in order to know what to do next. In other words, it can operate independently.

Secure HyperText Transfer Protocol (HTTPS or Secure-HTTP)

This is a more secure version of HTTP and only allows one message at a time to transmit. **HTTPS** remains secure because it accesses a secure Web server.

Secure Socket Layer (SSL)

Unlike HTTP, this Internet security protocol can interact with all Internet tools and not just the World Wide Web. In **SSL**, the browser sends a public key to the server, and the server sends back a secret key.

doesn't depend on the commands that have already been given to figure out what to do. It takes each command it's given independently and executes them without referring to anything else. In HTTP, most of these commands are requests to see Web pages.

"Remember how Web pages get to your computer, Beta?"

"Yes, once the browser has the IP address from the name server, it asks the server to see the specific page. If the page is there and the viewer has permission, the server sends back the page information, and the browser will build the page."

"Yes, B. Now, what do you suppose the protocol **HTTPS** is?" Dr. F. was trying to trip me up again, but I remembered seeing that once when I was surfing the Internet. It was while I was looking at my meager savings account. (I probably remembered that because I almost had enough to get that new optical mouse I wanted!)

"Doesn't it have something to do with security?"

"Yes, B, it does. HTTPS is how browsers abbreviate **Secure-HTTP** when then they're using it in an address. Secure-HTTP is just a more secure version of HTTP. It only allows one message at a time to go through, but it does that fairly well. Frequently, Secure-HTTP is used with **Secure Socket Layer**, or **SSL**. SSL is another protocol that allows any amount of data to transmit securely over a connection formed between the client and the server. Online merchants, banks, and similar groups use HTTPS and SSL to conduct business as a way to ensure they don't give away their customers' bank account or credit card information—or even their names, addresses, or phone numbers.

"Now, B, for the big one. I mentioned **File Transfer Protocol**, or **FTP**, several times. FTP is used to download files off a server on the Internet. But you already know that HTTP can do that, albeit with some restrictions. However, FTP establishes a connection between two computers that also allows you to send files to the server. FTP is typically how Web sites get onto the Internet. Usually Web pages are built on the designer's computer and then the designer will use an FTP client to upload the files to his server.

"FTP usually requires that a user give a username and password when he connects. This is to help make sure that someone only has access to files or folders that he has the right to manipulate. Once this logon is established, a command connection is made. The command connection is how the client sends orders to the server and how the server sends errors or other messages back to the client. If you then try to download or upload a file with FTP, the server will also create a data connection. The data connection automatically closes once the file has been transferred.

"Another thing that's interesting about FTP is that the client has a lot more control about what files and folders are viewable. It won't display a Web page like a browser does; it only shows that the Web page file exists. But it will list all the contents of a folder, showing all the files that are present in that folder. It will also allow you to move to different folders without the need for a hyperlink. On the other hand, FTP clients won't allow you change what domain you're connected to without disconnecting and reconnecting to a different site.

"There are a number of FTP sites that don't require you to log in with a specific user name or personality. These sites are called anonymous FTP sites—partially because the person using the site is

> ### File Transfer Protocol (FTP)
>
> A protocol (set of rules) for electronically transmitting information without losing any of it over the Internet and other networks. **FTP** establishes a connection between two computers that also allows you to send files to the server you are connected to.

File Transfer Protocol

anonymous to the server, and partially because when you log onto these sites, the username and password used is typically 'anonymous.' These sites are typically used to distribute or gather files from the public.

"Most people use FTP with a client specifically designed for FTP use. But like I've told you before, most Web browsers will allow you to use FTP sites without having to do anything special."

I heard the sound of more scratching noises, indicating that Dr. F. was writing on a blueboard—a sure sign he was about to move onto something else.

"Now, I want to talk about one more way you can connect to other servers and work with the files that are there. **Telnet** is a **terminal emulation** protocol. Bert, I mentioned this earlier. Can you tell me what terminal emulation is?"

I sputtered for a moment, but then remembered when earlier while I was wearing that stupid hat he'd told me about dumb terminals. "Terminal emulation is where you use your keyboard and monitor, but are actually giving commands to a computer somewhere else!"

"Yes, B, that is correct. Telnet is a way of connecting to another computer and giving it commands. Usually when you connect with Telnet, you only have command line access. There isn't a graphical user interface that lets you click on images to issue commands. In other words, you have to type in the commands in the form of words. There are HYTELNET applications, however, which allow people to use a client that support hypertext interfaces on a telnet host, but that's a little beyond the scope of our discussion right now.

"The host, incidentally, is the computer to which you connect. The host can be running any operating system, but frequently it uses some sort of Unix or Linux operating system. With Telnet you can operate the remote computer exactly like it was in front of you, but to get there, you generally have to log in, just like you do with FTP. Usually the username and password have to be set

Terminal Emulation and Telnet

This process emulates, or imitates, a terminal and its processes in order to access its system/network. A **Terminal Emulation** protocol such as **Telnet** allows you to log onto a remote computer and use the programs from that computer.

up by the system administrator, but sometimes Telnet hosts will allow anonymous connections.

"Telnet is often used to make information available or to allow the owners of a Web site to make changes directly to files or move them around without having to connect with FTP or download the files first. Telnet is a very useful tool for getting work done from a distance."

While Dr. F. took a breather to make some scratches on one of his blueboards, I gloated for a bit. I'd managed to make it through this series of lectures without yawning once.

Chapter 14

Facilitating File Facts

"Bert, how much have I told you about file types?" Dr. F. asked suddenly.

"Uhm, let's see... You told me about HTML files. I think you also mentioned that the HTML files are separate from the image files that are in the Web page."

"Well, then, it appears that I've been neglecting an essential part of your education. We need to talk about the different types of image files that you will see on the Internet."

I liked Dr. F's use of the word "we." Somehow, I doubted that my half of that "we" would be doing much of the talking.

"I won't bother telling you about every single one, just the types of files that you will generally be able to see in most browsers. These files are the most common because most Web browsers support them. That is, most Web browsers are capable of displaying them without using a plug-in or helper program.

"The first image type we'll talk about is the **JPG**."

He pronounced that acronym as "jay-peg."

"The JPG is a common type of file used primarily for photographs. This is because JPG files can display millions of different colors. Photographs frequently have many different colors, more than you usually think. JPGs have limitations, however. The more you compress a JPG, the more quality you lose. I'll tell you about compression in a minute, Bert. First I want to cover the different kinds of images.

> **Joint Photographic Experts Group (JPG)**
>
> A JPG (or JPEG) is a graphics standard defining how a computer can compress a photograph. JPGs files can contain millions of colors, and as such are commonly used for photographs.

Graphics Interchange Format (GIF)

We use this high-resolution graphics compression technique for bit-mapped graphics files. **GIFs have an upper limit of 256 colors, but can achieve smaller file sizes than JPGs without losing quality.**

File compression

File compression is a technique that reduces the size of a file without appreciable loss of the information or quality of image. Various compression techniques exist such JPG, GIF, BMP, etc.

"Another image type is a **GIF** file."

This one was pronounced pretty much the way it's spelled, with a hard "G", like in "good".

"GIF files have an upper limit of 256 colors. However, they can also achieve smaller file sizes than JPGs without losing quality, so long as the image stays under those 256 colors. Why would smaller file size be important to someone making a Web page, Bert?"

I kept getting caught off guard by all these questions in the middle of his lectures. "Uh... because most people still use connections with low bandwidth."

"That's right, B. In the world of Web design, smaller is better. Most people get impatient if they have to wait too long for a Web page to display on their screen. You want to get files onto their computer quickly so they won't stop loading the page and look elsewhere. So, to make things transfer faster, **file compression** is used.

"File compression is a way of taking all the information in a file and expressing it in a way that will take up less space. There are many different methods of file compression, but the basic idea is this: when you look at the information used to communicate the contents of a file, you'll notice that certain combinations of information are used several times. A special mathematical formula is used to identify the repetitions, and then a symbol is used to replace those repetitions. That way, the repeated information is only used once, and the symbols representing it are used instead. This takes less space to communicate.

"Both GIF and JPG files use file compression. A GIF file keeps an index of the colors used in the picture, then identifies which color is used in a row and how many pixels of that color appear in that row. So, rather than identify the color of each pixel in the picture, point-by-point, it maintains a file that identifies rows of color.

"A JPG file is much more complex in the way that it compresses files, but it can shrink files down to very small sizes. In fact, the person who makes the JPG can control how much it is compressed. The more compression, the lower the picture quality, but the faster it will download. A lot of Web design is balancing quality with speed."

"So JPGs give the creator more control and allow more colors. Why does anyone use GIFs?" I asked.

"Because, my dear Beta, there are things that GIFs can do that JPGs cannot. For example, GIFs can use a transparent color. This is often referred to as using a 'transparent background,' which is often how images can be used over other images—like a background design—so that only the picture itself is displayed; most often it's the 'white space' around that picture that's transparent.

"GIFs can also be used to make animations that don't take up a lot of file space. The animations are not nearly as detailed as movies, and there are better ways to make animations, but GIFs are a cheap and dirty way to do it, and they're small, so they don't take a long time to load.

"Your question, however, leads me into a discussion of **Portable Network Graphics** files, or **PNG** files."

PNG was pronounced "ping."

"PNG files are a relative newcomer to the field of Web image types. Most older browsers do not support them. However, they have quite a few advantages over other JPGs and GIFs. PNGs are typically smaller than either and have a lossless compression type. JPGs are lossy, which means they lose data when they're compressed. That's why they start looking bad as you apply more compression. PNGs also allow more colors than GIFs or JPGs, although allowing more colors usually makes the image bigger. PNGs even allow you to use transparent colors and to create animations.

"PNGs started becoming popular recently because of potential legal problems with GIF images. CompuServe owns the file format for GIFs, and they have hinted recently that they might start charging the makers of graphics editor software that uses GIFs. The online community didn't like the idea and a movement began to get people to start using PNGs, which do not have those copyright complications."

"So why don't people just use PNGs?"

"Well, they were never intended to replace JPGs, and they still don't always display properly, even in the latest browsers. But technology is advancing rapidly, and it will be interesting to see if PNGs really do replace GIFs in common usage someday."

Dr. F. paused for a bit. Then I heard the chalk going on the blueboard again.

"Beta," he said finally. "While we're on the subject, we may as well talk about different ways to present text on the Internet. That is, let's talk a little bit about file types that present text information.

"Besides a normal HTML document, there are many other ways. One way is just to write up the information in a word processor and upload the file. The user will then have to download the file and open it in a word processing program on the local computer. This only works if the user has the right program, and it takes time to open the other program. There are two main types of files used to share textual information that most browsers can display without making the user store the file locally and open it from there.

"The first of these is a normal text file. These are files that have the ending dot-T-X-T. That ending is usually pronounced 'text,' B. I just wanted to make it clear. Text files use **ASCII** encoding."

Portable Network Graphics (PNG) Files

PNG files are a relatively new type of files that are not supported by some older browsers. **PNG files** allow more colors than JPGs or GIFs, are typically smaller, and do not lose quality when they are compressed. **PNG files** also do not have the potential legal issues that surround the use of GIF files.

ASCII was pronounced "ask-ee."

"ASCII is the acronym for **American Standard Code for Information Interchange**. That's just a fancy way of saying that it's a universal set of characters so that the characters aren't confused. Browsers can read ASCII and will display it right on the screen. You can't use hyperlinks in a text document, but text documents take up very little space, since they also don't need the tags that HTML requires. Text files are a 'no frills' way of displaying information. You have no control over the font or the formatting, and you can't include pictures.

"Text files are also very easy to download and edit. This makes it very simple to update or change for the owner. On the other hand, it's also very easy to take this information, even if it's copyrighted, and steal it for use somewhere else. HTML documents are also very easy to copy and paste information from.

"A company called Adobe has come up with a way to correct all the problems of text files. They invented a file format that is called **Portable Document Format**, or **PDF**."

For once, one of these file formats was pronounced the way it was spelled: just the three letters P-D-F.

"Web browsers can't actually read PDF files, but the program which can, called Acrobat, can plug into Web browsers. It works just like other plug-in programs; when it's needed the browser starts it up and runs the program as an extension of the browser.

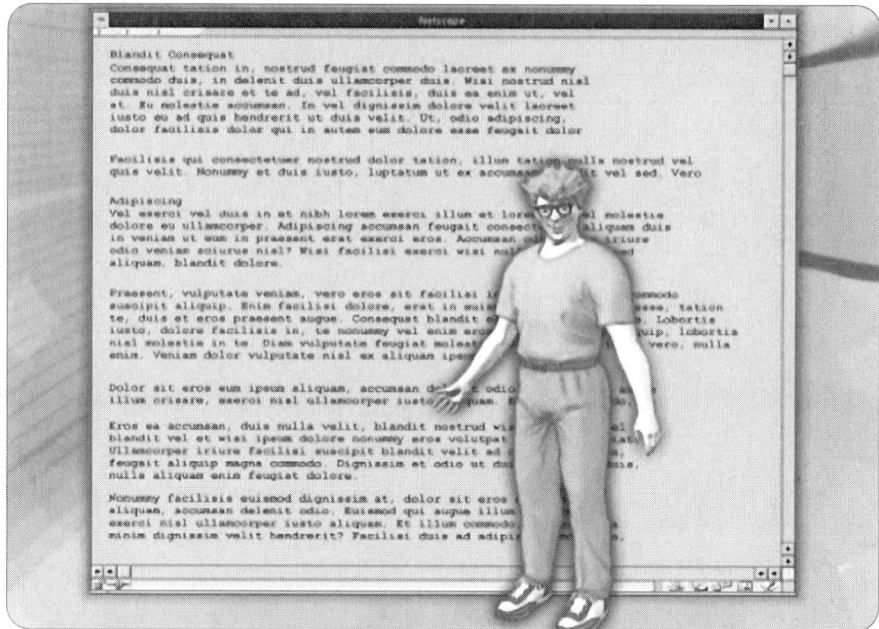

> ## American Standard Code for Information Interchange (ASCII)
>
> Created in 1968, this code increases the compatibility and communication between products made by different companies. **ASCII** uses 96 uppercase and lowercase letters and 32 non-displayed control characters.

"PDF files preserve their formatting and look exactly the same no matter what computer they're stored on. You can have it 'embed' fonts so that even if the reader doesn't have those fonts on his computer, he'll still see the ones you chose. HTML can't do that. If a computer reading a Web page doesn't have a font stored locally, then the person reading the HTML document won't see the correct font, and the browser will have to guess as to which one is similar when it displays a substitute font.

"PDF files can also contain pictures to go with the text. In fact, there are really only two problems with the PDF file format.

"The first problem is that PDF files are usually bigger than HTML files with the same information, and always bigger than text files. The other problem has to do with price. Acrobat Reader is a free program that will allow you to read PDF files and can plug right into your browser. However, to be able to create or edit PDF files, you have to buy the full version of Acrobat or one of the other programs Adobe makes that will edit PDF files. So it's costly to make or edit PDF files."

"Putting a Web page online is more complicated than it sounds," I said.

"It's not so much complicated as it is knowing enough about the concept to be able to plan how best to display the information so that your Web page communicates the message you wish to convey, and does it in a file size that takes the least amount of bandwidth possible to download."

Portable Document Format (PDF)

Adobe Acrobat software uses the **PDF** format for its documents.

I let that soak in. Whether one considers it complicated or not, I decided I was probably going to need to spend as much time considering my page design options as I spent preparing the content for my site—if I ever got home to where I could get to work on applying all of this newfound knowledge.

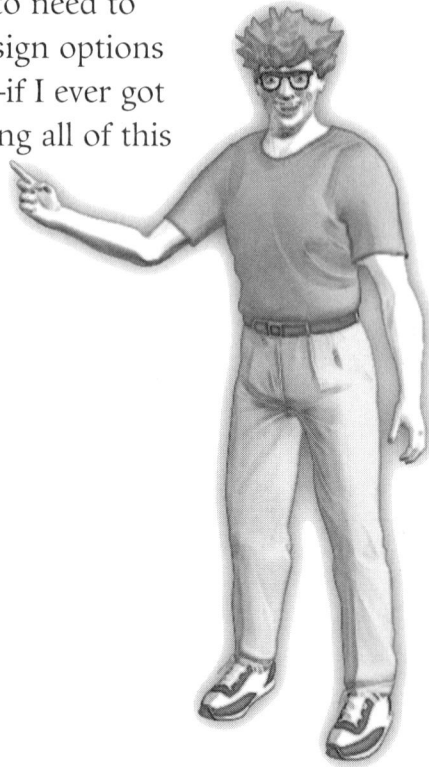

Chapter 15

Online Extras

"Bert, how much have I told you about **scripting**?"

I suddenly had visions of actors reading their parts for a movie. *What does that have to do with the Internet?* I wondered. "Not much," I said, and then gave voice to my thoughts. "What does scripting have to do with the Internet?"

"Quite a bit. But I'm not talking about movie scripts."

I once again thought that maybe Dr. F. could read my thoughts while I was in this computer.

"No, I can't read your mind, Bert, you're just very predictable."

I wondered if I should be insulted.

Dr. F continued, ignoring my discomfort as usual. "Bert, how much have you heard about **DHTML**?"

He still hadn't answered my question about what scripting had to do with the Internet. "Not much. Is it a special kind of HTML?"

"You could say that. You'd even be mostly right. DHTML stands for **Dynamic HyperText Markup Language**. Dynamic means that it changes and moves according to the actions of the person viewing the Web page. DHTML usually involves some sort of scripting," Dr. F. explained.

We'd come around full circle. "So what's scripting?" I asked, again.

"Don't get so worked up," Dr. F. said. (If he was trying to placate me, his voice didn't sound all that comforting.) "I was just going to explain that.

"In programming, there are full languages and then there are **scripting languages**. Full languages, like HTML, can do things without needing anything else except for a system on which to run. Scripting languages are usually used to augment other programming languages.

"In the case of HTML, scripting languages like VBScript and JavaScript are used to make a Web page do things that HTML can't make it do on its own. However, the scripting still has to be *in* a Web page to do anything.

> ## Dynamic HyperText Markup Language (DHTML)
>
> **DHTML** allows users to customize their own Web pages. In contrast, you cannot change a Static HTML page. By using **DHTML**, a Web page can be made to react to the actions of the viewer of the Web page, for example changing color or pictures as the mouse pointer is moved across the screen.

Usually, however, just a partial line of JavaScript language will be able to do something special. It doesn't take a lot of work to add just a little bit of a scripting language."

"JavaScript," I said aloud. I pushed the image of the actors from before—now drinking coffee—out of my head. "I've heard about Java."

"Not Java, B," Dr. F. must have decided it was his turn to be annoyed. "Java is a programming language. JavaScript is a scripting language that uses some of the same language as Java."

I was a touch embarrassed. "So what kind of dynamic things can scripting languages do?"

"Have you ever looked at a Web page where you move the mouse over a picture, and the picture changes?"

Here we go with the answering a question with a question. "Yes," I replied.

Maybe Dr. F. expected a longer answer. I suddenly found myself off on another JTCI, this time going through the routine of calling a Web page—specifically http://www.thelemur.net.

"Scripts are used to react to certain actions of the person viewing the Web page," Dr. F. said, while I watched as the red menu items on the right side of the page one-by-one changed from red to yellow and then back again.

"Basically, scripts are a prepared set of statements for how the Web page is supposed to react to different events, like clicking on an area or just passing the mouse over it. Scripts usually don't take up very much space and add a nice touch that pulls the user into the page by creating a more interactive experience.

"Did you notice the changing menu colors, Bert?"

"Yes," I replied as I felt myself moving once again. Within a split second, I ended up back in my all-too-familiar limbo state.

"It's JavaScript that does that. A little command called onMouseOver tells the picture to change when the mouse moves over it. Another one, onMouseOut, tells the picture to do something else—usually change back—

> ## Scripting language
>
> **Scripting languages** are usually used to augment other programming languages. **Scripts** are a prepared set of statements for how the Web page is supposed to react to different events, like clicking on an area or just passing the mouse over it, making the Web page a more interactive experience for the user.

when the mouse moves away. Commands that tell the browser to do something when the user does something are called **event handlers**. Event handlers actually only initiate events; they tell the browser when to act.

"JavaScript can do many other things, too, like make new windows, change the Web page being viewed, make random numbers, check information, and much more. It's a very useful yet simple tool.

"Of course, it's not the only scripting language. VBScript is another common scripting language. It's based on Visual Basic, and it can do things similar to how JavaScript can. VBScript is usually used to store information as the user changes pages on the same server. It's not used quite as often as JavaScript, however, and is not as simple. It has better capabilities for dealing with databases.

"A database is a way to store information on a computer. Companies often use them to keep track of customers or to control forms.

"Remember when I told you about FTP?"

"Yeah."

"Prove it. Tell me what it is," Dr. F. demanded.

"It's a method of transferring files back and forth from a remote location," I said smugly.

"Does it have any special limitations?"

"Well, you have to connect to an FTP server. And it doesn't allow you to look at files, only download and upload them. Also, you can't send files to the server using http, which is what Web pages use to view files."

"Very good, Bert," Dr. F. said. "I see that you do well under pressure.

"Scripting languages, as well as some programming languages, have the ability to send information to the server without using FTP. They take information that's provided by the user, and send it back to the server, where the server can process it. It doesn't send a whole file, just a piece of information. So it's not as powerful as FTP, but it can be more useful."

Event handler
An event handler is a program or command that instructs the browser how to begin or initiate a command from the user.

Plug-in

A **plug-in** is an auxiliary program that enhances a software program's capability, allowing it to do things it normally could not (such as read certain types of files, for example). A **plug-in** is often called a helper program.

There was a long pause, so I started stretching out. All this lecturing was giving me a headache. I still wondered if any of these cables were soft enough to rest my head against. Probably not.

I heard chalk scratching sounds in the background, and I thought that I could at least be grateful that the chalk didn't screech. Only then it did screech, and so did Dr. F.

"B! I've been talking this whole time about plug-ins and I haven't explained what they are, have I?"

"No," I replied, upset that I wasn't going to get a nap. My stomach growled. I had almost forgotten about that. "No, you haven't."

"We must rectify that immediately. What is a **plug-in**, Bert?"

This time the image in my head was a movie camera being plugged into a wall. I noticed the hand doing the plugging belonged to one of the actors who'd been drinking coffee earlier. I guess my mind wandered too long (as I've said before, hunger makes my head swim—some pizza would help me stay focused) because Dr. F. grew impatient.

I heard Dr. F. clear his throat and he then continued as if I'd answered. Or maybe continued as if I hadn't. I guess it didn't really matter.

"A plug-in is a program that the Web browser uses to display file types the browser doesn't support by itself. The plug-in shows up inside the browser window. Plug-in refers to the behavior of the application: it plugs into the browser and acts like an extension of it.

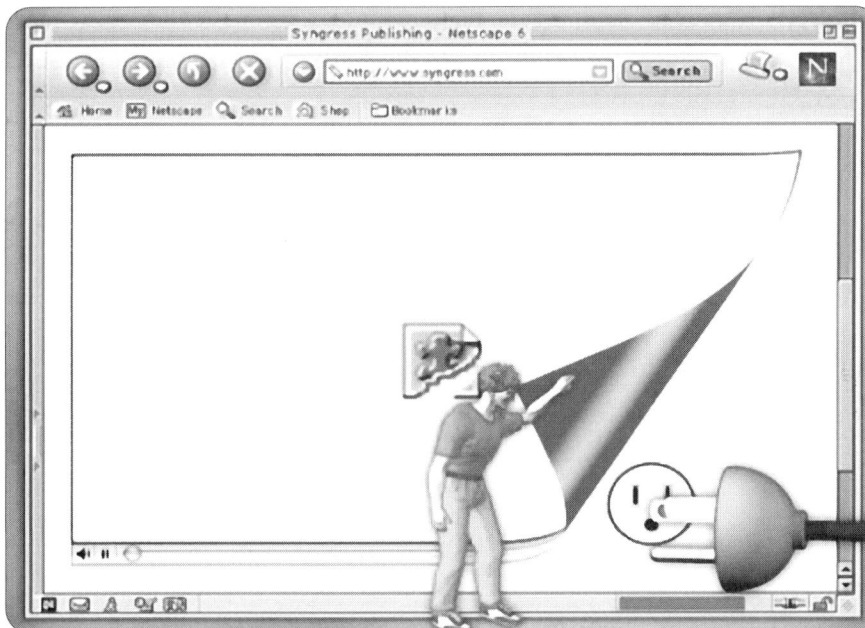

"Perhaps you could name some of the file types that require plug-ins, B."

I tried to set aside my thoughts about my gnawing hunger pains and come up with an acceptable reply. I could hear what I assumed was his foot tapping.

"PDF files! We just talked about that one!"

"Yes, B. What program plugs in to use PDF files?"

"Acrobat Reader," I answered.

"That's correct. Can you think of any other file types?"

"Well, didn't you say most movies need plug-ins? And music files, too?"

"Yes, most music needs a plug-in to be played. And all movies need plug-ins. Windows Media Player, QuickTime, and Real Player are three examples of movie players that plug into your browser. The function of a plug-in is to expand the func-tionality of your browser. Frequently, browsers are built to be small and fast, so that they can do their job quickly. I think I've mentioned before how users don't like to wait long to see their Web pages dis-played.

"That's why browsers aren't designed to do a lot of work. They don't support a lot of different file types, just the basic files that most Web pages use, like JPG, GIF, and of course HTML. There are other file types, like PHP and ASP that are used to build a Web page in a way that the server actually interprets it and sends it to the browser, where the information is then used to build the page. Plug-ins aren't needed for any of these file types.

But when you want to look at an AVI or an MOV or an SWF file, you need a plug-in.

"Plug-ins help you see more and do more over the Internet without forcing you to save a file first and then open another program to look at it."

With a squish and whoosh I was back on another JTCI. I knew I was heading for a Web site, because I could see what I thought were pictures. I started to slow down, so I realized that I must be getting closer. There *were* pictures, and I could make them out now.

I got excited. It sure looked like I was at starwars.com, because I could see all of the characters. Then, I stopped (and so did the squishy feeling).

I looked around.

"Hey this is the page where you see the trailer for the next *Star Wars* movie!"

"Yes, it is, Bert. Have you seen all of them?"

"Well, I don't own the DVD, so I haven't seen the special one."

"What sort of a teenage boy are you? Let me get my copy and we'll watch it!" A few moments later I heard Dr. F. slide something into what I figured must be his computer's DVD player and close it. "There," he said, "now click on it. We want to see the big one."

"Sure! But what does this have to do with the Internet?"

"Didn't you just tell me that movies, like this trailer, need plug-ins? Sit back and relax."

A few moments later I was more excited than ever to see information on another *Star Wars* movie due to come out soon. I only wish I'd had popcorn to eat while I watched that trailer. Or a hotdog. Or pizza. Actually, by that point I think I would have eaten anything.

"So, what did you notice about that?"

"When he jumped out the window to catch..." I started excitedly, only to be interrupted.

"This is JTCI, B, not a film appreciation class. What did you notice about how that worked?"

"Oh, well, I had to choose how big the movie was going to be, and then I had options to pause or play again."

"Exactly, most sites with movies offer you several choices of size for the movie, so you know how long you have to wait for the movie to arrive so you can watch it. The controls for pause or play and such were actually part of the plug-in program. If I do this," Dr. F. said as he clicked the play button, "then the command is actually given to the plug-in, not to the browser.

"Most Web browsers are not programmed to show things like movies or sound files. They need another program to help them out. The plug-in, which is what this helper program is called, will show things right inside the browser window.

"The plug-in installed to work with your browser will automatically run whenever you want to see one of the file types that require more help than just the browser alone can provide. That way, you don't have to do any extra work to see the movie. You just have to click a link!"

Dr. F. didn't give me time to reply about how nifty I thought plug-in capabilities were. I'd also wanted to thank him for letting me see the *Star Wars* trailer. It was awesome! However, before I had a chance to collect my thoughts (let alone do what I'd really wanted to do—push play again), I felt another squish and soon found myself back in my hovering limbo state, where I awaited further instructions.

Chapter 16

Security Stuff

Dr. F. cleared his throat. "So, B. Now that we've talked a little bit about scripting, we should probably cover how security works on the Internet.

"Internet security is very important because there are many people, who for whatever reason, feel it's necessary to break into networks and steal information, or drop in viruses, or find other ways to be destructive.

"Because the Internet is very open, companies especially need to be very careful. Knowing about the pitfalls and potential security problems, however, is something about which everyone should be aware. This is why security measures have been designed and implemented to protect users and networks. What sort of security measures have you heard of, my little protégé?"

I had recently read William Gibson's story *Burning Chrome*, so images of *Star Wars*-like devices shooting down Internet connections popped into my head. I think if I had some food my head wouldn't wander like that. Then something I'd heard of in the real world popped into my head. "Well, I've heard of **firewalls**," I said, "but I'm not really sure how firewalls work. In fact, what are

> ## Firewall
> A **firewall** is a computer system or group of systems that polices traffic between an organization's internal network and its external network. It regulates who from the outside may enter the system and what network services they may access.

they anyway? Now that I think about it, I don't even really know what a firewall is."

Dr. F. chuckled. "Firewalls are a good place to start a discussion of security. They are a very common method of security for networks with a constant Internet connection. And what better way to learn about these things than seeing them close up?"

Uh oh, I thought. I knew what "up close" usually meant, and sure enough, I soon felt another squish. This one transported me to inside a computer. In this case, the computer was behind a brick, stone, and titanium wall, behind which flames shot up and out from all directions.

This time Dr. F. giggled. "Those *Star Wars* people aren't the only ones who can do impressive special effects," he said. "In a physical structure like an apartment building, a firewall is a reinforced wall that's built to a specific code. If there is ever a fire in the building, the firewall is there to contain that fire and keep it from spreading to other parts of the building. The wall is constructed of less flammable materials in the hope that the fire will burn out before it can pass through the wall.

"When someone on a network that uses a firewall wants to connect to the Internet, they have to pass through several routers that are a part of the network, before they even look at the outside of the network."

I felt myself move from inside the computer to where I abruptly stopped in front of the wall. Imagine my surprise—and horror!—when I saw a hangman's noose drop from out of nowhere. While I stared at the scary sight in front of me, I actually heard Dr. F's giggles progress to almost hysterical laughter.

"Got your attention with that one, didn't I?" he asked, his voice sounding more like hiccups as he evidently fought to regain his composure.

He didn't give me a chance to reply. *At least the flames have disappeared*, I thought.

"When somebody inside a firewall wants to access the Internet, the first router data being sent from the network encounters is an **internal screening router**, which is sometimes called a **choke router**." Dr. F. laughed again. "Get it?"

"Couldn't we just send me on a JTCI to someplace where they only frisk me and read me my rights?" I asked.

> **Internal screening router**
>
> The **internal screening router** prevents certain information (packets of data) from leaving the proscribed network and getting out into the Internet, etc. So, if the company does not want you surfing the Web for inappropriate material, it will use this router to stop you from doing so. An **internal screening router** is often also called a **choke router**.

The doctor ignored that question as well. "The internal screening, or choke, router looks over the packets of data.

"There are several ways of running a firewall this way, but what usually happens is that the router is programmed to block certain packets. How do you think it chooses those packets, B?"

"I guess I don't know."

"Think, B. What about packets could be used to screen them?"

I thought for a minute. "The header!?"

"Yes, B, the header. The header of every packet says where it came from, where it's going, and what it's doing. With that information, a lot of the bad stuff trying to sneak in can be separated and blocked. In fact, the network administrator can say that anything that is going by FTP can be blocked. He could tell the router to block everything but E-mails if he wanted.

"Another level of protection is what's called the **external screening router**, which is also known as an **access router**. It also screens packets between the network and the Internet and vice versa. This router protects the network in case there's a failure of some sort from the internal screening router."

I felt another squish—and felt relief to see the noose disappear—as I moved through the firewall and out through points on the Internet. After another squish, I did a U-turn. It appeared that I'd soon be headed back towards that point I'd started from.

"Well, that takes care of stuff going out of the network, but there is also a substantial risk of packets trying to get into the network. This is what a bastion host is used for. A bastion host is part of the network's firewall, and everything that knocks on the door asking for access to a network computer has to talk to the bastion host first."

> **External screening router**
> An external screening router prevents unwanted information from getting into a network. It is also called an access router.

A squish later, I found myself back at the firewall. This time I faced a huge door with one of those brass knockers in the middle of it.

"The bastion host gives the administrator a lot of control over what is let in. This host is usually very well protected and refuses to let anything come through. It's very strict about that.

"The bastion host is sort of a bouncer. Anyone who wants to do anything on the network has to talk to the bastion host first. Some packets get in, but many of them are refused."

"I hope I'm one of the packets the bouncer decides to let pass," I said. I tried to block any thoughts of some burly guy pounding me into the virtual pavement. I hadn't trained for physical obstacles!

"Bastion hosts can be programmed to act as **proxy servers** as well. Proxy servers are like a kind of firewall.

A proxy server adds an extra step to the connection process, but the step is usually worth it.

"With a proxy server on a network, the Web browser first talks to the proxy server. The easiest way to describe it is to say the browser almost pretends as if the proxy server is actually the Internet. It says: 'I want this page or that file.' The proxy server then connects to the appropriate server. Then, when it receives the information, it sends it back to the client that requested the file.

"That is, it sends it back *if* the file is permitted."

While I hung around in limbo outside the firewall, wondering whether or not I was going to have an unfriendly encounter with the bouncer, Dr. F. continued.

"In fact, the proxy server doesn't just add a step; it also provides a means to log every packet that goes into and out of the network. It can block forbidden areas or sites, as well as specific file types. You sometimes hear a lot about the freedom on the Internet, but to most private networks, complete freedom is dangerous. Network administrators want tight control over what goes in and out of their network. To do this, proxy servers can be set to block only one direction, or to disallow a connection either way.

"Proxy servers also help control how much bandwidth is used. The more bandwidth being used, the less bandwidth is available for other things. Proxy servers have ways to control bandwidth usage, and can clamp down if it exceeds too much.

> **Proxy server**
>
> A proxy server monitors and controls the flow of certain types of data into or out of the network. It can cancel or break a connection between a sender and a receiver. It can also be set up to regulate the use of bandwidth in a network.

"One way a proxy server controls the use of bandwidth is to cache pages. This means that it stores Web pages, usually ones that are viewed frequently, on the proxy server itself. It goes out and gets the pages and then stores them locally for everyone who wants to view these pages. This frees the network from constantly using bandwidth that connects to the Internet; it also speeds up the viewing of those pages.

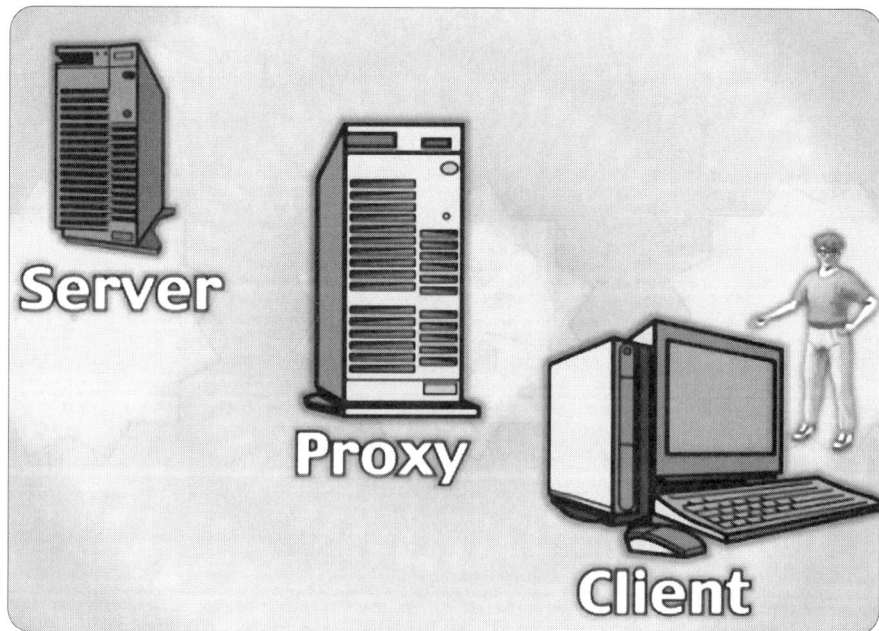

"So the extra step doesn't always hurt speed; sometimes it makes things faster!"

Encryption

Encryption is a system of rules for changing computer data into unintelligible and/or unreadable symbols so no one else can decipher them unless they have the password.

That said, I felt another squish, and the door opened and I moved through the firewall to where I was back on the other side. I didn't hang around inside that network for long though. After a series of more squishes, I was back in my limbo position, awaiting further JTCI directions.

"Now, Beta, what other sorts of security measures do you know about?"

"Well, when I use the Internet to check on my bank account, they tell me that it is secure, but that doesn't use a firewall or a proxy server, does it?"

"That depends, Beta. They may have a proxy or a firewall for other things, or even behind the scenes, but they're probably using **encryption** to secure the information.

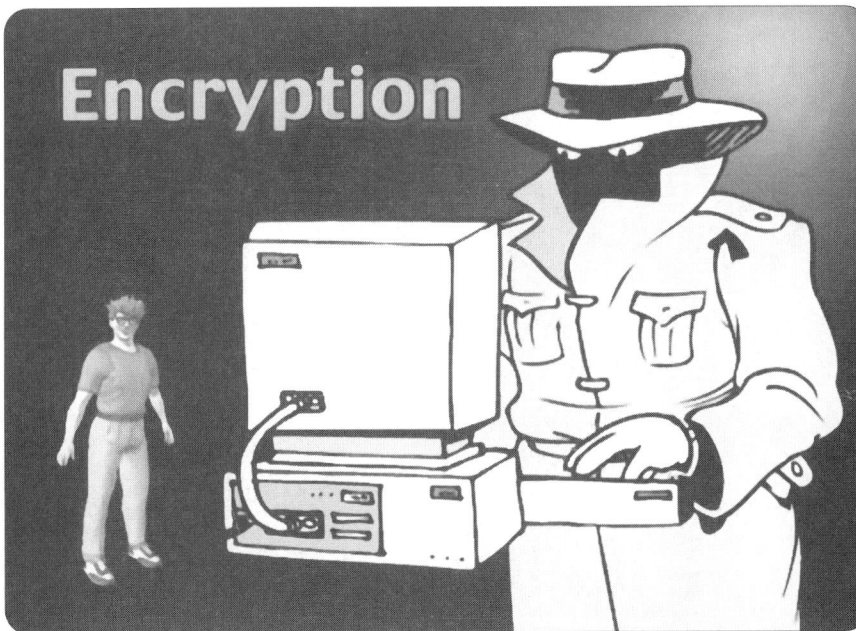

"Encryption can be very complicated, and that's good, because simple codes are easier to break. Encryption is exactly like the secret codes that you hear about in all those spy movies. On the Internet, there are both private and public keys for interpreting these codes. Generally, the public ones are made to encrypt and cannot decode the encrypted message, while private ones are used for both.

"What actually happens is the person sending the information will first encrypt a personal identifier using their own private key. They then encrypt that key and the information using a randomly generated key. Then everything—the random key, the message, and so forth—all gets encrypted using the public key of the person to which the information will be sent. When the information is all received the recipient uses his private key to decode it all. It was encoded using the recipient's public key, but since that is never used to decode, the recipient's private key is used instead. Then, the recipient has to decode the message with the random key that the sender used. Finally, the recipient can decode the original personal identifier using the private key. The personal identifier helps the recipient know that the message came from the right source and was not tampered with.

"Like I said, it gets pretty complicated. If you didn't follow all that process, just remember that encrypted information actually has several layers of protection, so it's very difficult for information to be understood or secretly changed by someone who manages to intercept it along the way.

"Encryption is used when you need the information to go through, but you need to make sure it gets through correctly. Proxy servers and firewalls only protect the network from what comes in and out. They don't protect the information that actually goes through the transfer.

"Now, all this discussion of security brings up another concern: privacy. What do you know about Internet **cookies**, Bert?"

"I've heard they're bad. They tell other sites all about who you are so they can get information about you."

"Well, that's partially true.

"Cookies are small files that are used by Web sites to track information about users who view their Web pages.

Cookies

Cookies are Web site-created text files. They identify you as a specific visitor to a Web site and companies often use them for shopping cart and personal home page information.

These are viewed as a threat because they can report information to the Web server about which sites the browser viewed and what the user did. This information can be used to decide what pages on a site are the most popular, to determine what kind of person visits the site most frequently, and so forth. This is information that businesses use to improve their products and their Web sites.

"In fact, the most common use for cookies is to make things easier for the user. These cookies store information about your user name and password on certain sites, so you don't have to type it in every time. This may sound very insecure, but only a Web site that sent you a cookie can read the cookie. And if you're still worried, browsers let you determine whether you want to accept cookies or not.

"Cookies are sent to a client computer the first time that client visits a Web site. Then, every time afterwards, your computer will look to see if there is a cookie for that Web site; if there is, it sends the cookie to the server and the server will customize the display you see—perhaps calling you by your login name or something similar.

"This is how shopping carts on Web sites work as well. These sites send a cookie to your computer, which records what you're buying and so forth. The cookie is replaced every time you tell the server you want to buy something else or you change your mind about something and change your order. It's a very effective way to keep track of this information. It's also secure because you sent the information to them; they didn't request it. Plus, like I said, you can always tell your browser not to accept cookies or to ask you for each cookie that is offered."

I heard more of those scratching sounds that indicated that Dr. F. was writing more stuff on one of the blueboards.

As I hung around waiting to find out what things I'd learn about next, I decided being in limbo wasn't such a bad thing after all. In fact, I was sort of glad the doctor hadn't decided to encrypt me. After that encounter with the noose, I didn't feel like fretting over whether or not Dr. F. would lose the key necessary to get me unencrypted and back to my semi-normal state. I do have to admit, though, that some cookies sure would have been nice at that point. The soft sugar ones like my grandma makes—with the sugared walnuts on top. And a nice cup of hot cocoa with marshmallows on top.

Chapter 17

Setting Up Your E-Mail Client

Suddenly I felt the familiar squish again.

I sped through some cables until I found myself looking at a big E-mail setup screen. I knew what it was because at the top of the panel it said: "Set up an E-mail account."

"Well, Beta," I heard the distant, reverse-megaphone voice of Dr. F. say. "Now we're going to do some practical work. To help you understand E-mail a little bit better, I'm going to walk you through setting up an account. What do you think goes here?"

The screen I looked at had a big blank space with a blinking cursor. To the left of the space were the words "Full Name."

"I guess it wants my full name. Is that like my full log-in name or my E-mail address?"

"No, Bert, this is your full real name— or, at least, the name that you want everyone to see when they get E-mail from you. There is nothing technical about this field. By the way, a field is what all the blank spaces into which you're to add information in this set-up procedure are called. All this field does is attach your name (or whatever you type in) to every E-mail you send out so other people know who those messages are from."

I typed in "Albert." There was no reason to put in my last name. I only use my E-mail for casual correspondence, so I decided to help protect my identity by not revealing my last name.

Post Office Protocol, version 3 (POP3)

This protocol allows you to send and receive e-mail. POP3 is not as sophisticated as IMAP.

Internet Message Access Protocol (IMAP)

A more sophisticated protocol than Post Office Protocol, version 3, IMAP is able to hold any messages until the users come and get them by logging into their server. Also called Internet Messaging Access Protocol.

When I was done, Dr. F. changed the screen. This time the field asked me for my E-mail address. "What's my E-mail address, boss?"

"Oh yes, I forgot to tell you that I got you a new one. You can have the address: bert@webosaurus.net."

I had visions of the big skeleton I had ridden earlier as I typed in my new E-mail address. "How is this field used?" I asked.

"This actually serves the same purpose as the full name. The server will use other information that we'll enter in a minute to find your actual account. This is just to let the E-mail client of someone reading your message know where to send an E-mail reply to your message.

"Let's move on now that you have that entered."

The screen changed again. This time, the screen had two fields and a drop-down menu I could make choices from. The drop-down menu was labeled: "Type of incoming mail server." I could choose between POP3 or IMAP servers. "What do these choices mean?" I asked.

"Very good question," Dr. F. replied. "These two types of servers handle mail in very different ways. The first part is **Post Office Protocol**, usually called **POP3**, which is the most common, but far from the exclusive method. With POP3, you actually download the information from the servers before you can read the messages or make any changes to them. This is common because Internet providers like to send that information on to your computer instead of storing it on their servers. It also means that you have control over what happens to the message. For example, if the server breaks down, you still have copies of all your E-mail on your hard drive.

"**Internet Message Access Protocol**, or **IMAP**, allows you to set up folders as well as read and move messages around while they're still on the server. This is convenient if you don't have very much hard drive storage space on your own computer."

"So which do we have?"

"Webosaurus runs a POP3 server," Dr. F. told me. "You'll want to choose that so the E-mail client knows how to treat the messages that it finds when it talks to the server."

I made the appropriate choice and looked at the next field. "Incoming mail server:" was the label on this one. "What do I put here? 'Webosaurus?'" I remembered he'd called the server 'Webosaurus' earlier.

"No, you have to put more than the name of the computer where the server runs. You have to put in an Internet address. This field is where your E-mail client will look to find the messages for you to read. Usually this is a domain name prefixed by a sub-domain such as 'mail' or 'pop.' What it actually is called depends on what the server administrator decides. The sub-domain will point at the server software for your incoming E-mail. The entity that is pro-viding you with E-mail service will have to supply this information for you."

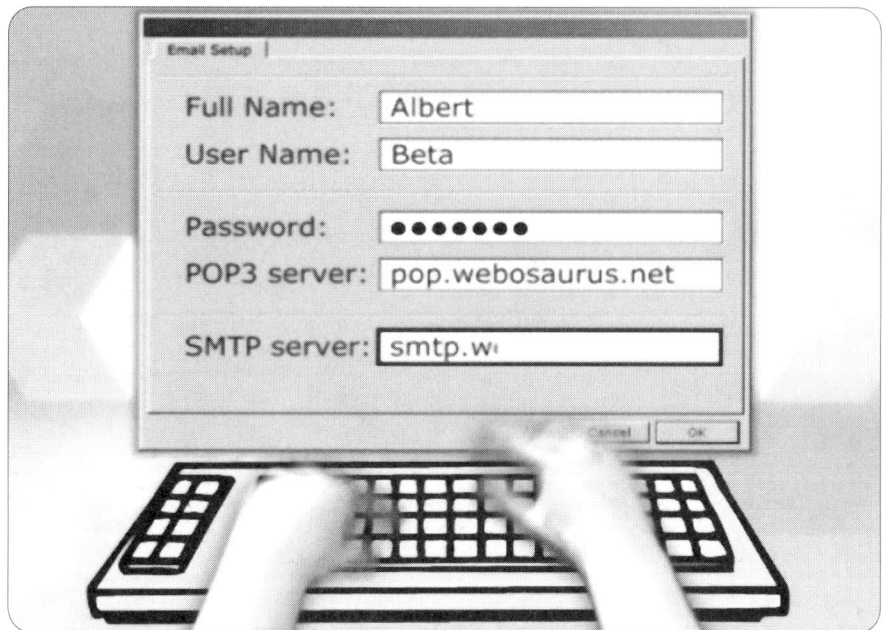

Email Setup	
Full Name:	Albert
User Name:	Beta
Password:	●●●●●●●
POP3 server:	pop.webosaurus.net
SMTP server:	smtp.w

"So which one do I use as the address for the Webosaurus POP3 server?" I asked.

"Oh, yes," Dr. F. said. "I nearly forgot to tell you. In your case, the POP3 server field information will be pop.webosaurus.net."

"Thank you," I said as I typed it in. "The next field is 'Outgoing server.' What do I put there?"

"This will be the 'send mail to people' protocol," Dr. F. said as he started snickering. When he calmed down he told me, "Sorry, that was a private joke. 'Send Mail To People' is a mnemonic device I give people to help them remember the initials for **Simple Mail Transfer Protocol**, or **SMTP**. This is the outgoing server. 'Send Mail To People' is simply a way of remembering that SMTP is the protocol used to send mail to other people, not how you get mail. SMTP sends mail from your computer to the server, and it is also used to send mail from server to server. The SMTP server on Webosaurus is smtp.webosaurus.net, which is different than some servers." I started typing as he spoke. "Some server computers use the same address for the incoming and the outgoing mail, such as 'mail.webosaurus.net.' This just means that their mail server can function as both a POP3 and SMTP, depending on what it's asked to do."

The screen changed again, and the first field on this screen asked for my account username. I remembered that Dr. F. had told me (several times, in fact) that the account name for logon was usually the same as the first part of the E-mail address. I typed in "bert" and waited for Dr. F. to tell me if I was wrong. After a few moments I cleared my throat.

"Yes, what?" Dr. F. asked. "Why aren't you moving on?"

"Because I don't know if this is right."

"Oh, yes. Yes it is. Didn't I tell you the username is usually the first part of the E-mail address?" He didn't wait for an answer. "Yes, I suppose I did; after all, you've got that information there already, so I guess you learned it from somewhere—and you're learning most of this information from me, after all.

"Keep in mind that not all servers use the first part of the E-mail address for the username, it is just a very common convention. The username is how the E-mail client identifies the person for whom it wants messages from the server. Without this, the server will never know what messages to give you, and it will ask for more information. The server never looks at the E-mail address itself when a client tries to log in. It only asks for the username and password.

Simple Mail Transfer Protocol (SMTP)

SMTP is a protocol, based on TCP/IP, that aids in transmitting e-mail.

"Now, Beta. What would you like for a password?"

I told him and he started typing something.

"You see, most E-mail providers let you tell them what you want your password to be, although some of them generate one randomly. The password is how you confirm your identity to the server. Since it is so common to use the first part of the E-mail address as the username, most people could guess what your username is fairly easily. Just like I could go get a passport and tell them my name was Bert. But you have to prove that you are who you say you are when you get a passport. In that case you provide documentation attesting to that fact, such as a certified copy of your birth cer- tificate. In the case of E-mail, the password is how the E-mail client proves it's legitimate when it asks for your messages from the server.

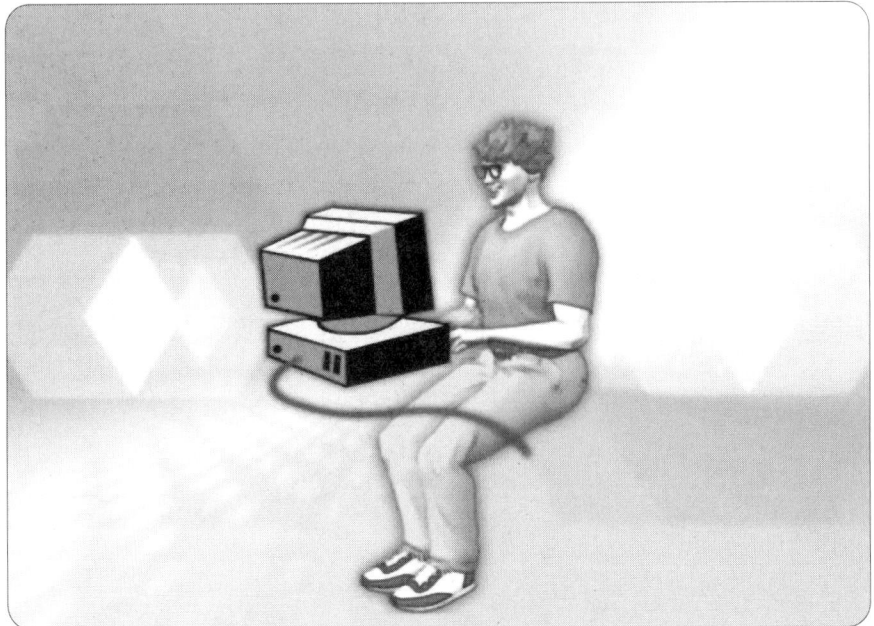

"A good password will have nothing to do with the E-mail address and probably not have anything to do with your real name or birthday or anything else someone could guess very easily. Once you choose a password, the administrator will have to configure your account on the server to recognize the password, which is something I have just done for you."

The screen disappeared.

"There, Beta," Dr. F. said. "We're done setting up your E-mail client. It's now ready to receive your E-mail any time you poll the server and request your messages."

"Is there a way I can access my E-mail account while I'm *inline*?" I asked.

"Inline?" Dr. F. asked.

Wow, I thought. *I've finally stumped the good Doctor!* "Well," I said, "when you connect to the Internet, you go 'online.' In my case, however, you literally zapped me into the Internet for my JTCI, so I've been kind of thinking of myself as being *inline*."

Dr. F. actually chuckled. "No, Beta," he said. "I haven't set up things so that you have access to your E-mail while you're on your JTCI."

I'd hoped for more specifics, but that was all he said, so I was left wondering just how long it'd be before I was back *offline* so that I could go *online* and access E-mail sent to my new account, and read it while I sat at my computer chowing down on one of my favorite snacks.

Chapter 18

Newsgroups and Other Nifty Online Stuff

"Now that we've talked about E-mail quite extensively," Dr. F. said, "let's discuss some other methods of communicating over the Internet. First, I'd like to talk a little bit about **newsgroups**. What do you know about newsgroups, Bert?"

"Aren't those the things that are identified as fluffy.bunny.alt.news or similar names?"

Dr. F. started to laugh. Loudly. For a long time. When he finally got himself under control, he addressed me. "Oh, Bert! That's very funny," he said. "Yes, that is sort of how newsgroups are organized on **Usenet**.

"Usenet is the main home for newsgroups on the Internet. Usenet is a collection of servers dedicated to providing a forum for electronic discussions. Each newsgroup is a discussion on a specific topic, but the groups are all divided by more general topics.

"There are a score of categories, abbreviated to a three or four letter combination. For example, the Recreation category is REC and the Alternate category is ALT. This first section is then subdivided into more specific areas. REC is broken into things like Arts, Sports, and so on. The subdivision keeps happening, getting more and more specific. For example, you could have a news thread on Molly Ringwald at rec.arts.cinema.actresses.ringwald, or you could have a general discussion of film at rec.arts.cinema. It all depends on how broad or how limited you want the subject matter to be. The newsgroup about your fluffy bunnies would probably be at sci.bio.rabbits.

"Now, as I mentioned, Usenet is a network of servers that host forum discussions, but not every server will host every forum. The administrator of each server decides what forums will be hosted on that server.

"When you connect to a Usenet server, you must use a special client to read the messages. Most clients allow you to read messages as **threads**. Threads are a series of messages that are responses to each other or to a common original message. They are usually displayed in

---

Newsgroup

A newsgroup an online discussion group devoted to a single subject. Those reading the messages can read, post, and/or reply to a message.

Usenet

A collection of servers that make up a world-wide network, **Usenet** allows people to post messages and notes on a variety of topics, allowing for the creation of a large number of different newsgroups. Originally **Usenet** used a protocol known as UNIX-to-UNIX Copy (UUCP), but today it uses the Network News Transfer Protocol (NNTP).

Thread

A thread is a series of messages and responses about a particular subject in a newsgroup.

a hierarchical pattern. In other words, the first message on a subject will be to the far left. Then all messages that respond to it will appear underneath the first message and offset from the left by a little bit. The responses to those messages will appear underneath them and slightly to the right a little bit more, and so on. Original messages will always appear on the far left.

"What happens when you submit a message to a newsgroup depends on whether the newsgroup is moderated or unmoderated.

"In an unmoderated newsgroup, the message is sent to the server, and the server posts the message. The message is also copied to every other server on Usenet that hosts the newsgroup and is finally sent to every subscriber of the newsgroup.

"In a moderated newsgroup, however, there is an additional step involved. When you submit a message to a moderated newsgroup, a person called a moderator will first review the message to make sure it is suitable. This way the newsgroup can stay on topic and the moderator can make sure that the content of the messages remains in accordance with the newsgroup's standards and format. Once the moderator has approved a message, then it is posted to the server, distributed to the other servers, and downloaded by the subscribers."

Dr. F. finally stopped talking for a moment, presumably to catch his breath. Then he dove right into another lecture.

"Another method of communicating on the Internet is to use an online chat forum, usually referred to as a **chat channel** or **chatroom**.

"Chatrooms are a way of sharing what you type with more than one person. Chat rooms operate in real time, which means that people see what you have to say right away without having to download the information. By far the most popular way to chat on the Internet is **Internet Relay Chat**, or **IRC**.

"To use IRC, you have to download a client designed to connect to IRC. There are IRC clients available for use on every operating system, so this isn't usually a problem.

"Beta, do you remember what is meant by the term 'client'?" Dr. F. asked.

"A client is a user program, isn't it?"

"Exactly!" Dr. F. replied. "The most popular client for IRC chat is a shareware program known as mIRC. It's a program written by Khaled Mardam-Bey and is available at www.mirc.co.uk.

"Once you have the client working, you must connect to a server. The server you join determines which network you will be on. Not every IRC server talks to every other server; they are collected in groups called networks, although IRC networks aren't really the same as other networks. Being on an IRC network just means that the server is running IRC server software and talks to a specific group of servers.

> ## Chat room
> A chat room is a particular computer/network area where people can write to each other and get immediate responses. In essence, they are chatting to one another using the computer, but they do not hear each other's voices. Also called a **chat channel**.

These networks usually have interesting names like Undernet or Dalnet.

"To be precise, IRC servers don't even talk to every other server on the same network. The servers only talk to some of the other servers, but they talk to enough that eventually a hop or two to every other server connects them.

"Once you're connected to an IRC network, you will have to join a specific chat room, or channel, to be able to chat with everyone. Channels on IRC are usually a descriptive word or phrase preceded by a pound sign, like #Authors or #Webosaurus. Joining a channel in one network, say the Undernet, allows you to talk to other people who are in the same channel in the same network. The channel #Authors on Undernet is different, however, than the #Authors channel on Dalnet. If you want to talk in both of them, you'll have to run two clients at the same time.

"Most IRC client software splits a window that represents the channel you have joined into three parts. The part on the right allows you to see a list of the nicknames, or nicks, of people who are connected to the same channel. The smallest space along the bottom of the display is where you type in the messages you want to send to everyone. The main part of the window displays all the messages that you and everyone else send to the channel. This is also where you usually see important information about people who join the channel.

"When you send a message to an IRC channel, the message then goes to the server, and the server distributes it to all the other servers it talks to, and they send it to the servers they talk to. The message is then sent to all the people who are logged into the same channel as you.

"A chat message will always be sent to a person or channel by the shortest path possible. This means that some people may see a message a few seconds before others, depending on which server to which everyone is connected. Sometimes the lag between when you type a

Internet Relay Chat (IRC)

An **IRC** is a particular channel (chat group) on the Internet. Everyone who belongs to that channel can read the messages you leave there. You can "chat" with someone or many people simultaneously, much as in a conference call.

message and someone else sees it can get quite long. When this happens, you have three options. Quit IRC, wait for the servers to improve their communication, or try to connect to a different server to decrease the number of hops between you and the people with whom you are chatting.

"Oddly enough, the number of hops isn't always shorter if you join through a server that's geographically the closest to you. When I use the Undernet, I often have less lag when I connect using a European server such as diemen.nl.eu.undernet.org or espoo.fi.eu.undernet.org than I do if I use a server in the United States, such as chicago.il.us.undernet.org or austin.tx.us.undernet.org.

"By the way, you don't have to remember the server information. Most chat clients already have that information there for you. For example, in mIRC you go to the *File* menu and choose *Options*. In the *Options* menu, there are drop-down menus for server types and server locations. The ones I mentioned would be found under all of the servers listed for the Undernet.

"IRC also allows you to do many other things as well. You can send or receive files with other people, send private messages, or find out information about the other users.

"It is very important that you follow certain rules of conduct when you use any of these methods to communicate on the Internet. These rules of conduct are called Netiquette, and they're basically the description of how to be polite. I'll talk more about Netiquette in a little bit. Before we go there, I want to tell you about **instant messaging**.

"Instant messaging, or **IM**, is a way to talk to one of your buddies. Instant messaging is popular, possibly because people think IM systems are easier to learn than IRC. IRC has the advantage that it doesn't matter which client you use; you can still join all the different servers. IM systems do not work together. If you use the ICQ IM client (ICQ is a clever set of letters meant to pun with

> ## Instant Messaging (IM)
> A method of talking to one another (similar to IRC) via the computer. Unlike IRC, a particular **IM** client cannot connect to all servers because **IM** systems put out by different companies do not work with one another.

the words 'I seek you') then you won't be able to talk to someone who is using Yahoo! Instant Messenger. You can run more than one IM client on your computer at the same time, but that tends to take up a lot of RAM and processor space, so most people don't do it, instead choosing a favorite or the one that all their friends use. Sometimes an IM system is used in an office environment. In this case, you'd better use the same system as everyone else does!

"No matter what IM system you use, the process is basically the same. You start by logging onto the server, which will verify your username and password. Once it has done that, the IM client will display a list of all your friends who are also logged into the system. You can then use this list to choose which friend to send messages to. Some IM systems also allow you to send pictures and other files to your friends. Of course, these friends have to use the same system, and you have to tell the system who your friends are first. You create your 'buddy list,' adding those people to it with which you're most likely to want to chat. Most chat and IM systems also let you 'block,' or ignore, those you wish to avoid.

"When you send an instant message, it first travels to the server, and the server sends it to your friend. The friend can then reply or look at more information about you. Most clients allow you to see the history of what you've written and what you've received. Some of them even keep a log of the conversations.

"As an additional feature, many IM systems also have an option where you can search for someone you've never met but has common interests. In this case, the person must have filled out the information form, which a lot of people don't want to do for privacy reasons. But you can meet some interesting people this way that you may have never known any other way!

"I'm sure you've used some form of chat online, Bert. Is there anything I'm leaving out?"

I thought for a minute. "Well," I said, "it sure seems to me that it could be risky talking to people I don't know, like if I were to meet them by using one of those information forms you mention."

"Good point, Beta!" Dr. F. said. "While you're online and chatting, there's a 'buffer' of sorts between you and the person to whom you're chatting. By buffer, I mean that person doesn't see your real name; they only see your logon information or nick. In addition, some servers also show a small amount of geographical information, such as where your ISP is located. That's why it's important that you not divulge your real name when you're chatting online.

"Always use caution when participating in an online chat. Unfortunately, not everybody is honest when they do. For example, somebody may tell you that he's a teenage boy but you really have no way of knowing that for sure. Predators can be very efficient at 'fishing' for information. Say, for example, you mention in conversation that you just got back from a school trip. A predator trying to learn your true identity might ask you something innocent-sounding like: 'Oh, what school is that?' How would *you* answer that question, Bert?"

"I'm not sure," I said. Dr. F. had finally managed to stump me. "I wouldn't feel comfortable telling a lie."

"That's what a predator is counting on, Beta," Dr. F. said. "There are ways that you can keep your answer vague, however, without resorting to lying. For example, you could answer that question by saying 'the only one

here in town,' if that's the case. If the person continues to ask probing questions that make you uncomfortable, tell him or her that you'd rather not discuss personal information. If he or she persists, end the conversation and put that person on the blocked list of users, or on 'ignore.'

"I'm not trying to make you feel paranoid or cause you to live in fear, Beta, but on the other hand, I also want you to learn how to protect yourself.

"As long as you keep your chat answers to strangers vague—such as saying 'I did some work with my neighbor who's a research scientist,' instead of volunteering that you live next door to me, or answering something like 'here in the eastern part of the United States,' instead of volunteering the name of your town and state, you'll be ensuring that your Internet experiences are safe ones."

Dr. F. made some good points. Sometimes it seems like adults can worry too much, but there's usually a good reason for certain advice. Like "look both ways before you cross the street," most rules are meant to protect us from harm. It can sure get difficult sometimes dealing with what can seem like meddling from my parents or other adults when I know I'm old enough now to know these things on my own. I had to resist the temptation to advise Dr. F. that I know how to take care of myself. Instead, I just keep reminding myself that he meant well.

I still look both ways before I cross a street; getting older hasn't changed that. And I suppose one never gets too old to learn about safety stuff, either.

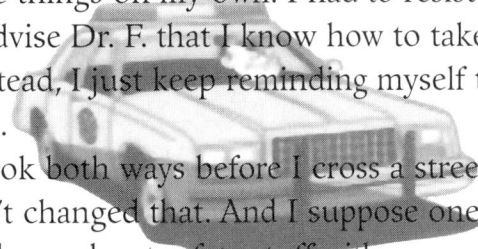

Chapter 19

Netiquette

"Bert," Dr. F. said, interrupting another one of my in-limbo-state thoughts of hunger. "There's more to Internet interactions than just being concerned about your own safety. You also need to be considerate of others."

Oh great, I thought. *More rules.*

"Bert, I told you I was going to tell you about **Netiquette**. You may recall that Netiquette is the word used to describe the rules of the road: the guidelines of behavior on the Internet. It's a contraction of *Net* and *etiquette*, because Netiquette consists of the guidelines for being polite on the Internet. Following these rules as you interact with other people on the Internet will mean you're doing your part to keep people friendly towards you.

"To understand Netiquette, you need to understand how the social dynamics of the Internet work. In other words, you should understand what the expectations and normal behaviors are for people who are on the Internet.

"The first people on the Internet were very technically proficient. They expected everyone to know how to do things and to read up on problems before asking questions. From this developed a large number of conventions that slowly evolved into the conventions of today.

"However, these people were still just ordinary people, and for the most part, the rules are just extensions of behavior expected of normal social interaction in the real world. It is important to remember that there is a technological aspect to Netiquette. Things such as bandwidth, files sizes, and other hardware and software aspects can have a huge impact on how comments are received or made. These things have the same sort of impact that real world elements like room size, crowds, and spare time have on face-to-face conversations.

"However, there's more that can affect how a message is sent and received on the Internet than in real life, because most things in real life can also impact interactions online.

Netiquette
This is an agreed-upon set of rules of etiquette when posting messages or sending E-mail to anyone.

"There are a number of things that affect interactions on the Internet with which you don't normally have to deal in real life. For starters, the people you talk with aren't in the same room. They might not even be in the same time zone or continent! This has a couple of effects. Firstly, they may have vastly different religious, ethical, or moral beliefs than you do. They feel they're just as right as you think you are. Respect those differences, just as you'd respect somebody's difference in opinion on a movie.

"Another thing to remember is that if somebody is in a different time zone, he or she may not be able to respond right away. It may be morning for you when you send that E-mail, but it may be 2:00 A.M. for the other person. You have to give time for people to respond to messages that are not in real time.

"Secondly, malfunctioning technology can color responses. That guy who won't answer your question may have lost his connection and not been able to re-establish it. It's also possible that you have been disconnected, and your client hasn't figured that out yet! You should also be aware of the possibility that information can get lost or corrupted.

"Thirdly, one thing that separates the Internet from other interaction is that the Internet is an anonymous medium. People use aliases and nicknames a lot when they post to message boards or chat. It is inappropriate to ask for personal information from people unless you have spent some time getting to know them and have a friendship. People resent being asked for their sex, age, or location when first meeting others. The Internet is a great place for being able to be someone new. You can pretend to be something else and no one cares. All that matters are your ideas and how you treat others.

"On the other hand, while the Internet is a largely anonymous medium, it is not a license to impersonate someone else. Don't pretend to be somebody else, or even worse, someone else who belongs to the same forum.

"Finally, remember that you aren't talking to someone face to face. People who read what you've written on the Internet don't have your gestures, voice tone, or expressions to clue them in to your intentions. Sarcasm isn't always understood. Nor is anger, happiness, sadness, or boredom. You have to make sure your words alone communicate your message.

"A long list of general suggestions and guidelines can be found in 'Request For Comments 1855.' You can find this document at http://www.dtcc.edu/cs/rfc1855.html. Besides these basic issues, out of which many, many specific rules are extended, there may be site- or group-specific rules. Most Internet message boards, chat channels, IM systems, newsgroups, or other interactive forums will list a set of group-specific rules somewhere. This document may be called a **Frequently Asked Questions** file. **FAQ** can either be spelled out loud or pronounced as one syllable. It is inappropriate to pronounce the first two letters as a syllable and then pronounce the Q.

"FAQs will tell you any specific rules a group or site has about posting advertisements, confidential information, 'adult' material, topics, or other rules. If a FAQ file exists for your group, you should always read this document before participating in the group. You should also read the messages for a while before posting. This will help you get a feel for the personality of the community.

"These are all some good general guidelines to help you know how to treat others. But there are also some specific things that you should be aware of on the Internet that you may not be able to figure out just from these rules. These are major issues that everyone needs to be familiar with no matter what the forum is.

"The first of these is **flaming**. Flaming refers to comments that are intended to be provocative or incendiary. Basically, anything that will make people angry. You should neither start a flame nor continue a flame war.

> ## Frequently Asked Question (FAQ)
> **Frequently Asked Questions** are a series of postings that help users solve problems and establish rules for using particular interactive forums.

> ## Flaming
> When you **flame** on the Internet or in a forum of some sort, you are ranting, raving, and complaining in an impolite way. **Flaming** is the use of language in a message that is meant to be provocative.

Often, anything that is obviously emotionally intense can be considered flaming. One way to avoid flaming is to wait overnight before responding to an inflammatory comment. If you still must comment on something in a very emotional way, be sure to tell people you are about to do so.

"Another no-no is **spam**."

Suddenly, it seemed we were back to discussing food again. For some reason, this particular comment failed to make me hungry at all.

"Spam is any message that is unsolicited and intrusive—particularly messages that are trying to advertise something off topic from the rest of the forum.

"You may have gotten E-mail about stock offers or vacations or X-rated web sites. These tend to make people very angry and they are bothersome. You should never engage in this type of activity; there's a time and place for advertising and unsolicited e-mail isn't one of them.

"Another important thing to remember is that when you type in a chatroom, message board, or other forum, make sure to use mixed case. In other words, don't type your whole message in capital letters. In the online world, typing in all capital letters is like yelling in someone's ear. It's considered to be rude behavior."

"I once sent a message to a chat channel and then discovered I'd hit the caps lock key by mistake," I told Dr. F.

"Did you apologize for your behavior afterwards?" he asked.

"Absolutely," I replied.

"That's good, Bert," he said. "Most people understand the difference between an honest mistake and intentional, rude behavior.

"Speaking of rude behavior, akin to flaming, is being abusive. Just like you should never call someone names or be vulgar in person-to-person interactions, you also should never use this type of language on the Internet.

Spam

Spam is an unwanted and unsolicited message, especially an unwanted advertisement.

It's rude. Considerate people just don't exhibit that type of behavior.

"There's also the issue of what language you speak. The Internet is a worldwide phenomenon. People from all over the world will post information to message boards or send E-mails or show up in chat rooms. While American English is considered the official language of the Internet (although there's been some controversy about that), not everything you encounter online will be in English. Usually any given forum will have an official language. It is inappropriate to speak Greek when everyone else speaks Spanish, or vice versa. You shouldn't expect others to meet your demands if it is their forum. It's like whispering during a conversation. If you can't say something so everyone else will understand it, then you need to say it privately. Don't use foreign languages as a code or try to make other people use your native tongue. This will generally get you banned from a forum.

"Another thing to avoid is **flooding**. Flooding is taking too much time or posting messages that are far too long. You flood the channel or message board with your own thoughts without allowing anyone else to speak.

"Have you ever been in a conversation where only one person does all the talking and he doesn't let anyone else say anything?"

Like this one? I thought.

"It can get boring, can't it? And rude. The same thing can happen in a chat room or on a message board. Let other people have their turn. If you have something very long to say (or quote), get the permission of everyone else to do so first.

"Now, suppose you are in a chat room and someone starts flooding you with inflammatory statements. What should you do?" Dr. F. asked.

"I guess I tell him to stop," I suggested.

> **Flooding**
> **Flooding** refers to sending an overly long message (or series of messages) to a channel or message board.

"But what if he doesn't? And what if the moderator of the chat room isn't paying attention? Then what?"

"I'm not sure."

"You'll remember from our discussion on online safety that most IM systems and IRC clients have an option that lets you put someone on an 'ignore' status. When someone is on ignore, you will not see anything they try to send you. Usually this is the best way to deal with these sorts of people."

"But what if it's on a Usenet group?"

"Then you can just skip any of their messages. It sometimes doesn't seem fair, but often responding to flames or abuse or flood may just cause more of the same. In fact, before you know what happened, often you are guilty of the same crimes. The best solution is usually just to ignore the person who is being offensive.

"Now, Bert. Remember how I said that people on the Internet like to use abbreviations? Well, the same is true in online communication forums. These abbreviations aren't usually for technical terms, but they mean things that people say a lot. What would you think if somebody sent you a message that said 'LOL'?"

"Lots of luck?"

Dr. F. chuckled. "No, Bert. 'LOL' means 'laughing out loud.' I'll give you some of the other most common examples: 'rofl' means 'rolling on floor laughing,' 'BRB' means 'be right back,' while 'bbiab' means 'be back in a bit,' and 'ttyl' means 'talk to you later.'

"Others you're likely to encounter are 'OMG,' which means 'Oh my goodness!' and 'otoh' means 'on the other hand.' There are a great many of these abbreviations, and you can find a list of their meanings on Webosaurus.net. It helps speed up a conversation when you know what these chat acronyms mean; if you're in doubt, however, most people are usually happy to explain what an abbreviation or acronym means, especially if it's one that's unique to that forum."

I heard some of the scratching noises that indicated Dr. F. was now writing on one of his blueboards. I wondered where we'd be headed next.

"Beta," Dr. F. said. "We've now discussed the types of forums you can join online and the netiquette you should use when you participate in them. How do you suppose you go about finding such information so you'll know where to join in the first place?"

"I imagine in the same manner that one would look for any other information online," I answered. "By using a search engine or directory."

"Exactly!" Dr. F. said.

I guess that means I don't have to wonder what we'll be doing next, I thought.

Chapter 20

How to Find Information Online

While I was speculating about what Dr. F. would have me do next, I couldn't help but wonder whether or not I'd have to be divided up into packets to do it. I had no idea how I would be handling online searches from *inside* the Internet! For that matter, knowing how changeable Dr. F. could be, I didn't even know for sure if I would be doing any searches.

Squish followed squish as I zoomed about the Internet, hitting several servers and heading to who knows where. Well, Dr. F. knew where, I guess. At least, I hope he did.

After a while I stopped and I saw... library shelves. That was kind of boring. He could have taken me to a food page or some sort of pizza delivery Web site.

"So what's all this?" I finally asked. (It sure looked to me like I was on some sort of detour.)

"This is an object lesson. This site is just a file server, or a site that hosts a bunch of files for other people to download. I've programmed it to look like a library for a simple reason. What do you think that reason might be, Beta?"

I'm sure I have no earthly clue, I thought. What I actually did, though, was ask him this question: "Because we're going to 'check out' some files by downloading them?"

"Well, you've caught on to the idea, but you're not quite right. I'm making a comparison here. I'm saying that this file server, like any Web site or any Internet server, is like a library. How do you think that is so, Beta?"

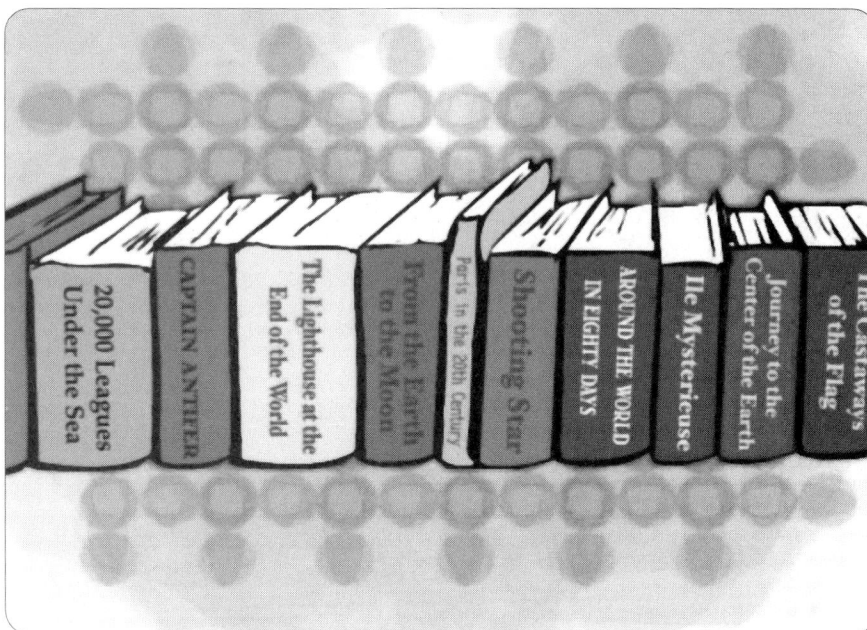

"Well, you already said that borrowing books is wrong. So I guess I don't know."

"Admitting you don't know is the beginning of wisdom, B. Socrates said that. Or at any rate, Plato said he did. Or something to that effect. But that's not what is important here. What is important is that I didn't really say you were wrong. Downloading files is sort of like borrowing books from the library. You can get to them so long as you have access, which is usually free but sometimes requires registering, and you don't have to buy them.

"However, there are some very important differences. What do you think those might be?"

"Well, you don't get a physical book to lug around if you get the 'book' from the Internet."

"Well, that is a difference, but it's not that important. At least, it's less important to the understanding of how the Internet works. Everyone should know that you don't actually get any printed paper from the Internet unless you make it yourself with your printer. But that's beside the point. What I'm getting at, apparently ineffectively, is kind of an extension of what you said. How many copies are there of the classic Chinese novel, *A Dream of Red Mansions,* at the public library in town?"

"I don't know. I don't read Chinese." I sometimes get sarcastic when I'm hungry.

"Well, let's find out." There was another squish and in a moment I was looking at a list of books at the public library. I searched through the titles and found the book he had mentioned.

"It looks like they have 3 copies. One is an abridgement," I said.

"Very good, B." Another squish came. I found myself waiting in line with a bunch of packets for a while. When I finally got to the front, there was another squish and then I was in front of the original virtual bookshelves I had seen. "Now, what's different about this Internet library?"

"There's only one copy of each of the documents," I had thought about this while I was waiting with the packets.

"But..." Dr. F. led me.

There's more? Dang! I thought for a little bit more. "But," I started after a pause, "there's no limit to the number of people who can access the document!"

"Not entirely accurate, but you get the idea." Dr. F's praise was always reserved. "The number of copies of a file does not limit how many people can look at it at the same time. An unlimited number of people accessing the Internet through different browsers and clients and such can read the file at once. In fact, as you read a file online, at least while using a Web browser, you make a copy of the file when you access it. The original file stays on the server, but the browser reads it and makes a copy of it on your hard drive or in the RAM. It usually only stays on a temporary basis, but it's there nonetheless.

"However, Beta, there is a limit to how many people can see it at once. Two things will prevent too many people from viewing the book at once. The first is bandwidth and intervening traffic. Remember how you had to wait in line with all those packets? I already told you that sometimes there is too much information passing through a router and packets have to wait to be processed and sent in the right direction. This can cause some delay in receiving a document.

"The other detail that will limit the number of people who can read a document at once is the amount of processing the server has to do. Computers are wonderful things, but they aren't infinitely powerful. Servers are just like any other computer. They have a processor and memory. The more stuff that a computer has to do the slower it gets. Eventually, there comes a point where the computer just can't do any more than it's already doing. When this happens, people trying to access any documents on the server will get an error message saying that the server is busy. That's what happened when we first tried to come here. Popular file servers can get really busy sending files out to people, so sometimes you have to try several times to get in. That's why it took so long but you didn't wait anywhere. I just kept trying until it was free enough to let you in."

I took a moment to look at the documents on the shelves. The files that this server had were special missions for a game I liked to play. I set a couple of them to download to Dr. F's computer. I could burn them to a CD and take them home from there. After all, Dr. F. had much more bandwidth than I did.

As I continued to look over the files, I was amazed. There were all kinds of neat things here to make my game play different or look better. "I wonder why I haven't seen this site before," I wondered aloud.

"Probably because you never looked for it," Dr. F. spoke up. "It's a very popular site. A simple Web search with the right keywords would have brought you right here."

"Oh, I guess I never did much Web searching," I admitted.

"Then I guess I'll have to tell you all about it." Dr. F. steeled himself for the task.

"There are two ways to search the Internet. You can use an index—sometimes called a directory—or a search engine. It's probably easier to use an index, so let's talk about that first. An index is a large list of Web sites. When you search an index, you start by choosing a broad category and clicking that. You'll then be showed a list of sub-categories that fit under that broad category. You narrow it down until the index starts displaying Web sites in your area of interest; this display is usually accompanied by a brief description about each site. Then, you look through the Web sites listed to see if any of them are likely to fit your needs. This method depends on someone updating the index.

"You can also use a **search engine** to find what you want. With a search engine, you have a bit more control over the terms for which you are searching. You don't have to wonder how the index has been organized. You simply enter the terms and tell it to start the search.

"A search engine is just a big database of all these Web sites. It doesn't actually search the Web when you perform a search. This has already been done.

"Search engines periodically send out agent programs called **crawlers** or **spiders** to cover Web sites and index the information on them. Not all search engines search for the same things, but information a search engine might pull from a page includes the size of the document, the text or keywords from the text, the title, and the header. This information is all saved in the search engine's database and when you perform a search the engine merely needs to check out the information it already has.

> **Search engine**
> A search engine is an external application which examines parts of the World Wide Web to find articles, pictures, video, etc., to match your search request. A search engine is like a reference librarian who helps you find the information you need.

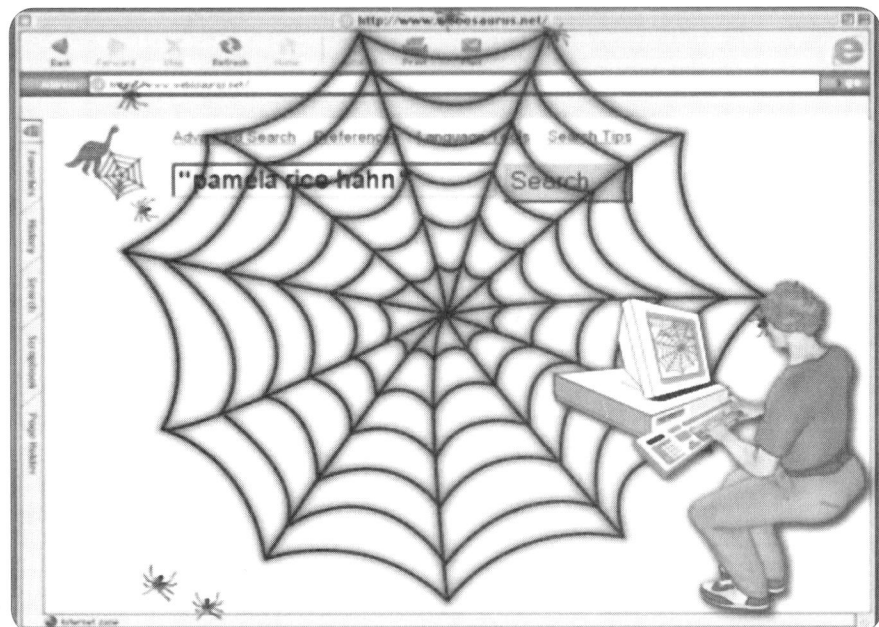

"When the search engine displays the information, it may prioritize the Web sites for you, calculating by some formula the pages from the list it believes are the mostly likely to give a result that you wanted.

"You can also find Web pages more successfully if you are careful about what words you put in the search and how you order them. Most search engines will provide better results for that which you're searching if you use special characters or connectors with your words. Each search engine will have an explanation page link to take you to information about what connecting words and characters will do for your search; it's worth your time to consult that page.

"Let me tell you one more thing about searches, Beta, and then we'll move on. If you really want to make sure you find what you're looking for you should perform a search on several search engines. After all, there are quite a few of them, and none of them have an identical database. They search for different elements, so they often come up with different results."

"Won't doing searches on a number of different search engine sites generate a lot of repeated results?" I asked.

"Good point, Beta," Dr. F. said. "There's a remedy for this problem. You can use a **metasearch engine**.

"A metasearch engine is a piece of software that resides on your own computer. You enter the words you want to search for into the metasearch software, and then it sends an agent to several different search engines. It then performs a search on each of these sites for you and returns the results. The metasearch software has been pre-programmed to understand how to make a search most effective with each engine, so you usually get fairly good results. When all the search results are returned to the software, the metasearcher will then compile those results, eliminating duplicate hits and prioritizing the findings in the order it will be most like to return results you can use.

"There are also metasearch sites on the WWW. One popular metasearch site is ProFusion at www.profusion.com. That site offers a directory index and search engine functions. The search engine searches

Crawler

A **crawler** is a program sent out by a search engine to index the contents of sites and update its knowledge of those sites. Also known as a **spider**.

Metasearch engine

A **metasearch engine** searches several other search engines for a particular topic, allowing for a much more thorough search.

more than 1,000 other search sites. This site lets you do a simple keyword search. It also has an 'advanced' page that explains how to do a more detailed search.

"You think you can find what you're looking for now, Beta?"

"Well," I said, "I at least now know where to start doing my searches."

"Sometimes knowing where to find information is just as important as knowing facts and figures," Dr. F. said. "Any idea why this might be, Beta?"

"I imagine it'd be important when I need to document my sources for a report. Prepare a bibliography and stuff like that."

"I'm proud of you. That's exactly the answer I was looking for!"

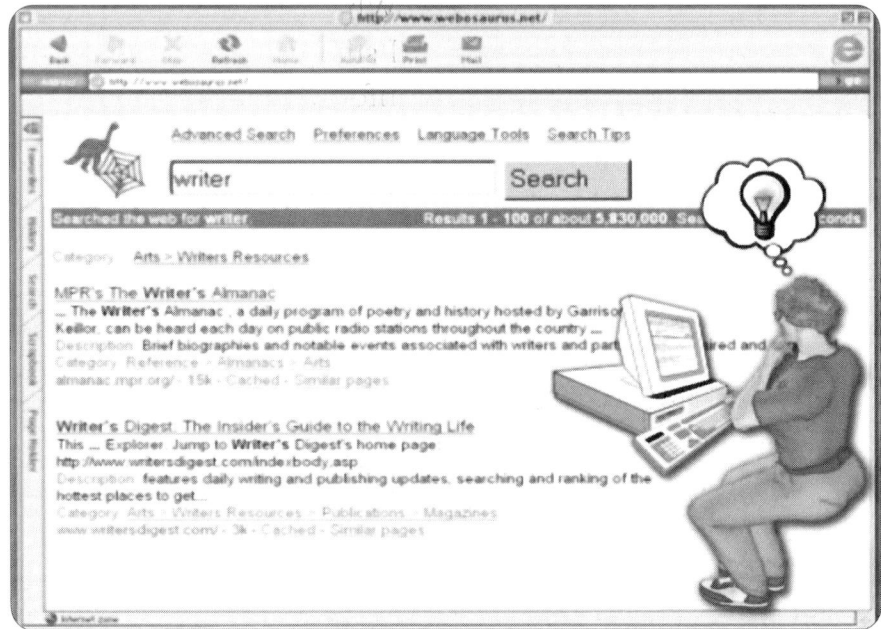

I felt a squish and soon found myself at Google.com.

"See anything there on which you want to comment?" Dr. F. asked.

"I suppose if I were going to comment on something, it'd be the amazing number of Web pages Google has in its database," I answered.

"Very observant, Beta! With almost two billion pages in that one search engine alone, you can imagine the importance of being able to narrow a search.

"Let me show you what I mean. Pick a general word or topic."

I thought for a minute. "How about 'journey'?" I asked.

"Good one," Dr. F. replied. "Enter that word into the Google search bar."

I did as I was instructed. "Whoa!" I said. "Google got over five million hits on that topic."

"It'd take you quite awhile to load and read through that many pages to find the 'journey' information you wanted, wouldn't it? Let's narrow that search. Now type in 'Journey to the Center of the Earth' and put quotation marks around that phrase."

Again I did as I was instructed.

"What do you see now, Beta?' Dr. F. asked.

"I still got over 11,000 hits," I said, "but it looks like the information I'd want is at the top of that list. I see a link to where I can go to find a copy of that book online."

I felt a squish and soon I was back in my limbo state, awaiting further instructions from Dr. F.

"I'd recommend that you spend some time reading about advanced searches," he said, "but I'm impressed with the great start you have on learning how to do efficient Web searches.

"In fact, I'm so impressed, I think it's time you had some fun."

Fun sounded good. Maybe not as good as eating, but Dr. F. did make me curious about what I'd be doing next.

Chapter 21

Online Audio, Video, and Other Stuff

I felt a squish and suddenly found myself in a virtual concert hall. I must say the acoustics were great. Unfortunately, I can't say the same for all of the music. The quadraphonic sounds coming at me were a blend of John Williams conducting the Boston Pops (interspersed with pop and show tunes) combined with one-liners from movies and cartoons, along with a disconcerting blend of what sounded like *The Greatest Muzac Hits from the Dentist's Office and Your Favorite Local Elevator*.

Suddenly, Dr. F's voice boomed at me through one of the speakers, interrupting a musical effort that sounded like it was about to rupture Celine Dion's diaphragm. "Now, Bert," he said, "there are many ways to listen to sound on the Internet. Most of these involve downloading a file first—like an mp3 or a wav or a midi type. Even when a sound file is embedded in a Web page, the entire file is downloaded into your computer before you listen to it. Audio files of any sort tend to be rather large. What does that mean, Bert?"

"I guess it means that they take a long time to download."

"Right. And what sort of consequences does that have?"

"What do you mean?"

"How does the length of the download affect a user?"

"Well, if it takes a long time, they may get bored and not wait for the file to finish."

"Exactly, and if the user doesn't look at the site, then the person who made it also has a problem! No one is

> **Streaming audio**
> This is an audio signal transmitted over a network. An audio file sent through **streaming audio** will begin playing before the entire file has been downloaded.

hanging around long enough to look at his Web page. Because of this sort of problem, a new technology was invented: **Streaming Audio**!

"You may recall what we discussed when we talked about browser plug-ins earlier. Streaming audio allows you to start listening to the sound before the whole file is on your computer. This means the user has to wait less time, and that he is entertained while the file comes. It makes sound a lot easier to use both for the Web page designer and for the person who views the pages.

"Here's how it works. When you click on a link for a streaming audio file, the browser starts the plug-in software associated with the file type. No browser can play streaming audio without a plug-in file at this point. You probably also recall that the plug-in program usually started is Real Player, QuickTime, or Windows Media Player. These programs will do the actual playing and interpreting of the file.

"Once the program has started, the file then begins to download to your computer. Streaming Audio files typically use the **User Datagram Protocol**, or **UDP**, to transfer instead of the normal TCP method. UDP is very similar to TCP, except that it doesn't resend missing packets. If the server kept re-sending packets, then the playback would be interrupted frequently, and it wouldn't sound very nice. Instead, the player skips over bad packets.

"The player doesn't start as soon as the file starts arriving, however. It waits until a certain amount of information is in the cache first. The cache, as I've mentioned,

> ## User Datagram Protocol (UDP)
>
> This protocol is often used to send streaming audio files. **UDP** is similar to TCP except that it does not resend missing data packets.

is a temporary storage place for files, and is sometimes
called a buffer. The amount of information that has to be
in the cache varies. The faster the packets are transferring,
the sooner the player will start playing the sound file. If
you have less bandwidth, then the player will wait until
more packets have arrived. The idea is not to let the playback catch up with the download. There should always be
packets waiting to be played, so that the playback doesn't
get interrupted in the middle of a feed.

"It doesn't always work perfectly; sometimes the
player will guess wrong
about how soon it can
start playing, and it
plays all the packets in
the cache. In this case,
the player will wait
until the cache has
rebuilt itself before it
continues playing.
Usually, you will have
some control, and if
you don't believe that
the file is downloading
as fast as it is playing
back, you can use the
plug-in controls to pause the playback, or return to an
earlier point in the file.

"Now, remember when we watched the *Star Wars*
trailer a while ago?"

"Yeah, that was cool!" I secretly hoped we would get
to watch it again. Maybe this time I'd get some buttery
popcorn and a Coke. I also began to wonder why we had
started talking about videos instead of streaming audio.

"Did you happen to notice the progress indicator
while we were watching it?"

Dr. F. didn't wait for an answer.

"On some video playback devices, like the one we
used to watch that video, the progress bar will change

color to indicate how much of the complete file has reached your computer. In other words, when you have a third of the file in cache, one third of the progress bar will change color. When you have the whole file, the entire progress bar will have changed. Some audio players do this, too. But my point, Beta, is that you can stream video as well as audio."

Oh, well, I guess that makes sense then. I hated how sometimes things didn't make sense until Dr. F. was done explaining. But I guess that's why they needed to be explained in the first place.

Dr. F. proceeded with his lecture. "Streaming video works very much like streaming audio does. It piles up in the cache, transferring using UDP, until you have enough to play. However, most video files use a **codec** as well.

"With most kinds of files, software knows how to decode and use it according to the file extension of the streaming file. However, with video files, they are often compressed using different algorithms or mathematical formulas. The same type of video file may be compressed in many different ways, but they're all compressed. Video files contain much more information than audio files, so they're also much bigger. The compression helps reduce that file size so that they download, or stream, faster.

"Each file is compressed using a special codec, which is short for coder/decoder, to tell it how to make the compression. The codec also tells the player how to uncompress the file. However, the type of compression provides a problem for the player. If the player doesn't have the same codec to refer to when it decodes the file, it will be unable to play it back. Fortunately, if the codec is not already on your computer, most video players will search on the Web for a codec that will work."

"So is streaming video what was used when I watched that concert in New York over the Internet?" I asked.

"Probably not, actually. What do you think would happen if a hundred thousand people tried to download

Codec

Codec is short for coder/decoder, and is a piece of software that compresses signals/data so the file is smaller and travels more quickly. The coded software also tells the receiving computer how to decompress the file.

the same file from the same server computer all at the same time?"

We had just talked about this. "Oh, I guess the server would be too busy to send it to everyone. So how do they do it?"

"For major events like this, the solution is usually to do a **multicast**."

"What's a multicast?"

"Be patient and I'll explain," Dr. F. said, as if I hadn't been patiently hanging around this place listening to him for quite a while already.

"Multicast is a way to send a signal to several locations at once. Normally, the Internet can only send one signal to one person. To accommodate the needs of multicast, the Multicast Backbone, or MBone exists. The MBone is a high-speed backbone that understands the special protocol of multicast broadcasts.

"A multicast starts when someone digitizes a sound or video performances and sends it over the Internet. It is only sent once, but it has a special header that lists all of the destinations it needs to reach. The multicast packets eventually reach a number of different hosts. These hosts will then split the signal and send it to everyone who is connected to the host. This way, all the bandwidth is used up locally, instead of across the Internet. This also reduces the stress that is placed on the hardware of any one server by quite a bit, because several different servers are sending the information. Does that make sense?"

"Yeah, it does." And actually, it sounded kind of neat, too. Now I knew what would be happening behind the scenes the next time I watched a rock concert online.

"Good. Then there's one more thing I want to talk about that concerns audio-video online. Let's talk for a minute about Web cameras. Web cameras, or Webcams, are commonly used to show what's currently going on in a location without actually showing a video, streaming or otherwise. Instead, the camera takes pictures and displays them. The subject of a Webcam can be just about any-

> **Multicast**
> **Multicast** is a method for sending a signal over the Internet to several locations at once. Data packets in a **multicast** are sent to several different hosts, who then send them on to everyone who is connected to that particular host.

thing. Some people use them to show what's going on in a lab. Others show the progress of a structure under construction, or just the scene outside. Some even just focus on the person who is sitting at the computer to which the Webcam is attached. Some Webcams are very popular because the audience is interested in the subject. Some are popular for no reason whatsoever. Either way, they're here to stay.

"The Webcam is programmed to take pictures at regular intervals. Some are set to take a picture every second, some only once a day. A more common interval is about every twenty to thirty seconds. The picture is then immediately transferred to the computer, which encodes the picture into a Web compatible format, usually a jpeg. Once the file is saved, it is uploaded to a server where the owner has a Web page, and the picture is made accessible by anyone who knows the URL. The entire process is automated and you can usually see what's going on in a room within a few seconds of it happening.

"Most Web pages that feature a Web camera also automate a refresh rate. That is to say, they automatically reload the image every half minute or so. This way, the person viewing the Web page doesn't have to keep reloading the page to see what's happened."

Now I know why Dr. F. has that Webcam on top of his computer back in the lab, I thought. *I doubt that many of them walk back and forth across the monitor on tiny little legs though.*

I doubt that many of them send innocent, hungry victims off on a JTCI either.

I heard some more of the now-familiar sounds I associated with Dr. F. writing on one of the blueboards. "Well, Bert," he said, "I think it's time we sent you into battle."

"To battle?" I asked, trying to keep the panic out of my voice. Maybe my earlier thoughts were prophetic, because it seemed I was about to become a "victim" in more ways than I realized.

Chapter 22

Unfriendly Fire

While I hung there in limbo, pondering my fate and worrying about exactly what kind of "battle" Dr. F. had been referring to earlier, he continued his discussion as if nothing had happened—or was about to happen.

"Bert, we've talked about a lot of wonderful things on the Internet," he said. "The technology is amazing and very helpful. The development of the Internet has been a great boon to many people and will continue to do so much for society.

"However, when I talked about Netiquette earlier, it was for a reason. Not everyone in the world is nice, and not everyone who accesses the Internet is there to help other people. There are people—usually called **hackers** (although true geeks resent that term)—who aren't so nice. You see, a hacker is actually someone who is interested in learning about systems with the intent of gaining more knowledge. Think of the malicious types as **crackers**; they're those who actually want to hurt other people and be as destructive as possible on the Internet. Some of them want to break into Web sites and steal information or rearrange the data; others have even more destructive activities in mind.

"There are a lot of options these people have to do their dirty work. Among other things, they can create **viruses**."

"So your computer can get sick?" I almost chuckled. It sounded awfully funny to me.

"This is very serious, B," Dr. F. said sternly.

"I'm sorry. I'll stop. Actually, I've heard a lot about computer viruses. What are they and how do they work?"

Dr. F. immediately cheered up. He seemed happy to have gotten a question from me, even if it was something he was about to explain anyway. "A virus is a malicious program that is written for no other reason than to cause damage to computers and even the Internet itself.

"Viruses are made in such a way that they look like part of another file. It used to be that they could only be

Hackers and Crackers

A **hacker** enters a computer system/ network and looks around without destroying files or causing damage. A **cracker** enters a computer system/network with the intent of stealing data or crashing the system.

Virus

A **virus** is a piece of software designed to infect a computer or its peripherals and cause damage of some sort to the computer or its files.

activated by infecting a program, but these days a virus can be activated by opening any file, such as a word processing document, for example. Another common way a virus can be distributed is through what is called an executable file. We won't go into all of the inner workings of such a file. Just suffice it to say that if anyone ever sends you an E-mail attachment that has an .exe file extension, never ever open or double-click on that file until you've first checked it with your anti-virus software!

"You see, a virus can only be activated by opening the file—at least so far, so there are some preventative measures you can take. If you know a file is infected by a virus, don't open it. That's a rule you should never break.

"Viruses can enter your computer any way that a file can enter your computer, like from a disk. There have even been cases when a virus has infected CDs that software manufacturers have made to install programs. But the most common way that viruses enter your system is by way of E-mail. We didn't talk much about attachments, but most E-mail clients allow you to send and receive files. The file you send or receive in this manner is called an **attachment** because it is connected with the message itself.

"Viruses either come as an attachment or they may come as an infection of a file that is sent to you. Some viruses are even programmed to send themselves to everyone you have listed in your E-mail address book. They're very sneaky.

Attachment

An **attachment** is any type of file that you attach to an E-mail which the receiver can open with similar software.

"When you activate a virus, either by double-clicking the virus or opening a file that is infected by a virus, the virus then goes to work. Usually the first thing the virus does is replicate, or copy, itself. As I mentioned before, it may do this by using your E-mail client; or, it may simply be programmed to start infecting other programs and files on your hard drive. Either way, pretty soon there can be dozens—even hundreds—of viruses all over your computer and all your friends' computers."

He paused and started writing on one of his blueboards, so I thought for a second and came up with a question. "I assume viruses take up space, but besides that, what harm can they do?"

"What harm?" Dr. F. sounded upset. "For starters, that's plenty of harm! Any virus, no matter how small, could potentially replicate itself enough to fill up all of your hard drive! Not to mention how it takes up CPU processes and memory to do its dirty work. But that's not the only thing that viruses do.

"Viruses can be programmed to do many things. At the very least, most viruses make the files they infect work oddly or not at all. More often, they are actually programmed to set up processes that will soak up all your system's resources, from processor power, to RAM, to storage space, or to start actually deleting other files. There is nothing nice about viruses.

"Viruses also have a cousin called a **Trojan horse**. Do you know what a Trojan horse is?"

> **Trojan Horse**
> A Trojan horse is a program that appears to perform a valid function but instead contains hidden instructions that damage a computer or network.

"Yeah, that's something the Greeks used way back in ancient times when they were fighting Troy. They made a giant horse and gave it as a peace offering to the Trojans. Only they had a bunch of soldiers hide inside the horse, and when the Trojans took it inside the city walls, the soldier came out, opened the city gates, and attacked the people." I'd paid attention in school when they had talked about this. I was pretty proud of myself for knowing it. I didn't know what this story had to do with computer viruses, but for the sake of my hungry stomach, I stopped asking questions that might slow us down so we could finish faster.

Dr. F. seemed a little bit surprised. "Why, yes, B," he said. "That's very good, but it doesn't have anything to do with the Internet, does it?"

Dr. F. can be too literal at times, if you ask me! He didn't ask me, though; he continued with his lecture.

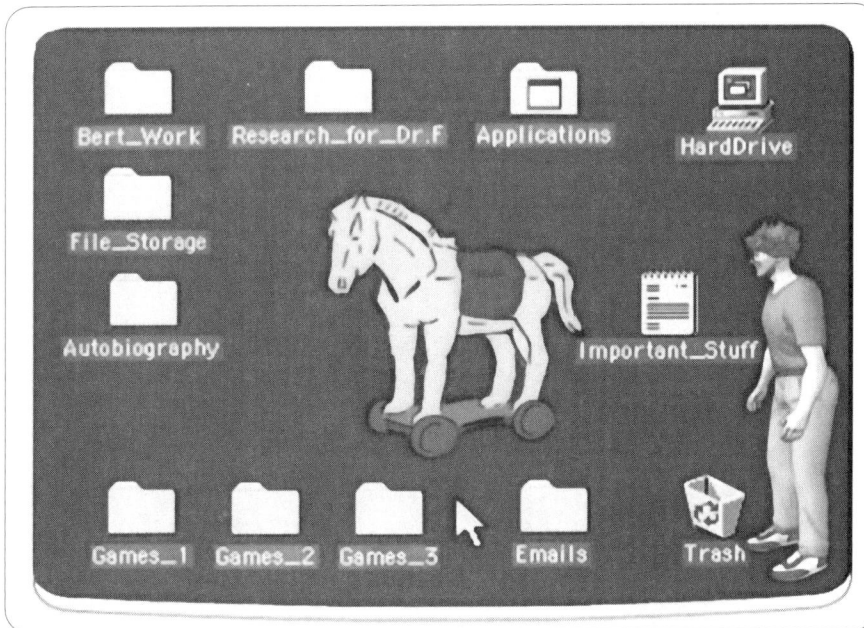

"A computer Trojan horse is named after the horse in that story; however, on the Internet, a Trojan horse is a program that is disguised as a helpful or a fun program. It may look like a game or a financial calculator. But when you try to run the program, it starts to do other things.

"A Trojan horse may delete or damage data on the infected system, or may break security measures. It may even introduce viruses to the system. Fortunately, Trojan horses are a little different than viruses in that Trojan horses don't replicate themselves. However, they can still do a lot of damage.

"A third variety of malicious code, called a **worm**, is also very similar to a virus. Worms try to replicate themselves and move from computer to computer on a network—remember that the Internet is really just a big network. There is a very important difference between worms and viruses though. Worms don't infect other programs; they work as a single program (like Trojan horses do) and stop computers from functioning.

"Because there are so many programs that can be so harmful, there are also programs designed to detect and stop viruses, Trojan horses, and worms. These are generally called anti-virus programs. You'll recall that earlier I mentioned using your anti-virus program to check files about which you're uncertain.

"The most popular such programs are made by McAfee, Norton, and Trend. The primary function of an anti-virus program is to detect viruses and the like and keep you from running them. These days, however, most anti-virus programs can do a lot more than that. Many will delete Trojan horses and worms and even clean a file infected of a virus. If the anti-virus program can't clean a file, it will isolate, or quarantine, the file so you don't accidentally open it and damage your system.

> **Worm**
> These virus-like programs move from computer to computer on a network, causing the computers to shut down or stop functioning correctly.

"It is a very good idea to use an anti-virus program at all times. These programs can do a scan of your entire computer, or they can be set to scan any file that opens or any file that gets added to your computer. Almost all anti-virus programs will have some sort of automatic protection mode that will scan all E-mail messages as they arrive, as well as any other files you download off the Internet. If you find that you have a virus and cannot remove it, you should look for help from a software manufacturer. Norton runs a help center that is free even to non-Norton Antivirus users at http://www.symantec.com, and McAfee does the same with their site at http://www.mcafee.com as does Trend at http://www.antivirus.com/.

"The last thing I want to talk to you about that concerns destructive activities found on the Internet has many names. **Denial of Service**, or **DoS**, attacks are often called ping attacks or ping flooding; they used to be called smurf attacks too. Whatever you call them, they use pings to keep people from accessing a network or to keep the network from doing anything at all."

"What's a ping?" I asked.

"A ping is a very simple, very small signal that is sent from one computer to a second in order to confirm that the second one is available on a network. As I said, the piece of information that asks for this response is small so it can travel very quickly.

"You'll recall that a cracker is someone who hacks into a computer with harmful intent in mind. In a DoS attack, a cracker will start sending pings to a specific computer, a router, or a host that will block the access of many other computers. When the attack actually starts, however, the cracker will disguise the ping. Pings have to have a return address so they know who to tell when they find the server for which they're looking. A cracker will forge this return address, usually to another computer on the network he is pinging. This way, the computer that receives the ping sends the response to the wrong computer, and this new computer sends a response to the first. Often, the ping is even disguised so the server will do this with many of the computers on the network. The computers keep sending information back and forth, and the cracker keeps sending more pings into the network. Eventually, one of two things, and sometimes both, will happen.

"First, the bandwidth the network has will be completely used for these pings and nothing else. This prevents anyone from doing anything on that network. No one on the network can talk to any other computer on the network or on the Internet. This also means that other people from outside the network can't access it. If the network hosts a Web site, that Web site will not be available.

"The second thing that can occur is the pings could potentially use so many hardware resources that the computers on the network start to crash. Usually the DoS attack is ended before this point, but it's a possibility.

"Stopping a ping attack can be difficult, but measures have put into place on most networks to prevent that eventuality. Preparing these measures can be very complicated and are best left to administrators who have a lot of experience and expertise on the matter."

Dr. F. paused and I heard those blueboard-associated scratching noises.

I decided to get brave and ask him the question I'd feared most. "How exactly does this mean I'll be going into battle?"

Dr. F. laughed. "You shouldn't always take what I say so literally," he said.

Chapter 23

Bert Returns

"Well, Bert," Dr. F. said, "now that you've learned you don't have to fight all of your battles yourself, especially when it comes to computer viruses and other destructive files, how about if we have you spend some time doing some fun stuff?"

"Fun sounds great to me," I said. "You know, I often find a lot of ways to have fun while I'm eating," I added as a hint.

"Then you're going to love what I have planned for you to do next," Dr. F. said.

"Great!" I had to show some enthusiasm. That was the best news I'd gotten in a long time. It sounded like I might get to eat soon.

Instead, Dr. F. started another lecture. "The Internet has revolutionized the way many people shop," he said. "You'll soon see how a lot of the things we've discussed already made—and continue to make— this revolution possible.

"For example, database technology makes it possible for a wide assortment of stores to exist online. By keeping track of products within a database, a shopping site can be set up to generate the HTML necessary to display information on a product in a company's inventory. This automatically generated Web page usually gives a description of the product, shows pictures of it, and has price information."

I felt a squish and soon found myself staring at the Webosaurus Books Web page.

"Online shopping sites also use their databases to keep track of customer information," Dr. F. said. "Some let you register at the site even before you've chosen anything to buy. Others wait until you have items in your shopping cart—something we'll discuss in a minute—

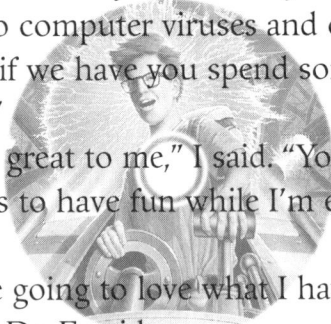

before they send you on to a secure area of the Web site to fill out a personal information form.

"Once you've completed the form on the secure site, your information is encrypted as it's sent to the company database, where it's unencrypted and stored. Likewise, that encrypted information is also sent to your credit card company's site where it's unencrypted so that the company can verify that it's a valid credit card.

"If you also verify your order at this time—in other words, you tell the Web site that you're indeed ready to make a purchase—that information is forwarded to the area of the site where you complete the transaction. Once there, you choose the shipping method you prefer and complete the 'shipped to' address information as well.

"Most often the Web site then sends you an E-mail confirming your order. The company's transaction server then forwards your order to its warehouse, where your order is completed and shipped.

"You get to do all of this without leaving the comfort of your computer chair," Dr. F. said. "A very convenient way to shop, wouldn't you say?"

"Is it a safe way to shop?" I asked.

"Absolutely," Dr. F. said. "In fact, it's far more secure than reading off your credit card numbers and other information to an operator over the phone."

Dr. F. paused for a minute, then asked, "What method of transportation are you enjoying now, Bert?"

I didn't actually think I was enjoying it. In fact, I felt a bit uncomfortable seated here with my legs sprawling out over the sides. There was also very little support for my back. "I appear to be sitting in a shopping cart," I answered.

"That's exactly what you're in, Bert," he said.

"There are a number of different ways that a Web site shopping cart can work, but basically what happens is that once you complete the online shopping site's registration form, that site sends a cookie back to your hard disk. That cookie is used to identify you to that Web site.

"Once you decide you're ready to buy something, you click on an item—or a designated link established for that purpose. This sends your request to the Web server, which in turn adds that information to your cookie, and then that item is added to your shopping cart. Once you've made all of your selections, much like you would at any local store, you proceed to the checkout area. Here you confirm the transaction, verify your credit card information, and select your preferred method of having that item or items shipped. In other words, you check out.

"Now that you know how online shopping works, I'm about to give you an experience most people only dream about, Bert."

Before I could question what he meant, I felt a squish and I literally felt like I was on a roll as the cart started to move.

"I'm going to give you momentary *carte blanche* with my credit cards," Dr. F. continued.

"*Carte blanche*?" I asked.

"That's a term that means you can use my credit cards without any restrictions."

"You mean you're going to let me charge stuff to them?" This was starting to sound like something I'd enjoy very much. I guess I'd been wrong earlier. I didn't care how I traveled as long as I'd get to spend somebody else's money while I did it!

"That's exactly what I mean," he said. "What better way to understand how an Internet shopping cart works than by traveling in one and using it?"

What better way indeed!, I thought. "Then let's get started," I said.

I felt a squish and I rolled around in the book section. I clicked on an entire assortment of titles I'd wanted to read and then proceeded to the area where I could find the CDs and DVDs I wanted.

I moved on to the electronics equipment. I clicked on the latest and greatest computer system I could find, and added some video editing equipment as well.

I was about to add the newest Weezer CD to my cart when Dr. F. interrupted me. "You do realize that there are food sites on which you can shop, too, don't you?" he asked.

Food!, I thought. I hurried and clicked on the CD. I then felt another squish and found myself on a site that offered any type of fruit I could imagine. *I'm really enjoying this now!*

My mouth watered as the cart rolled on to another site offering gourmet baskets and then to one with chocolates and other candy. I found a popcorn site and some with steaks and lobsters, too. For good measure, I even clicked on some of the types of tea that Dr. F. was so fond of.

"You do know that you can also order pizza online, don't you?" Dr. F. asked.

"Pizza!" I shouted. "Squish me there!"

"Squish?" Dr. F. asked, then chuckled. "Good description."

I felt the cart zoom to another Web site where I started clicking on toppings at random. If I continued to have this "carte blanche" stuff Dr. F. had promised, this was going to be the biggest, most deluxe pizza I'd ever seen. Or—with any luck—eaten!

"I think that pizza's fancy enough now," Dr. F. said. "Besides, there's one more thing I want you to see."

I guess all good things must come to an end eventually, I thought.

"Online auctions are another popular Internet phenomena.

"Some online auctions install a cookie on your computer once you register as a bidder or a seller; others utilize a username and password system.

"Auctions are set up so that a program or script accepts bids on each item for sale. Bids are accepted until

a predetermined time at which the auction is closed, or is over. At that time, the auction database checks to see which bidder placed the highest bid. That bidder wins the auction. Procedures are then in place for the winning bidder and the seller to contact one another to complete the transaction, which means the bidder finds out how he or she is to pay the seller and the seller then ships the auction item to the winning bidder once that payment is received.

"It's pretty straight-forward and simple. And, it can be a lot of fun. Here, let me show you!

"Most auctions have a search feature for the site. This lets you search by keyword for items that you're interested in bidding on. For example, type in 'comics' in the search box."

"Do I still have that 'carte blanche' stuff?" I asked once I saw all the auction choices available to me.

"For a bit longer, you do," he said. "In fact, if you'll excuse me a minute, I'm going to see what I can find on 'blue roses' while you look at the comics."

I clicked and bid as fast as I could. There were so many auctions and I felt sure I had little time. That proved to be too true. I soon felt a squish as the shopping cart sped ahead, only to come to an abrupt halt, which hurled me out of the cart and into cyberspace. I felt myself turning somersaults, which were soon interrupted by another squish, which triggered my JTCI dismount. Then imagine my surprise when I found myself

standing in front of the computer back in Dr. F.'s lab—the one I'd started my JTCI from in the first place.

I nailed my landing, by the way! Olympics gymnastic team, here I come!

"Welcome home, Bert," Dr. F. said.

I tried to answer, but I could only stare. I saw a lot more writing on the blueboards in Dr. F.'s lab. But I also saw many more things that held my attention.

Almost every countertop and available surface held a package of some sort. Over in one corner were my comic books I'd gotten at auction, stacked neatly in their plastic holders. Beside those was a tea set with a blue rose design on it.

I saw my video editing equipment!

I saw boxes of apples and peaches and oranges and lots of other fruit. Lobsters inched their way around in a tank set in another corner of the lab. Beside the tank were tins holding popcorn and caramel corn.

I saw containers of every kind of roasted nut you can imagine. There were all sorts of baskets that I knew my mom would love and they held fancy-looking packages of cheese and crackers.

It took all of my resolve to keep myself from drooling.

Then I noticed an aroma that had the same affect on me that Pavlov's bell surely had on those dogs. Pizza!

"Don't you want a slice?" Dr. F. asked. I noticed he already had a plate in front of him and was proceeding to fill it up. I figured I'd better get over to that table fast if I was going to get any for myself!

"Do you even have to ask?" I pulled up a chair and started filling up my own plate—after I'd taken a bite out of the first slice I picked up, of course.

"You notice anything else?" Dr. F. asked.

"Wow!" I said as I looked at the soft drink in front of me. "You're letting me drink some of what you call that 'nasty fizzy stuff.'"

"I think you've earned it, Bert," he said. "But it's back to herbal tea and fruit juice after this."

I had my mouth too full to answer.

"You've learned a lot on your Journey to the Center of the Internet, Bert," he said. "During your journey, we discussed how the technology is amazing and very helpful. The possibilities are endless. The Internet not only provides a great wealth of information for anyone doing research, but it's also opened up a way for people to interact socially with others throughout the world—something especially of value to those with limited mobility because of disabling conditions. Those are just a few of the reasons why the development of the Internet has been a great boon to many people and will continue to do so much for society. I know I'm certainly anxious to see what the future has in store."

Of course I agreed completely with what Dr. F. had just said, but I only nodded. I had other important considerations at the moment. My mouth was full and my tummy soon would be.

What a perfect ending to a wonderful journey, I thought.

Glossary

401 error   You will discover this error message while surfing the Web. It indicates this Web site/page has not authorized your entry.

403 error   Similar to a 401 error, a 403 error message means the site/page has forbidden you access.

404 error   You will discover this error message while surfing the Web. It indicates it cannot locate the Web site/page you want. If this happens, either the spelling of the site/page is incorrect or the site/page has disappeared.

Accelerated Graphics Port (AGP)   An AGP is a high-speed port between a display device and memory. The AGP works at twice the speed of a PCI bus.

Acrobat Reader (Acroread)   A software package from Adobe Systems, Inc., which reads PDF files (files created by Adobe software products).

Address bus   The address bus is an electronic pathway in the computer that receives/sends the location of information.

Adobe Systems, Inc.   Founded in 1982, Adobe helped graphic and visual designers by making desktop publishing easier and making more fonts available.

Advanced Research Projects Agency (ARPA)   The ARPA was a department within the Department of Defense and helped begin development of the Internet in 1969. *See also* Defense Advanced Research Projects Agency.

Advanced Research Projects Agency Network (ARPANET or ARPANet)   ARPA personnel and others developed ARPANET, which they subsequently divided into MILNET (the network for military use) and ARPANET. ARPA, Honeywell, and others launched ARPANET in 1969 by connecting four sites: University of California in Los Angeles (UCLA); University of California in Santa Barbara (UCSB); Stanford Research Institute (SRI); and University of Utah. By 1983, they had connected 300 computers. ARPANET led the way to the Internet.

America Online (AOL)   Now merged with the communications conglomerate, Time Warner, AOL is the world's largest information service for online users. AOL offers Internet access, e-mail, chat rooms, databases, and other services.

American Standard Code for Information Interchange (ASCII)   Created in 1968, this code increases the compatibility and communication between products made by different companies. ASCII uses 96 uppercase and lowercase letters and 32 non-displayed control characters.

Anti-virus program   This program defends your computer against incoming viruses sent purposely or by accident.

Archie (ARCHIvE)   This utility searches for file names on the Internet via nearly three dozen Archie servers.

Asymmetrical Digital Subscriber Line (ADSL)   This technology uses twisted copper wire pairs to support broadband transmission. ADSL does not transmit information as quickly as Symmetric DSL but can transmit farther distances. However, ADSL can receive information more quickly than Symmetric ADSL if you are using the Very-high-bit-rate DSL (VDSL) variety. Also called Asymmetric Digital Subscriber Loop.

At (@) sign   We use this symbol to separate the username from the ISP in an e-mail address. Suppose Joe Johnson is a photographer and uses Southwestern Bell (SWBell) as his ISP. If he wants a username of Photographer, his e-mail address would be photographer@swbell.net.

Attachment   This is a file you attach to an e-mail that the receiver can open with similar software.

Backbone   A backbone is considered to be the network that handles most of the electronic/information traffic either across a large area or within a company. *See also* Backbone Network Service; Very high-speed Backbone Network Service.

Backbone Network Service (BNS)   A BNS is a fast set of wires that serves as the main connection to the computers that want to interact with the Internet or one another.

Bandwidth   Bandwidth measures the capacity of an electronic medium (wire, cable, network, etc.) to transmit information. We measure bandwidth three ways: bits per second, bytes per second, and Hertz (cycles per second). The greater the bandwidth, the more quickly information travels.

Baseband   Baseband is a process whereby you send an electronic signal without changing its modulation. Baseband only works for transmissions of short distances. Unlike broadband, baseband only allows one transmission at a time since it consumes the full bandwidth of the transmission line.

Basic Input/Output System (BIOS)   BIOS is the software coded into computer chips for various purposes. The BIOS on the motherboard of Windows-based computers is the program used to boot (or start) and control the computer.

Basic Rate Interface (BRI)   BRI is two 64-Kbps B channels, used for data or voice, and one 16-Kbps D channel, used by the carrier for control and signaling. Each B channel can make a second connection, or you can use the channels together.

Bastion host   A host computer in a network that is secured and fortified against illegal entry and attack.

Baud   A measurement of how often the frequency or voltage changes (the number of transitions) within a line. This measurement is identical to bits per second at slower transmission speeds.

Bearer channel (B channel)   This communications channel can send/receive information at 64 Kbps when using an ISDN.

Bit   A bit is the smallest amount of computer storage needed. Each bit is either a 0 (zero) or a 1 (one). We deal with binary options all the time: yes and no; red light or green light; up and down, etc. The word bit stands for BInary digiT.

Bits Per Second (BPS)   The speed at which we can transmit information (measured in bits), dependent on the transmission line, equipment used, etc. One bps only equals one baud at slower transmission speeds.

Blue Screen of Death (BSD; BSoD)   A Windows error that locks up (or freezes) your computer and shows an error message in white type on a blue screen. Usually, your only option is to reboot (or restart) the computer by turning it off and then on.

Bookmark   A program in Netscape Navigator that allows you to mark a Web site or page to find more easily the next time you want to visit it. We call this function a Favorite in Internet Explorer.

Broadband   Baseband is a process whereby you send an electronic signal over long distances. Unlike baseband, broadband allows multiple transmissions at a time (for example, phone, computer, etc.) since it does not use the full bandwidth of the transmission line.

Browser   This is a software program that allows you to examine a file or files of data. *See also* World Wide Web browser.

Bulletin Board System (BBS)   Like a bulletin board on the wall in which everyone can communicate with others, this electronic system performs the same function over the computer and network. Various Special Interest Groups (SIGs) often have their own BBS on which their members and others can leave messages, comments, and thoughts for all to read.

Bus   A bus is the pathway inside the computer within which information travels. A bus is usually 16 bits wide (like a 16-lane highway) or 32 bits wide. *See also* Address bus; Data bus; Expansion bus; Internal bus; Universal Serial Bus.

Byte   A byte is eight bits of memory. Each letter, space, punctuation, or character you type on the computer is one byte in memory. The previous sentence used 89 bytes or 8 x 89 bits (712 bits) of memory. Images, graphics, etc., use much more memory. *See also* KiloBytes; GigaBytes; MegaBytes.

Cache   A temporary storage area on the hard drive for frequently used information. Web browsers, the computer's operating system, and the system memory use a cache. The more cache you have, the more quickly the computer can process information. This word is pronounced cash. Also called a buffer.

Central Processing Unit (CPU)   This chip (or processor) controls the operations of the computer. Current CPUs also contain an Arithmetic Logic Unit (ALU). In one analogy, the CPU is a traffic cop controlling the flow of the cars (data) at an intersection (inside the computer). You will find the CPU inside the computer on the motherboard.

Chat room   This is a particular computer/network area where people can write to each other and get immediate responses. In essence, they are chatting to one another using the computer, but they do not hear each other's voices. Also called a chat channel.

Checksum   To ensure we can transmit data accurately, we add a value with each block of data. When we receive the data, the computer matches its calculated checksum against the checksum sent with the data. If the values match, no error has occurred.

Client   In a network, the client is the computer/workstation that connects to the network to request files, information or services. The client connects to the server, which is the computer(s) that controls the network.

Clipboard   An application that comes with various versions of Microsoft Windows. The clipboard holds information temporarily and allows you to cut, copy, and paste information between applications. All data held in the clipboard disappear after you have turned off the computer's power or are replaced after you have saved something else to the clipboard.

Clock (and clock speed)   This timing device inside the microprocessor sends pulses to the CPU to help keep the data flow synchronized. For instance, inside a 900 MegaHertz (MHz) computer, the clock emits 900 million pulses (or cycles) per second to the Central Processing Unit (CPU). The more quickly the clock can send pulses to the CPU, the more quickly the CPU can process data at the right time.

Cluster   When a drive is formatted, the spaces or blocks on the drive that contain storage space for files and applications are the clusters. More technically, a cluster (or allocation unit) is the smallest possible amount of storage the operating system can handle. For newer computers, a cluster is 4 KiloBytes (KB).

Coder/Decoder (Codec)   This software compresses signals/data so the file is smaller and travels more quickly. The coded software also tells the receiving computer how to decompress the file.

Compact Disc (CD)   This disc contains digital information in various formats, for instance, CD-ROM, CD-R, etc. The CD you use holds about 75 minutes of music and we began using them in 1982.

Compact Disc Read Only Memory (CD-ROM)   A compact disk read-only optical storage technology. CD-ROM disks are often used for encyclopedias and software libraries. A CD-ROM can hold text, video imagery, audio, and graphics.

Cookies   Cookies are Web site-created text files. They identify you as a specific visitor to a Web site and companies often use them for shopping cart and personal home page information.

Cracker   A malicious hacker who breaks into systems/networks and causes damage.

Crawler   A search engine often sends out a program to index the contents of sites and update its knowledge of that site. We call this program a crawler or spider.

Data   Any type of information in any format. Data can be numbers, dates, names, images, etc., or all of these.

Data bus   The data bus is an electronic pathway in the computer that receives/sends the information back and forth.

Dedicated line   This is a transmission line used for one purpose. Hence, it is dedicated to doing that one job.

Defense Advanced Research Projects Agency (DARPA) This research branch of the Department of Defense helped fund the creation of the Internet. The Department of Defense had originally named DARPA the Advanced Research Projects Agency (ARPA).

Denial of Service (DoS) This attack floods a network with so many messages/requests that the network can no longer handle the volume and shuts down. Sometimes, we call a DoS attack a Ping attack.

Dial-up access This is how you connect to another computer/network, for instance, the Internet, with a modem-equipped computer.

Digital Subscriber Line (DSL) DSL is a technology that brings high-speed connections to homes and small businesses using standard phone lines. DSL allows you to make a phone call and connect the computer to the Web on the same phone line at the same time. Also called Digital Subscriber Loop. *See also* Asymmetrical Digital Subscriber Line.

Digital Versatile Disk (DVD) A high-capacity optical disk used to store everything from large computer applications to full-length movies. Though similar in physical size and appearance to a CD-ROM, a DVD is technologically more advanced. Originally called digital video disk.

Disk Operating System (DOS) A Microsoft operating system, or control program, for personal computers, especially earlier versions of Microsoft. A modified version of DOS was included with Windows 95 and Windows 98.

Domain name A domain name is the name/address of each Web site. The domain name farthest to the right of an Internet address is the most general or Top Level Domain. So, .com specifies a company and syngress specifies the name of the Web site for the company, Syngress. Together it becomes the syngress.com address.

Domain Name System (DNS) This software keeps a domain name database (collection of data) to make it easier for us to find a specific URL instead of using the IP address' numbering system.

Driver A software program that allows the hardware peripherals to talk to the computer and vice versa. This program tells the peripheral (mouse, keyboard, etc.) what your instructions mean (for instance, when typing the letter A or moving the mouse and clicking). Also called a device driver.

Dumb Terminal (DT) This monitor (display capabilities only) has no ability to process information. It merely displays the information. An example of a DT could be an Automated Teller Machine (ATM), which can do nothing unless attached to its network.

Dynamic HyperText Markup Language (DHTML) This HTML process allows users to customize their own Web pages. In contrast, you cannot change a Static HTML page.

Dynamic IP address We assign dynamic IP addresses as floating addresses. For example, individual home computer users do not need a permanent, or static, address. Therefore, their ISP can give them a new one each time they log onto the Internet. *See also* IP address; Static IP address.

Dynamic Random Access Memory (DRAM)   DRAM is one type of RAM chip. Since it contains a capacitor, you must refresh the DRAM's memory every 30 nanoseconds (30 ns), which is 30 billionths (0.000000003) of a second. In a computer, this can seem like an eternity and is three times slower than a Static Random Access Memory (SRAM) chip. Though a DRAM requires less power and space than the SRAM chip, it is slower than the SRAM. *See also* Static Random Access Memory.

Electronic mail (E-mail)   This is the message that you send to another person or organization via the Internet. You can attach files of text, pictures, etc., when you send the message. You can also simultaneously send the message to multiple parties.

Electronic mail (E-mail) address   The electronic address of the user comprises the user's name (username), the at (@) sign, and the ISP. Suppose Joe Johnson is a photographer and uses Southwestern Bell (SWBell) as his ISP. If he wants a username of Photographer, his e-mail address would be photographer@swbell.net.

Electronic mail (E-mail) client   A program you can use to read and send e-mail.

Encryption   A system of rules for changing computer data into unintelligible and/or unreadable symbols so no one else can decipher them unless they have the password.

Enhanced Integrated Drive Electronics (EIDE)   A standard built on the original Integrated Drive Electronics (IDE) standard. EIDE is an improved hardware interface (between the drives and a computer). It increases the allowed hard disk size from 504 MegaBytes (MB) to 8 GigaBytes (GB), more than doubles the data transfer, and doubles the number of drives (to four) a computer can use.

Event handler   An event handler is a program or command that instructs the browser how to begin or initiate a command from the user.

Expansion bus   You can find this input/output bus on the computer's motherboard. The bus, with its multiple slots, can connect many peripheral devices to the computer. ISA and PCI buses are expansion buses.

External screening router   This router prevents unwanted information from getting into a network, for instance, spam, pornographic material, etc. Also called an access router.

Favorite   A program in Internet Explorer that allows you to mark a Web site or page to find more easily the next time you want to visit it. We call this function a Bookmark in Netscape Navigator.

Fiber-optic cable   Cable used for fiber optic transmissions. Fiber optic transmissions lose less signal strength than copper cable over longer distances.

File compression   This compression technique reduces the size of the file without appreciable loss of the information or quality of image. Various compression techniques exist such JPEG, GIF, BMP, etc.

File Transfer Protocol (FTP)   A protocol (set of rules) for electronically transmitting information without losing any of it over the Internet and other networks. FTP establishes a connection between two computers that also allows you to send files to the server you are connected to.

Firewall   A firewall is a computer system or group of systems that polices traffic between an organization's internal network and its external network. It regulates who from the outside may enter system and what network services they may access.

Flaming   When you flame on the Internet or in a forum of some sort, you are ranting, raving, and complaining in an impolite way. Flaming is the use of language in a message that is meant to be provocative.

Flooding   This refers to when you send an overly long message (or series of messages) to a channel or message board.

Floppy disk   Unlike a hard disk, which is inside the computer, a floppy disk is a removable storage medium (called a diskette). Older formats of floppy disks were 5.25 inches and 8 inches wide. The only one available now is 3.5 inches wide and holds about 1.44 MegaBytes (MB) of information.

Frequently Asked Question (FAQ)   These postings help users solve problems and establish rules for using particular interactive forums.

Gateway   A point on a transmission line at which a computer converts one protocol to another for different types of networks and/or applications.

GigaBytes (GB)   We use GB to measure the amount of memory in the computer's hard drive. For instance, most current hard drives can hold between 20 GB and 80 GB with larger ones available. A 60 GB hard drive can hold approximately 1 billion words or 43,000 floppy disks of information. Note: We normally do not capitalize the B in Gigabytes when spelling the word out. We capitalized it here so you could see where the B comes from in the acronym.

GigaHertz (GHz)   We use GHz to measure the speed of the clock and/or CPU in billions of pulses (or cycles) per second. For instance, a 1.7 GHz computer has a clock inside it, which sends 1.7 billion pulses per second to the CPU. For comparison, most people can hear from 20 Hertz to 20,000 Hertz (or 20 KHz).

Gopher   This Internet program searches for file names, documents, and resources in a hierarchical form via over 6,500 Gopher servers.

Graphical User Interface (GUI)   An overall method that makes interacting with the computer easier and more consistent. GUI can involve pull-down menus, dialog boxes, on-screen graphics, and a variety of icons.

Graphics card   A graphics card, also called a display adapter, converts digital image signals into usable signals so you can see images and graphics on your monitor.

Graphics Interchange Format (GIF)   We use this high-resolution graphics compression technique for bit-mapped graphics files.

Hacker   A hacker enters a computer system/network and looks around without destroying files and/or computers. He or she merely wants to prove he/she could break in.

Hard disk   The hard disk is the metal platter(s) inside the hard drive on which the information is stored, written, and rewritten. The more disks inside the hard drive, the greater the memory.

Hard drive   A hard drive is a storage device (usually inside the computer) that holds information, programs, etc., for the computer and you to use. Hard drives are rated by how much memory they can hold, measured in bytes, for instance, megabytes, gigabytes, or terabytes. Part of this measurement depends on how many hard disks are inside the hard drive.

Head end   This is often the beginning point of the transmission just before reaching you. Two examples are the computer that runs the network or the satellite dish that receives the transmission that goes to your television.

Header   A header is the first part of a message with data telling the recipient the type of message coming, the level of priority, etc.

Home page   A Web page used/created by an individual or organization to provide visitors with an introduction and basic information. On this home page, the Web designer may provide links to other pages with more specific information.

Hop   A hop is the link between the nodes of each network. Each node contains the appropriate software/technology to process the information to hop to the next node in the network.

Host   This computer can perform many functions or wear many hats. A host can be a depository for information (accessed by other computers), a server (used by many clients), a mainframe, etc.

Hub   A device that connects all necessary computers and communications devices together as the hub of your bicycle connects all the spokes of the wheel. Some hubs are passive in that they allow information to pass without altering it. Active hubs increase the strength of the data signal, important for transmissions covering many thousands of miles.

Hyperlink   This is a clickable icon, graphic, or word in a Web site/page/document which takes you to another Web site/page/document. If the hyperlink is a word, you will see it underlined.

HyperText Markup Language (HTML)   HTML is a programming language used to design a Web site. This language helps a programmer/designer mark the site and hyperlinks in it. *See also* Dynamic HyperText Markup Language.

Hypertext REFerence (HREF)   In this line of Web design code, you insert the hypertext address of the HTML document. So, after the equals sign in HREF=, you add the address.

HyperText Transfer Protocol (HTTP)   HTTP is a set of standards or protocols. As parties exchange information on the World Wide Web, HTTP ensures the information arrives to the receiver in the same condition it left the sender.

I Seek You (ICQ)   You use this program for chat room conferencing. It can alert you to arriving e-mail, files transferred into your computer, etc.

Industry Standard Architecture (ISA)   An ISA is an expansion bus that allows cards for peripherals, for instance, video cards. Most personal computers use a combination of ISA buses and PCI buses.

Input queue   A queue that holds the packets of information as they enter the receiving point of a router.

Input/Output (I/O)   A way of looking at information. When a peripheral sends information to a computer (specifically, the CPU), the information leaving the peripheral is output but the same information entering the computer is input. An analogy would be if people leave their country to come to America. They would be emigrating from their country but immigrating to America.

Instant Messaging (IM)   A method of talking to one another (similar to IRC) via the computer. Unlike IRC, IM cannot connect to all servers because IM systems put out by different companies do not work with one another.

Institute of Electrical and Electronics Engineers (IEEE)   Not-for-profit U.S. engineering organization that develops, defines, and reviews standards within the electronics and computer science industries.

Integrated Device Electronics (IDE)   An IDE is a hard drive interface. Because of its simple instruction set and short route between the controller the drive, IDEs are a quick and easy type of drive to use. The Enhanced IDE (EIDE) has replaced the IDE because it can handle larger hard drives.

Integrated Services Digital Network (ISDN)   ISDN allows you to make phone calls, connect the computer to the Internet, and move information over the Web more quickly than Digital Subscriber Line (DSL). ISDN is more expensive than DSL and was expected to replace the Plain Old Telephone System (POTS).

Internal bus   Like an external bus, an internal bus is a pathway for information to navigate. Unlike the external bus (between the CPU and peripheral devices), the internal bus is a pathway between the CPU and memory within the computer.

Internal router   This is a router that works inside a company's or organization's internal network and works in conjunction with its firewall.

Internal screening router   This router prevents certain information (packets of data) from leaving the proscribed network and into the Internet, etc. So, if the company does not want you surfing the Web for inappropriate material, it will use this router to stop you from doing so. Also called a choke router.

Internet   The Internet is a global network, a connection of networks throughout the world. The Internet is one part of the World Wide Web; it is not the same thing. Internet stands for *Inter*connected *Net*work.

Internet Architecture Board (IAB)   This volunteer organization was initially called the Internet Activities Board in 1983. Its major purpose is to support and resolve conflicts for the IETF.

Internet Corporation of Assigned Names and Numbers (ICANN)   Created in 1998 by Joe Postel, ICANN is a non-profit organization which administers the Internet name and address system/process.

Internet Engineering Task Force (IETF)   This volunteer organization identifies problems in the Internet network. Since 1986, it has proposed many technical solutions for the Internet making it more efficient and easier to use.

Internet Message Access Protocol (IMAP)   More sophisticated than Post Office Protocol, version 3, IMAP is able to hold any messages until the users come and get them by logging into their server. Also called Internet Messaging Access Protocol.

Internet Network Information Center (InterNIC)   This organization is responsible for registering the domain names. If you go to the InterNIC Web site, you can usually determine who owns a particular domain name. If no one owns the name yet, you can purchase it.

Internet Protocol (IP)   One of the many protocols designed to transmit information across networks. *See also* Serial Line Internet Protocol; Transmission Control Protocol/Internet Protocol.

Internet Protocol (IP) address   This is the Internet address for a Web site or page. This address is a series of four numbers (from 0 to 255) separated by three periods. Since most people have trouble remembering numbers, we changed the number sequence to a written address, such as www.syngress.com, which is also known as the URL. An analogy would be dialing your friend by using his or her name instead of phone number. *See also* Dynamic IP address; Static IP address.

Internet Registry   A stored and maintained registry (compilation of data) of domain names and their information. An Internet Registry stores the domain's information under a top-level domain heading along with the IP address for each domain.

Internet Relay Chat (IRC)   An IRC is a particular channel (chat group) on the Internet. Everyone who belongs to that channel can read the messages you leave there. You can "chat" with someone or many people simultaneously, much as in a conference call.

Internet Service Provider (ISP)   The ISP is the company that connects you and your computer to the Internet. This company provides service to the Internet.

Internet Society (ISOC)   This international organization's purpose is to support the Internet by enhancing its functions and extending its capabilities. Since 1992, it has worked alongside the IETF and other associated groups.

Java   We use Java, a programming language, to create Java applets (small programs used to add various aids, banners, and information).

JavaScript   This is a script language with short programming commands that, among other functions, gives buttons a pressed appearance when you roll over them with a cursor. These commands can also detect a person's browser type, computer platform, and all kinds of other information.

Joint Photographic Experts Group (JPG)   A JPG (or JPEG) is a graphics standard defining how a computer can compress a photograph. JPGs files can contain millions of colors, and as such are commonly used for photographs.

Keyboard   A keyboard is the typewriter part of the computer. Here, you type your letters and numbers, click on various function keys (F1 through F12), and employ other useful functions, such as Page Up/Down and Delete.

Kilobits per second (Kbps)   A transfer rate of information per second. Each kilobit equals 1,024 bits. Do not confuse Kbps with KiloBytes Per Second (KBPS).

KiloBytes (KB)   We use KB to measure the amount of memory in the computer's floppy drive or to measure the size of a file. Note: We normally do not capitalize the B in Kilobytes when spelling the word out. We capitalized it here so you could see where the B comes from in the acronym.

KiloBytes Per Second (KBPS)   A transfer rate of information per second. Each KBPS equals 1,024 Bytes (8,192 bits or 8 Kilobits) per second.

Local Area Network (LAN)   A LAN is a network of computers and communication devices that connect multiple users together. The difference between a LAN and a Wide Area Network (WAN) is the distance between the users. Users in a LAN are closer together than in a WAN.

Login name   We use a login name to identify ourselves when entering a system. A login (or logon) name can be the same as a username depending on the system.

Lossless compression   This compression technique compresses a file by almost one-third without damage or data loss to the file.

Lossy compression   This compression technique greatly compresses a file by discarding some of the data. This lost information does not appreciably affect the quality of the file/image.

Megabits per second (Mbps)   A transfer rate of information per second. Each Mbps equals 1,048,576 bits or 1 Mb. Do not confuse Mbps with MBPS (MegaBytes Per Second), which is eight times larger than Mbps.

MegaBytes (MB)   We use MB to measure the amount of memory in the computer's floppy drive or to measure the size of a file. For instance, a floppy disk is 1.44 MB, which is 1,440,000 characters, spaces, etc., of information or approximately 800 pages of text. Note: We normally do not capitalize the B in Megabytes when spelling the word out. We capitalized it here so you could see where the B comes from in the acronym.

MegaBytes Per Second (MBPS)   A transfer rate of information per second. 1,048,576 bytes or 1 MB (8,388,608 bits or 8 Mb).

MegaHertz (MHz)   We use MHz to measure the clock and/or the CPU in millions of pulses (or cycles) per second. For instance, a 900 MHz computer has a clock inside it, which sends 900 million pulses per second to the CPU. For comparison, most people can hear from 20 Hertz to 20,000 Hertz (or 20 KHz).

Memory   Inside a computer, the memory is total of all the (Random Access Memory) RAM chips. The more memory you have, the more programs you can use simultaneously. Memory can also be permanent (Read Only Memory or ROM).

Metasearch engine   A server/software that searches other search engines. These metasearch engines examine other search engines (on the World Wide Web) instead of one at a time.

Metasearch program   This program, usually a metasearch engine, searches other programs, such as the abilities of a metasearch engine, for purposes of research, information gathering, etc.

Microchip   This is nothing more than a chip on a microscopic scale. One example of a microchip is a CPU.

Microprocessor   A microprocessor is a combination of a Central Processing Unit (CPU), its power supply, memory, and an internal clock.

Military Network (MILNET)   ARPA personnel and others developed ARPANET in 1969. They subsequently divided this network into MILNET (the network for military use) and ARPANET in 1984 for security reasons. *See also* Advanced Research Projects Agency Network.

Millions of Instructions Per Second (MIPS)   We use MIPS as another to measure the speed of a computer (in addition to MegaHertz and GigaHertz). An analogy might be measuring how quickly you can read a page and process its information.

Moderator   A person/system that reviews and approves/disapproves all messages on a BBS is the moderator.

MODulator/Demodulator (modem)   This is a shortened form for MODulator/DEmodulator. This devices takes digital signals, converts them to analog signals (for phone line use), and reconverts them to digital signals once it reaches another computer.

Monitor   This hardware device is the screen on which you see text and images. Most monitors are a Super Video Graphics Array (SVGA) format able to display many colors with a fine resolution.

Motherboard   Part of every computer system, the motherboard is the largest printed circuit board in your computer. It usually contains the central processing unit (CPU) chip, the controller circuitry, the bus, and sockets for additional boards (called daughtercards). The motherboard is also called a logic board.

Mouse (Mice, pl.)   A mouse is a peripheral (input device) that allows you to control the cursor's location, click on various icons and hyperlinks, and control various commands, all without using the keyboard.

Multicast Backbone (MBone)   This system delivers real-time audio/video signals on the Internet. It allows for sending multiple transmissions while using few network resources.

Multilink Point-to-Point Protocol (MP)   MP allows multiple physical links to appear as a single local link over which data can be sent and received at a higher throughput than if going over a single physical link.

Multitasking   The computer's ability to run two or more programs simultaneously. This ability depends on the computer's operating system, amount of memory, CPU capability, etc.

Name server   A network uses many types of servers. One such server, a name server, provides names or directories.

National Science Foundation (NSF)   Established in 1950, this independent agency now has responsibility for investing over 3 billion dollars in over 19,000 research and education projects along with promoting science and engineering projects throughout the United States.

Netiquette   This is an agreed-upon set of rules of etiquette when posting messages or sending e-mail to anyone.

Netscape Navigator   A Web browser created by Netscape (now owned by AOL/TimeWarner).

Network   A system of connections that links users, computers, and organizations together. Think of all the homes or apartments in your town/city connected to the electric company; that is a type of network. A company may have hundreds or thousands of computers linked together in one vast network. The World Wide Web is another type of network. *See also* Local Area Network; Wide Area Network.

Network Access Point (NAP)   This is a junction/intersection where ISPs cross paths like the major intersection of two highways. Also called an Internet Exchange (IX), we have about a dozen of them now in the United States. In 1995, we had only four of them in San Francisco, Chicago, outside New York City, and in Washington, DC.

Network administrator   This person maintains the network within a company, corporation, or organization. Many networks are large enough to require several network administrators, who handle security, firewalls, software upgrades, technical difficulties, day-to-day activity, etc.

Network card   This printed circuit board plugs into a computer and connects users together throughout a network. We also call this card a network adapter.

Network Interface Card (NIC)   Also called a network adapter, this card regulates the information flowing between clients and servers within a network.

Network Solutions, Inc.   Acquired by VeriSign, Inc., Network Solutions aids in the process of domain name registration.

Network Working Group (NWG)   This is the group responsible for completing the initial host-to-host protocol used in ARPANET.

Newsgroup   An online discussion group devoted to a single subject. Those reading the messages can read, post, and/or reply to a message.

Node   This is a junction within a network. A node is wherever lines meet and join, e.g., a workstation, in a network.

Online service   An online service is an ISP that offers its own Web site and services, such as America Online (AOL).

Open architecture   This design allows other companies create software and hardware for the computer. Companies, like Microsoft, makes much of its technology proprietary meaning it does not let anyone know the details of its various systems. Apple, on the other hand, made its design available to others, for example, third-party vendors, so they could create software and hardware to match the new computer's needs.

Optical Carrier (OC)   An OC is a level of service within the SONET system and specifies the speed at which a digital signal travels through the fiber optic medium. The choices range from OC-1 (51.85 Mbps) to OC-768 (38813.12 Mbps or 38.81312 Gbps).

Packet   In order to send information efficiently, the computer packages it into packets much as we put our letters in an envelope to send through the mail.

Packet INternet Groper (PING or ping)   This software determines whether an Internet Protocol address is online and functioning, as when the telephone technician checks to see if your line is active. Ping software sends out a data packet and waits for a response.

Packet switching   This is a technology designed to divide information into smaller segments, called packets, send them through a WAN to their destination. Packet switching sends the information and the destination address so the information knows where to go.

Parallel port   A parallel port is a socket/connection on a computer that allows peripheral devices (for instance, a printer) to send information back and forth simultaneously.

Password   Any alphanumeric combination that allows you access to a system. The system could be your computer (e.g., screensaver password), the Internet (ISP password), etc. This password allows the system to keep out unwanted visitors, hackers, and so on. If you need a password, do not use your name, address, social security number, or any other information a person could easily obtain. Instead, use some more obscure detail that is still easy to remember, such as the name of the hometown for your grandfather.

Peer-to-peer (P2P) network   This is an equal network in that all the computers connected to it can act as servers to the other computers. In most networks, one computer, or set of computers, acts as a server and all the others act as clients.

Peripheral   This is any hardware device connected to the computer, such as a mouse, monitor, keyboard, etc.

Peripheral Component Interconnect (PCI)   A high-speed bus (or pathway) used in personal computers. A PCI connects the CPU and all its peripherals, allows for Plug and Play capability, and allows Interrupt ReQuests (IRQs) to be shared. Most personal computers use a combination of ISA buses and PCI buses, both being expansion buses.

Personal Computer (PC)   A PC is the computer (microcomputer) you use at home or in an office.

Plain Old Telephone Service (POTS)   This has the same meaning as your telephone system. Computer people do not like their telephone service because they consider it too slow.

Plug-in   This auxiliary program enhances a software program's capability. Often called a helper program.

Point of Presence (POP)   This is the point (in a WAN or long distance carrier) where the local phone call (the line) provides access to the network.

Point-to-Point Protocol (PPP)   This is one of two protocols for dial-up access to the Internet. The other is SLIP. PPP performs better but is more expensive than SLIP. For instance, PPP can retransmit garbled data packets, which SLIP cannot do.

Port   A connection point in the computer allowing you to attach a peripheral to the computer for communication between the two. A port can be serial (information travels only one way at a time) or parallel (information can travel both ways simultaneously) between the computer and the peripheral. *See also* Parallel port; Serial port.

Portable Document Format (PDF)   Adobe Acrobat software uses this file format for its documents.

Portable Network Graphics Files (PNG)   PNG files are a relatively new type of files that are not supported by some older browsers. PNG files allow more colors than JPGs or GIFs, are typically smaller, and do not lose quality when they are compressed. PNG files also do not have the potential legal issues that surround the use of GIF files.

Post Office Protocol, version 3 (POP3)   This protocol allows you to send and receive e-mail. POP3 is not as sophisticated as IMAP.

Power supply   As with any electrical device, the power supply converts Alternating Current (AC) from your local power company into Direct Current (DC) for your company.

Printer   A printer is the device that prints the pages you want. Some printers print only in black and white (with shades of gray); others can also employ colors. Two popular types of printers are laser printers and inkjet printers.

Protocol   A protocol is a set of standards/rules designed to control the flow of data. *See also* Internet Protocol; Transmission Control Protocol/Internet Protocol.

Proxy server   A **proxy server** monitors and controls the flow of certain types of data into or out of the network. It can cancel or break a connection between a sender and a receiver. It can also be set up to regulate the use of bandwidth in a network.

Queue   A temporary storage place for memory/data. *See also* Input queue.

Queue length   The amount of memory/data the queue can hold. If the queue length in a router is full, it cannot accept any more packets of information until the router has processed what it already has.

QuickTime   This plug-in program allows you to listen to audio signals using your computer.

Random Access Memory (RAM)   A special type of memory managed by the operating system software. Unlike the hard disk drive, RAM stores information in active electronic circuit patterns, allowing much quicker access to information; however, the information is lost when you turn the power off. *See also* Dynamic Random Access Memory; Static Random Access Memory.

Read Only Memory (ROM)   The ROM chip is inside the computer and permanently stores instructions and data for the computer. The user cannot alter these data.

RealPlayer   This plug-in program allows you to listen to audio signals using your computer.

Regional network   A regional network, covering more area than an ISP, controls and maintains access to the Internet in a predetermined area.

Registry   This is a listing of the domains included in each Top-Level Domain.

Request For Comment (RFC)   These documents are recommendations for changes to and enhancements needed for the Internet. Each RFC concerns itself with a particularly technology used within the Internet. Groups like the IETF use RFCs on a continuing basis.

Router   A device designed to send data (or packets of data) from one network or area to another. Routers decide what is the most efficient way of sending information much as when a delivery person must decide which streets drive on to save the most amount of time. *See also* Internal router.

Routing table   This database in a router contains information describing the topology (or interconnection pattern) of a network.

Satellite link   A signal travels from earth to a satellite and back to earth. This is the link between the satellite and earth.

Scripting language Scripting languages are usually used to augment other programming languages. Scripts are a prepared set of statements for how the Web page is supposed to react to different events, like clicking on an area or just passing the mouse over it, making the Web page a more interactive experience for the user. Some common scripting languages include JavaScript and VBScript.

Search engine   A search engine is an external device that runs software, which examines parts of the World Wide Web to find articles, pictures, video, etc., to match your search request. As an analogy, a search engine is the reference librarian who helps you find the information you need. Another type of search engine is a metasearch engine.

Sector   A sector is the smallest storage area on a floppy or hard drive disk. Typically, a sector is a segment of a concentric track encoded on the disk in a low-level format; it usually contains 512 bytes of information. If drawn, a sector would look like a slice of a pizza. The other way to measure memory storage is a track.

Secure HyperText Transfer Protocol (HTTPS or Secure-HTTP)   This is a more secure version of HTTP and only allows one message at a time to transmit. HTTPS remains secure because it accesses a secure Web server.

Secure Socket Layer (SSL)   Unlike HTTP, this Internet security protocol can interact with all Internet tools and not just the World Wide Web. In SSL, the browser sends a public key to the server, and the server sends back a secret key. Also called Secure Sockets Layer.

Serial Line Internet Protocol (SLIP)   This is one of two protocols for dial-up access to the Internet. The other is PPP. SLIP aids in gaining access to the Internet via dial-up access, especially to TCP/IP networks. This protocol defines the transport of data packets through a telephone line and allows non-LAN computer connections to the Internet. SLIP is less expensive than PPP but does not perform as well.

Serial port   One of many ports allowing the attachment of devices to your computer via a cable. A serial port sends and receives information over the same wires in the cable. This means that while information is traveling in one direction, the returning information must wait until the first transmission is complete, much like cars entering a one-way tunnel from opposite directions.

Server   A server is a computer used by other computers in a network to provide a variety of services. *See also* Proxy server.

Shareware   A method of selling software that allows the user to copy and distribute software without permission. Users pay a modest fee to the software authors and promise not to alter the software in any way. Sometimes, shareware will continually prompt you for payment before starting (nagware) or will stop working after a certain time period unless payment is received (crippleware).

Shopping cart   This is a collection of the items you plan to buy over the Internet while shopping at one Web site.

Simple Mail Transfer Protocol (SMTP)   This set of rules, based on TCP/IP, aids in transmitting e-mail.

Small Computer System Interface (SCSI; pronounced skuzzy)   A standard for hard drives, scanners, and CD-ROM drives. SCSI gives you the ability to add up to seven new devices to your computer. Computer users first employed SCSI on the Apple Macintosh computer.

Smurf attack   This is a type of DoS attack, which uses the pinging process with the response sent to another Internet address.

Socket   Wherever we plug in a device, that point of connection is the socket. This socket could be in the wall for power or the phone, at the back of the computer for a mouse or monitor, etc.

Software   A program or set of instructions created to do a certain function.

Sound card   This printed circuit board plugs into a computer; it records and plays back sound, supports MIDI, and allows the sound to reach speakers. We also call this card an audio adapter.

Spam   This is an unwanted and unsolicited message, especially an unwanted advertisement.

Spider   A search engine often sends out a program to index the contents of sites and update its knowledge of that site. We call this program a spider or crawler.

Splitter   This device splits a signal so it can travel along two cables simultaneously. Often, the splitter sends a low-frequency signal for use in the telephone and the high-frequency signal for use by the computer.

Stateless protocol   This protocol does not keep track of nor depends on commands already given in order to know what to do next. In other words, it can operate independently.

Static IP address   Static, in this definition, means permanent. We assign a permanent IP address servers within the TCP/IP network, just as you have a permanent home address for where you live. *See also* Dynamic IP address; IP address.

Static Random Access Memory (SRAM)   SRAM is one type of RAM chip. Since the SRAM does not contain a capacitor (the DRAM does), you can access the SRAM's memory in less than 10 nanoseconds (10 ns), which is 10 billionths (0.000000001) of second. This speed is three times quicker than the speed of a DRAM. Unfortunately, the SRAM chip requires more power and space. *See also* Static Random Access Memory.

Streaming audio   This is an audio signal transmitted over a network. An audio file sent thruogh streaming audio will begin playing before the entire file has been downloaded.

Super Video Graphics Array (SVGA)   An SVGA monitor is an improved VGA monitor able to display over 15 million colors. SVGA resolution is also superior; it can run from 800 by 600 pixels up to 1,024 by 1,280 pixels.

Synchronous Optical NETwork (SONET)   A fiber optic system designed for transmission of high-speed digital signals. The SONET is specified by various speeds/capabilities called Optical Carriers.

T-1 line   The telephone companies use this transmission line because of its speed (1.544 Mbps). Since a T-1 is a dedicated line and more expensive to use, companies and ISPs are usually the only ones to use it. One of its advantages is its ability to handle 24 64-Kbps channels simultaneously.

T-2 line   A dedicated line a little more than four times faster than a T-1 line (6.312 Mbps). It can provide 96 64-Kbps channels simultaneously.

T-3 line   A dedicated line a little more than seven times faster than a T-2 line (or 28 times faster than a T-2 line). This line can handle 672 64-Kbps channels simultaneously.

Telnet   This program allows you to log onto a remote computer and use the programs from that computer.

Terminal emulation   This process emulates, or imitates, a terminal and its processes in order to access its system/network.

Text-only browsing   The ability to browse a Web site's text information and exclude any graphics, images, and video. Usually, you click on a hyperlink which takes you to a text-only Web page.

Thread   A thread is a series of messages and responses about a particular subject in a newsgroup..

Throughput   The measured speed at which the computer processes information is its throughput.

Time Division Multiplexing (TDM)   This technology weaves slower signals into one accelerated signal and sends them together. This type of multiplexing allows you to send multiple signals simultaneously.

Top-Level Domain (TLD)   Within a URL, this is the most important or largest category in the Internet naming system. We designate TLDs with .com, .org, .net, etc.

Tower   A tower is the cabinet which holds the motherboard and various peripherals you use while working at the computer, such as a hard drive, DVD player, modem, etc.

Track   A track is one of the concentric circles on hard and floppy disks within a sector. They can also be the spiral tracks on CDs and videodiscs or parallel lines on audiotape. Track is one of the ways of measuring memory storage; the other is a sector.

Transmission Control Protocol/Internet Protocol (TCP/IP)   A common method of sending information over a computer network linking dissimilar computers. TCP/IP insures the accuracy of the information transmitted and received by breaking down the information into small packets and checking that all characters in each packet arrive in the same form that they were sent.

Trojan Horse   This program appears to perform a valid function but instead contains hidden instructions that damage a computer/network.

Uniform Resource Locator (URL)   URLs are the computer/electronic addresses of Web sites. An example of a URL is www.washingtonpost.com, which is the URL for the Washington Post newspaper.

United States Department of Commerce (DOC)   A government act created the DOC on February 14, 1903, which first called itself the Department of Commerce and Labor. Over the years, the DOC created various boards, branches, divisions, and departments. The DOC "promotes job creation, economic growth, sustainable development, and improved living standards for all Americans by working in partnership with businesses, universities, communities, and workers…" (from www2.osec.gov.doc/public nsf/docs/mission-statement).

Universal Serial Bus (USB)   USB is an interface for peripherals. You can disconnect this low-speed hardware device supports digital video without turning the computer off.

UNIX   An operating system, as is Windows, developed at AT&T in 1969 by Ken Thompson.

UNIX shell account   With this UNIX account (registered with an ISP), a customer can employ the UNIX system/commands to send/receive e-mail and any attached files.

Usenet   A collection of   servers that make up a worldwide network, **Usenet** allows people to post messages and notes on a variety of topics, allowing for the creation of a large number of different newsgroups. Originally **Usenet** used a protocol known as UNIX-to-UNIX Copy (UUCP), but today it uses the Network News Transfer Protocol (NNTP).

User Datagram Protocol (UDP)   This protocol is often used to send streaming audio files. UDP is similar to TCP except that it does not resend missing data packets.

Username   We employ a username as our personal identification in our e-mail address. Some people use their name; some do not. Suppose Joe Johnson is a photographer and uses Southwestern Bell (SWBell) as his ISP. If he wants a username of Photographer, his e-mail address would be photographer@swbell.net.

Very high-speed Backbone Network Service (vBNS)   vBNS connects high-speed computers to service the Internet and Internet2. The National Science Foundation (NSF) and MCI Communications Corporation are cooperatively running vBNS.

Video Graphics Array (VGA)   A monitor developed by IBM that can display up to 640 pixels by 480 pixels. If you reduce the resolution, you can increase the number of colors. Super Video Graphics Array (SVGA) replaced this standard. *See also* Super Video Graphics Array.

Virtual memory   Sometimes a program is too large for a computer to run. If that happens, a computer will simulate more memory than is available. With the larger hard drives now for sale, this problem appears less often.

Virus   A piece of software designed to infect a computer or its peripherals. As many biological viruses goes inside the host, a software virus embeds itself inside the host program. Upon entry, the virus will activate immediately or may wait. Viruses cannot attach themselves to data. They must hitchhike with a program; once you activate the program, you launch the virus.

Visual Basic Script (VBScript)   We use this programming language for a variety of Web design applications specific to Microsoft.

Web browser   This is a program that allows you to examine files on the Internet and/or World Wide Web, such as its pages, images, videos. Web browsers allow you to bookmark a site, so you can find more easily next time you want to visit it.

Wide Area Information Server (WAIS)   This Internet database contains indexes that point to various documents (text files).

Wide Area Network (WAN)   A WAN is a network of computers and communications that connect multiple users together. The difference between a WAN and a Local Area Network (LAN) is the distance between the users. Users in a WAN are farther apart than in a LAN.

Windows Media Player   This plug-in program allows you to listen to audio signals using your computer.

World Wide Web (WWW or Web)   The Web is a vast network or facility and links documents (Web pages), images, audio/video information via hyperlinks, a Web browser, and HTML tags.

World Wide Web cameras (Web cameras or Webcam)   These are cameras showing events as they occur. The person/system responsible for the camera broadcasts the video/audio signal via the World Wide Web.

World Wide Web Consortium (W3C)   Founded in 1994 and hosted at Massachusetts Institute of Technology (MIT), this group of industry leaders develops standards for the World Wide Web.

Worm These virus-like programs move from computer to computer on a network, causing the computers to shut down and stop functioning correctly.

Zip drive   A storage device that uses floppy disks able to hold much more memory than the standard 3.5-inch disks. A zip drive should not be confused with a zip program that compresses a file(s) to free up memory elsewhere.

Index

@ (at sign), 71–72

A

abbreviations, online communications and, 185
Accelerated Graphics Port (AGP), 11
access routers, 154
address buses, 11
addresses, IP. *See* IP addresses
Adobe PDF files, 140–141, 148
ADSL. *See* Asymmetric Digital Subscriber Line (ADSL)
Advanced Research Projects Agency (ARPA), 21, 22
Advanced Research Projects Agency Network (ARPANET), 22–24
.aero domains, 116–117
AGP. *See* Accelerated Graphics Port (AGP)
American Standard Code for Information Interchange (ASCII), 139–140
analog signals, transformation of by modems, 40
animation, GIF files and, 138
anonymity, online communications and, 181–182
anonymous FTP sites, 132–133
anti-virus programs, 210–211
AOL, 25, 32
Archie, 25
ARPA. *See* Advanced Research Projects Agency (ARPA)

ARPANET. *See* Advanced Research Projects Agency Network (ARPANET)
ASCII encoding, 139–140
Asymmetric Digital Subscriber Line (ADSL), 41–42, 43, 100
at (@) sign, 71–72
attachments, e-mail, 207–208
attacks, online, 206–212
  Denial of Service (DoS), 211–212
  protecting against, 210–211
  Trojan horses, 208–209
  viruses, 206–208
  worms, 210
attributes, HTML tag, 124
auctions, online, 217–219
audio, online, 148, 198–200, 202
AVI files, 149

B

B channels (Bearer channels), 98
backbone, Internet. *See* Internet backbone
Backbone Network Service (BNS), 29
baseband connections, 13
basic input/output system (BIOS), 9, 10
Basic Rate Interface (BRI), 98
bastion hosts, 154–155. *See also* proxy servers
BBIAB (be back in a bit), 185
BBS. *See* Bulletin Board Systems (BBS)
Bearer channels (B channels), 98
Berners-Lee, Tim, 26, 35

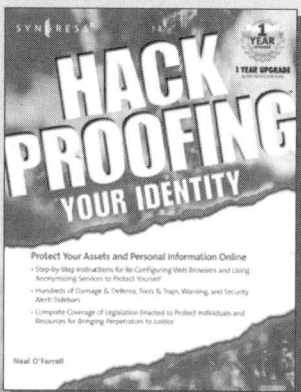